The Chronicles of
Big Money
SONNY 305

"The Beginning"

Copyright © 2024

All Rights Reserved. No parts of this book may be reproduced in any form without the express written consent of Publisher/ Author, except in the case of brief quotations embodied in relevant articles and book reviews for print ad electronic media.

TABLE OF CONTENTS

Preface 1

Chapter One: It's Time To Go To Trial 3

Chapter Two: The Insurance Man 9

Chapter Three: Poetic Injustice 35

Chapter Four: Convicts 59

Chapter Five: Her Brush with Life and Death 89

Chapter Six: I Can Snort Up Peru 121

Chapter Seven: Are You Smart or Intelligent? 147

Chapter Eight: Project Chick 159

Chapter Nine: Fat Pimp 179

Chapter Ten: Sonny's Bridge is Falling Down 203

Chapter Eleven: My Brother's Keeper 211

Chapter Twelve: The Feds 227

"Albert Campbell courageously opens up his head, heart, and life in a way that enlightens, empowers, and inspires. It is a must read for youth growing up in the urban core and who America too often believes are destined for prison, poverty, or an early death. His story of struggle, strength, and tremendous sacrifice is not only a cautionary tale, but serves as a story of hope, love, and redemption."

Congratulations!! This will be a blessing and gift to the world...

Best wishes!

Dr. Steve Gallon III, Author of "When Morning Comes" and School Board Member of Miami-Dade County Public Schools

PREFACE

I decided to write "The Chronicles of Big Money Sonny 305" to shed light on my situation and why I am the way I am. To some degree, it may even be a tribute to my faults, my virtues, or the dire straits I've endured over the years to tell the world my story live and in living color. The question that should be asked, about my story, is, as harsh as it may seem, "is it unique?"

Some would reason that several thousand children grow up in projects every day in exactly the same, and sometimes even worse, circumstances as I did, but weren't murdered or ended up in prison. However, notwithstanding the primacy of their argument, I beg to differ. You see, it's true we're all a product of our environment in so inherited by a society that wishes us to change, but what separates mine from those of the norm is my ability or disability to adapt to my own love of oneself, one's God, and one's family.

Now, I speak in terms of a righteous brother who found these qualities or inequalities when I was at the lowest point in my life, serving a thirty-five-year prison sentence. Nonetheless, it took me some years to create a platform of which I was comfortable with to tell my story. I'm grateful to the nature of literature for providing me with the necessary tools to do it with, and Dr. Joy Riley of Joy A Riley Publishing to produce my story into this form you now possess. Also, I would like to acknowledge Phoenix rise Publishing for editing.

Children, and in this account more specifically me, are a product of their environment. There were times in my life when murder, drugs, and the raw ghetto life were things I only saw on the news. To keep it Gutter, like we do in the hood, those were the things I related to. As I grew older and entered my teenage years it was common to see children my age, twelve, thirteen, or fourteen-years old selling drugs. Therefore, it was also common for me to desire those traits that I looked upon as royalties.

I knew from a very young age that I would never go to college. College was for squares, dudes who tried to elude the plight of the ghetto because they either were too soft or too green. Thus, in general terms, I was predestined by my environment to die young or end up in prison. That's more so a question rather than a statement. Nevertheless, what I witnessed growing up from the window of my apartment was the life I became a part of. I was a "CONVICT", an individual not so much blemished at birth but one who evolved into this man the "white" world looked upon as degenerate.

There are four types of people that come from the ghetto. First, there is the one that is unable to survive the ghetto and dies spiritually, physically, and mentally. Then, there's the one that ends up poor and unable to sustain himself but is willing to keep trying no matter what the outcome may be. Next, there's the one that didn't let the ghetto swallow them in its Gutter. This person becomes successful in all areas and still strives for better, only using the hard times to motivate him or her. Last but certainly not least, there's the one that ends up in prison because the ghetto's arms have captured him or her. Their crime was simply trying to live the fast life.

This is my story. I wrote this story in an effort to not only bring exposure to my case but to bring ease to some of the struggles of life that have burdened my family since I've been away. "The Chronicles of Big Money Sonny 305" is a real-life experience. It entails the struggles that my family and I faced while living in the ghetto, the experiences I've had to endure since a very young age, and the outcome of my bad decisions.

To all of you out there that are reading this book, please don't let the ghetto be an excuse to end up like me. Let this book be your eyes, ears, a mental, and spiritual guide for whatever it's worth. With those words, I leave you with my blessing that God will always guide you through your own trials and tribulations. I won't hold you up any longer. Get to reading!

CHAPTER ONE

IT'S TIME TO GO TO TRIAL

- 1994 -

I could still hear my lawyer's voice. It was sort of soft and consoling, yet cunning when he said, "Albert, they don't want you. They want him ... Butler Campbell," my lawyer pleaded with me as he fixed the rimmed glasses on his face. I peered into his dark, blue eyes somewhat confused, somewhat not understanding what the hell he was talking about. "Butler Campbell," I thought. "What did he have to do with this?" I started to think. I didn't have any idea what was up, but I was soon about to find out. My lawyer pulled his chair close to me and started to speak just barely above a whisper.

"Listen! Here is the deal. They don't want some guy that's running up and down the highway with a few kilos of coke. I don't know why they want Butler, but they want him bad, and if you can help them, they promised me they won't take anything from you. They won't indict your mother or any member of your family, and that includes your brother, Marvin, and your girlfriend, Samantha." He paused for a fraction of a second. I guess he was giving me a chance to digest his words. He kept smiling and grinning, or whatever the hell that is white people do when they're beguiling you.

"I could do something for them," my lawyer said.

"But I don't know anything about him selling no drugs," I said with a confused tone, interrupting him.

My voice was a little higher than his and had irritation in it. I was still a bit lost, but once again he offered me some clarity, at least as far as the way the F. B.I did things. To tell the truth, I thought the feds only messed with you if you were somebody like Bodily, Ike, or they had a case against you. I mean, I know I was making a little cheese, but it was nothing compared to some of the other players in the hood. He looked at me with this half smile half grin on his face and said, "Don't worry about that, Albert. They said they'll tell you what to say." Just like that, he let the words drop out his mouth.

Then he sat back in his chair like it was nothing. The wood from the chair scraped across the floor leaving an awkward sound, but it didn't seduce our conversation at all. I shot him a confused look like, "they'll tell me what to say? What do you mean tell me what to say?" Wow! Masons don't tell gambles, politicians aren't corrupt, and nuns don't lie unless God asks them to. So, what was my lawyer asking me to do, lie? Was he God or was I a nun?

For one thing, only women are nuns. I was a man, and my lawyer certainly wasn't a God, and that's all I was thinking. Now, I was getting hot at him, at them, and at myself for even sitting down with him to have this kind of conversation. I could feel my temperature rising like bubbles. Beads of sweat formed along my forehead despite the fact that the air conditioner, was on full blast. All I could think was, "I ain't 'bout to tell on nobody!"

"Albert, they've given you one plea agreement and I need to have an answer by five o'clock tomorrow, "my lawyer insisted, disturbing my thoughts. Then he paused again and looked down at his silver and gold Rolex, and I'm thinking, "Yeah, what's the deal?" It was like he was reading my mind. "From seventeen to twenty-seven years and that's with full cooperation," my lawyer said, still whispering nonchalantly. That's when I went slap off.

"What, buddy is ya' crazy?"

"Albert, calm down. It isn't that bad."

"I beg to differ."

Our meeting ended on a rough note. I have to admit for the most part he controlled the tempo of the conversation, but the next time he came I made up my mind. I was going to control the conversation, at least that's what I'd hoped for.

"Well, tell them I said do their damn job and screw 'em," I lamented before my lawyer could even put his briefcase down.

"No, they said they're going to screw you," he abruptly snapped back.

Now you tell me who won the next battle. From the moment I walked in the lawyer's booth I could tell he had something on his mind his facial expression and lawyer's tactics didn't faze me.

I had become immune to bad news. I mean, what else could he tell me that would be any worse than what he'd already said? At that moment I started viewing the whole ordeal as a chess game. Right now, I was down in pieces, and it was the government's move. I had one chance to stalemate the game. I was thinking if I refused to cooperate the government would have to start the game over, but if I cooperated, we both could be winners. I wasn't trying to go that route so I had to keep playing to see if I could catch the government slipping. I wanted to be the only one to win.

"The agent involved in your case told me yesterday he's not interested in you. He says they only want Butler Campbell. If you cooperate with them, they've assured me they'll do something good for Samantha, your brother, your co-defendant Ty, and yourself ... "my lawyer frankly said. He placed his briefcase on the table and started to open it. When he got it open, he pulled out a box of Tic-Tacs and placed one in his mouth. "Have one ... he offered. I refused. No special reason, I just did.

I took the seat across from him and the minute I sat down we exchanged looks. He had a look on his face of sincerity and my look was more so ashen. The government had made their move and now it was time for me to make mine. For a fleeting moment, I thought long and hard. My move had to be calculative. I could end it all with my next move and free a lot of people, or my next move could cause me to lose the game completely. The thing was I still had a chance to win the game. I kept telling myself I wasn't no snitch, and that's what I was going to live by.

"Tell them I don't know anything about Butler Campbell," I said nonchalantly. I felt like the government tried me. How in the hell were they telling me they'll give me seventeen to twenty-seven years with full cooperation? I told them, well I told my lawyer to tell them, I would plea out to whatever they wanted me to without cooperation if they would drop my family members off the case. A few days later the lawyer told me the original plea was the only plea they were offering, and I needed to make a decision before five pm. I told my lawyer he didn't have to wait that long. It was ten-thirty that morning and I was ready and willing to give them the answer right then. I just told him straight up - no deal!

When I got back to my cell I went straight to my bunk and laid down. I propped my hand behind my head and gazed into the top bunk. I never could go to sleep just like that. It took some preparation. Thinking always wore me out, and that's what I was doing, trying as best I could to assess my thoughts. While I drifted into deep thought a song, I used to hear on the radio all the time by Mr. Bigg ran across my mind.

It said, "Momma, call the lawyer cause it's time to go to trial ... "I reminisced about the song for as long as I could until I felt myself drifting off to sleep.

The days were winding down to trial. My lawyer started petitioning the court with all sorts of motions, but in the end, they would all be denied. Everything he filed the judge denied it like it was nothing. I used to get mail every day, with the exception of weekends, but it got to the point where I hated it when the officer called my name. Every time I got a letter from the court, I just knew the word "Denied" would be in bold letters on the last page. I stopped reading the brief and always just went straight to the last page.

"Mr. Campbell, the agents say they have statements saying you made drug transactions or exchanged money in the presence of your mother... as well as your girlfriend. They say that when you became aware that the federal agents arrested Billy Bob you started keeping drugs at an in-law's house, in which your girlfriend would make the drug transactions for you," my lawyer said. For a moment I struggled with everything he was saying. If arresting Samantha wasn't enough, now they were indicating they wanted to arrest my mom and Corenthia. At one time I thought the government was benevolent and unadulterated.

I never thought they would step over or across boundaries to where your family was, but now I was having second thoughts. My perception had been wrong, all the while. I now knew that the government was this body of people who formed a beggarly system that only sought to destroy you at any and every expense. Just because I was refusing to cooperate with them, they were willing to throw my entire family in jail, a family that had absolutely nothing to do with what I was doing.

Their pressure not only weakened me but now for the first time I was seriously contemplating cooperating because I could not see Samantha go to jail. I even tried as best I could to rationalize the situation. That seemed like it was the only way out. At that moment thin notes of defeat invaded my body followed by an unchanneled tear. Just one tear rolled down my face and dropped into my lap. I wondered what, if anything, the tear meant.

I wondered what, if anything, the hell I was going to do... barbecue or mildew? Shake or bake? I pondered all of that. Once we were young, energetic, and filled to the rim with hope and admiration. Now a fraction of my friends was dead, a fraction dying, a fraction without a clue as to what the hell was going on, and a fraction now shuffling awkwardly to life's off beats trying to win a life they never had. Somehow, I fit into the latter category.

My mother was with Samantha at the hearing, so when I got back to the county jail, she came to visit me. She said she wanted to see Marvin and me before she headed back to Miami. My mother brought Albria, my newborn baby, to the county jail with her. The first thing she told me when she sat down was that they released Samantha, but she didn't want to come inside the jail.

Shortly after they returned to Miami my lawyer came to see me again. I figured we had a lot to talk about, but the only thing I wanted to discuss was Samantha and why Corenthia's name was on the government's witness list. In truth, I didn't know what was going on. It seemed like the more I organized my thoughts the more dishevelled my life became. Things just kept happening! I remember when my lawyer first walked into the room and asked me was I ready to pay the piper. I was thinking in layman's terms that I didn't have any more money to pay anybody.

"No, Mr. Campbell. What I mean is, are you ready to tell whatever it is you know about Butler Campbell? You don't need to worry about Corenthia because the government is ready to lock her up at any time for contempt of court because they know she is lying. The one you need to worry about is Samantha," he said.

"Samantha ain't gonna' tell nothing because she don't know nothing," I protested.

"Listen here, Mr. Campbell," my attorney said, attempting to reason as he moved his body across the table towards my face. "I'm going to tell you one more time. The government has statements on your mother and Corenthia, and if you don't take the plea, they're going to lock both of them up. Remember, a lawyer can shape, mold, revise and cajole his client into saying what he needs him to say. My advice for you is to get on the bandwagon and let's play ball with these people," my lawyer responded in a voice a little above a whisper. He sat back in his chair and both of us played the eye game for a split second or two.

He was a relatively middle aged, affable, grey-haired man who appeared to have this channelled ego. He wasn't arrogant, but he wasn't shy either. I guess you could say he was one of those people who used his honesty to shape his personality and demeanour, to which at times if he lied or exhibited deceit or betrayal you couldn't rightfully say either emotion has a sense of evil to it. You had to think or believe he was honestly trying to help you even if you knew in your heart nothing was further from the truth.

I started losing weight. I was eating but somehow my body wasn't showing it. The government wanted me to cooperate when all my life I was taught a man should stand up and be a man irrespective of his situation. If he threw bricks at the chain gang, he had to face up when it came time to bid. In the hood, men were made by their bidding, and if you did a little time people respected you. The only thing the government was asking me to do was too much time, and they were asking me to break the rules while doing so.

I called my mother again and told her what my lawyer said. I had to let her know what the government was saying about how they were going to lock her and Corenthia up if I didn't cooperate. I hadn't anticipated her answer. It was my mother who truly defined who I was and was not when she said, "Boy, this is my last time telling you this. If they lock Samantha or Corenthia up, they have to deal with it, and if they come and get me and take everything you have then they'll just have to do that cause you ain't gon sell your soul to the devil. Stop trying to save everybody cause only God can save the world, not you! "

So, it seemed I didn't have a choice in the matter. My mother let me know by her being so strong, that she didn't raise any punks or snitches. I mean, even though I was still hurt by the situation, my mom's words reinforced my inner strength and spirit. All I could do now was inform the lawyer that I'd take a life sentence without cooperation if they spared my family, but when they denied my offer a trial date was set. The song appeared in my mind again, "Momma call the lawyer because it's time to go to trial... "

CHAPTER TWO

THE INSURANCE MAN

- 1971 -

Marvin and I were lying on the floor under our bedroom window while our mother and stepfather clung onto two Smith & Wesson .38 revolvers.

I'd never forget the gripping fear I was clinging to wondering what was about to go down. I had one of those cold kinds of sweats running down the center of my back which was accompanied by a constant shiver. Talk about being scared? I was past scared!

Marvin saw the frightened look on my face, or was it a look of confusion? He had to have noticed that I sensed danger by the way he kept staring as if he was lost. His eyes stayed glued on my face, but his stare moved me. I knew he wasn't lost because if there was anything he understood, he understood danger and its nature.

As my mother peeked from behind the curtain, I could feel the trouble she anticipated, and I was concerned. I looked at her, wanting to say something, but I couldn't get any of my words to form. All I could do was stare. Then out of nowhere, she eased all of my fears. She stared back at me with an assuring smile that somehow convinced me that no matter what happened she was going to make sure Marvin and I were safe and sound.

In fact, I remember my mother once told me, "You didn't ask to come here so it's my duty to take care of you, even if I have to sell myself to do so. We're tired of the insurance man taking our damn money," she cried.

A sense of desperation yearned in her voice as she continued to peek out from behind the curtains. I couldn't help but think, "The insurance man, huh?" I was so frustrated.

I don't know who my mom thought she was fooling by running this lame game, but I wasn't buying it. In actuality, the insurance man was no one other than the neighbourhood drug dealer that my mother and stepfather were in debt to. I mean, she may have had good intentions by trying to make. Marvin and I believe that it was the insurance man, but we knew what time it was. At least that's the conclusion I came up with.

That's why Marvin and I were cuddled beneath a windowpane watching two junkies, in the images of our mom and dad, battle with some strange type of destiny trying to figure out what the result of their life and ours was going to be. Watching my family go through these intense situations caused my body to react recklessly, and at times I would just pee in my pants.

It was the strangest thing because right before Marvin and I got under the window I didn't have to pee at all. It's like the urgency just came out of nowhere. The wetness and hot fluid dripped down my leg like a fountain, and the thing about it was I didn't even react. The hood called this behaviour "scary pee", and that meant whenever something was about to happen out of the norm, you all of a sudden had to pee, poop or fart. You were scared as hell!

My bladder was so full that it's a wonder why I hadn't peed right there in my pants. I guess it was because I had my little thingy clutched so tight between my legs it couldn't come out. I don't know what was going on but I was silently praying, "I'll be glad when this whole thing is over." I don't know what it was, but time must've slowed up on me.

It actually felt like we had been waiting on the infamous insurance man to show up for hours and it was nothing but a couple of minutes. I don't know how long we remained prisoners in our own home but thank God it became obvious to my mom and stepdad that the insurance man wasn't going to show up. They went to the other room.

"That brotha ain't coming by here tonight, Queen," my stepfather said in a relieved tone. As soon as they walked into the back room I took off to the bathroom because I couldn't hold it any longer. I think another second and I would have peed right there in my clothes. It ain't like I had never done it before.

I felt better than Kunta Kente escaping from his master releasing my urine into Big Mouth Shorty's mouth I know that. Oh. Big Mouth Shorty was the nickname Marvin and I called our- toilet bowl. On Marvin's account the opening of the bowl looked like a big mouth, but on my account, I said all the noise it made when it was being flushed made you think it was telling on you if you were trying to keep your usage of it a secret.

"Ahhhh"; I sighed, letting my urine ooze in the toilet, and watching it splash against the rim and make all types of noise. We had given the toilet the right name because that's all it did was make noise. Nevertheless, as I watched my pee-pee dissolve into the spinning water I could hear the muffled conversation of my mom and stepfather talking. Sheer panic was in their voices as they were trying to figure out what their next move was. I even heard them pacing back and forth.

"What are we going to do, Queen?" my stepfather whispered as if my mother had all the answers.

I guess they were planning on what to do next and I wanted to get my butt out of there before they came out and started looking at me crazy.

I never thought for a minute thing were over. That is after listening to my mother and stepfather talk, I knew sooner or later something was going to happen. So, as soon as I finished doing my thing with Big mouth Shorty I ran back to where Arvin was. All I wanted to do was make sure he was straight. When I saw that he hadn't moved from the window I knew he still had that sense of fear clinging to him.

So, I laid beside him and wrapped my arms around his lower torso. I embraced his as tightly as I could without hurting him and whispered in his ear that everything was going to be alright. I kept talking to him, and the more I talked the more I embraced. I just wanted to give him the same assurance from a brotherly perspective that our mother had given me, even if I didn't know what the hell was going to happen next.

"You think the insurance man is going to kill mommy?" Marvin asked scared out of his wits.

It was dark in the room, but I could see Marvin's big eyes lurking like headlights on a dark, country road. He discerned danger and was trying to make sense out of it all. I didn't know what to say to him because, on the real, I didn't know what was going to happen myself. I just kept hoping and praying that whatever it was it wouldn't be so bad. That night I thanked God that the insurance man never showed up. He probably knew that my mom and stepfather were waiting on him and thought he'd catch them when they were slipping.

I often remember seeing different people coming in and out of our apartment for short periods of time. There were different shades of blackness, light-skinned, caramel, jet black, blue black, pecan tan, and so many other colors pleasing to the eye. They had different attitudes. Some were loud and rambunctious, and others were obnoxious, calm, cool, collective or "simply red", meaning a mystery.

Yes, they were different, but they had one thing in common. They were all junkies strung out on the devil's potion, heroin, or boy. Girl is what they called cocaine, but whichever it was they were strung out on it. Or maybe they might have been strung out on life itself. At eight years of age, I didn't pay much attention to them. My main concern was my mom and stepfather trying to figure out why they did the things they did when they knew it wasn't getting them anywhere. I assumed my stepfather was a petty drug dealer because of the constant traffic coming in and out of our apartment.

They tried to hide what they were doing from Marvin and me, but they couldn't do it because I could always tell when they were high because they took on certain characteristics. Like wanting total silence and seeing things that weren't actually there, or they normally sat quietly with contorted facial expressions. Their faces used to be twisted out of shape, nose draining, and they would stare into oblivion like they were expecting the mother ship to come pick them up.

Before you knew it, they'd start nodding with their heads shaking and bobbing like bobble head dolls. Sometimes they would go into what appeared to be a deep sleep where they would be all slumped over and bent out of shape looking like they were about to hit the floor. Just before they'd hit it they would spring back up as if they had springs in their butts, and then they would repeat the same motion over and over again.

Now, I have to tell you Marvin and I used to get our laugh on watching them until we got caught, but that mess used to be so funny you couldn't help but laugh. I guess the flip side to my mother and stepfather's addiction was that even though we didn't have a nice car or live above the average ghetto family we never missed a meal, had nice clothing, and had plenty of laughs. Cecil always made sure of that.

LIVING IN THE STREET LIFE
- 1971 -

It's one of those hot days in "Da Bottom" that I'm all too familiar with and I'm slaving over a game of chance. Beads of sweat are protruding off my forehead and running down my armpits, but I'm not fazed at all.

Especially not when I have this dollar bet going on with Lil' Pookie and his cut buddy, Pee-Wee. Nothing else seems to matter when dead presidents are at stake, nothing but the bet anyway. I don't even have a dollar to jack up, but I'm willing to bet that little brotha on air, with nothing.

The worst thing that could happen is I might have to whoop Lil' Pookie up if I lose. If you knew me, you would know that ain't nothing but a thing to me. At my age not only am I the best marble shooter in the hood, but I am the second to the best fighter as well. The best fighter lived around the corner, and everyone called him Pretty Ricky. I called him Pretty Dickey when he made me mad. Anyway, Pretty Ricky was not an ordinary kid. He looked like a kid and talked like a kid, but he was different from a kid in so many ways. He had adult features like big hands, a big gut, and a big head.

What was most attractive about him was the fact that the brotha could throw down. Putting a shorty in check was his pleasure. He didn't have a problem with knocking the crap out of them and he would even wait for them to get their big brothers so he could do the same to them. The only thing about Pretty Ricky that disgusted me was the fact that people said he had a pretty face. Are you kidding me? I thought that he was ugly as sin.

What else was I supposed to think of him being I'm a boy as well? If I thought, he was pretty like all the girls then everyone would have thought it was something funny about me.

Pretty Ricky would never let you forget how pretty he was either. He would taunt you while beating you up by saying things like, "Ain't this face pretty?" and right after that he'd punch you in the eye. No, I wasn't about to fight Pretty Ricky, and if he had anything to do with this bet, I might have had to cop deuces. Hell, my stepfather always told me only pick fights you knew you could win.

Lil' Pookie was betting me that I couldn't shoot the red marble out of the circle at fifteen centimeters from the left. I'm thinking to myself, "This brotha must be crazy to think I couldn't do that or just plain stupid." He didn't know that for a dollar I would shoot the morning star out of the sky ten days before it was scheduled to arrive.

"Hey, I betcha can't," he yelled, slowly digging his forefinger up his nose and wiping it on his shirt.

"Boy, I'm so good at this game. Not only can I shoot the red marble out of the circle, but I can make it ricochet off the wall and land right back where it started," I hollered back.

"Well, put up or shut up," Pee-Wee said hoarsely. "I bet you can't do it."

"Oh, yeah? It's on," I thought, cutting my eyes at him.

As Lil' Pookie dug in his pocket for his dollar bill, I knelt down on my knees and commenced to align my body behind the circle and aimed at the marble I was intending to knock out. I had the beam down on it like I was a sharpshooter.

One of my eyes was closed and my tongue was hanging out the side of my mouth like I was in desperate need of a shot of water. I was thinking, to myself that I better make this shot, or someone was going home with a busted lip, and it was either me or Lil' Pookie. I had this though and was confident I could do it.

"You got this Sonny," I silently coaxed myself. I cut one of my eyes at the crowd watching in anticipation then put my attention back on the marble.

I was just about to let my cue marble soar across pavement when something caught my immediate attention and jacked everything up. I saw an army of men dressed in camouflage run up to our apartment and kick the door in. My heart jumped out of my chest. I saw me and Lil' Pookie duking it out because before I knew it my cue marble jumped out of my hand and sailed directly past my target. I hopped up off my knees and watched the army men in horror. What scared me the most was the fact that they had guns, and I'm talking about some big guns.

"Oh, please don't kill my mommy," I cried cogently. Then all of a sudden without warning I peed in my pants, just like that. I heard Marvin screaming and shouting and plus I heard Lil' Pookie saying something, but my mind wasn't registering anything. All I could see were images of people lying in puddles of blood, dying at the hands of another, and gasping for air like I was doing at that very moment. I was trying to catch my breath and make sense of what was going on at the same time. Things were happening so fast! "Please don't kill my momma," I prayed desperately as I ran past the army men.

All I could think about was the Insurance Man and his boys coming to collect what belonged to them.

I could have run to a relative's house that was close to mine, but I chose my Aunt Jean's house. My Auntie Jean was me and Marvin's favorite aunt and we loved her with a zillion strokes of passion or more.

I ran from Sixty-First street and Eighth Aveenue to Fifty-Third Street and Fourteenth Avenue as fast as my legs would allow me to run. By the time I got to Auntie Jean's house I was completely out of breath and gasping for air. As soon as I burst through the door our eyes came in contact with each other. "Girl, let me call you back," I heard her say before she hung up the phone. I knew she was looking for an explanation, but all I could do was point in the direction of our apartment and try to pull her towards the car.

I was hoping she would drive her car because I couldn't run another step. "Boy! What's wrong witcha?" Aunt Jean questioningly pleaded in her usually concerned way.

"Mommy... my momma," I cried between breaths, "... they gone kill her!" All I could remember as my aunt drove to our apartment were my mother's radiant eyes. I thought about how the birthmark between her eyes and her smile made my heart and stomach feel as though it had been invaded by a million butterflies. The way she hugged me as if to shield me, from life's bodily harm had the tendency to fill me with love. I saw our apartment approaching before we got there, and I couldn't wait.

Before my aunt, Jean stopped the car I jumped out dashing towards our apartment. I think I heard Aunt Jean scream that I was going to kill myself, but I didn't care. I needed to see my mother and brother and that was the most important thing to me at that moment. Even the possibility of me killing myself wasn't all that important. Not knowing exactly what to do, I ran to my stepfather as he was sitting in the back seat of a police car. I tried to open the door so I could talk to him, but the police ran me away.

"Where's my mommy?" I screamed at the top of my lungs. I was all hysterical. What made me even madder was my stepfather was sitting up there looking stupid and he wasn't saying anything. All he could do was point his head at the apartment.

The front door to our apartment was busted wide open. My Aunt Jean had already made it inside, but before I could move another muscle, I had to fully digest the condition of our apartment. I couldn't believe it; the place looked a mess. For a split second, I just stood in the doorway looking at its condition because the Miami SWAT team had torn everything up. It looked as though they had a vengeance against the apartment rather than anything else.

The furniture was turned over, clothes were scattered around everywhere, the floor was covered with flour and other debris that were tossed from the refrigerator, and the list went on and on. As I walked cautiously through the mess, I heard my mom telling Aunt Jean the police raided the house. I was like, "Yeah, anyone could see that," but I was relieved to hear her voice. I was still upset with the whole idea that our lives were in shambles, and this was one of those times I could use a dollar to take me away.

Actually, it sounded like my mom and Aunt Jean were arguing. I know I heard my Aunt Jean say something about, "One day you going to end up in jail or be killed if you keep up this foolishness!" Then I thought I heard her say something about my mother needing to leave Cecil alone. I was sure I heard my mom say, "You need to mind your own damn business!" Her statement made my Aunt Jean mad, and she stormed out the door.

I was thankful when I found my brother inside the bedroom sitting at the foot of my mom's bed. Both of their faces looked askew, but they were healthy and alive. I had to gaze at them for a moment, but after a while I couldn't help but notice the bedroom and the terrible condition it was in. It looked worse than any other part of the house. I took the time to process the situation and look around, out of nowhere tears ran down my face.

"Come here baby," my mom said, stretching her arms out toward me.

"They don' upset my baby," she said while giving me a kiss of passion.

From that instant, all seemed well.

FROM UGLY TO BEAUTIFUL TO UGLY AGAIN

Cecil spent a couple of nights in the county jail before Pre-Trial Release let him out, with stipulations of course. I think he was on house arrest. Apparently, the police found some drugs in our apartment. I don't recall how much it was, but obviously, it was enough for him to be concerned with the fact that he might end up going to prison. He kept complaining about not knowing how much time he would have to do if any, and if so, how long would it take him to get back on his feet.

I think he was thinking about not even going back to court or committing to any of the stipulations he agreed to in order for the Pre-Trial Services to let him out. He was talking about having his day in court on the streets.

"I'mma just let them crackers kill me," he often chanted.

THE INSURANCE MAN

It was a clear night with a slight breeze when my mother told us we were moving. There were five of us, me, my mother, Marvin, and Cecil. My mother had a baby girl as well, and her name was Tiffany. We traveled only a short distance to our new apartment, but it wasn't really new because my Uncle Ira used to live there, and we often visited him. When he found out we were having trouble he passed the apartment down to us.

My Uncle Ira was in the music business, and he had five young boys that he was trying to groom to be the next Jackson 5. Marvin and I weren't strangers to sharing a house with Uncle Ira because we lived with him once before in this same apartment. I don't quite know how that situation took place, but I'm sure it wasn't by his choice.

I don't know how long we stayed with him, but he found a way to get rid of us. He sent us back to our mom one day when he claimed he was missing twenty dollars out of his pants pocket. He accused Marvin of taking it and I felt bad, so I confessed to it, and he kicked us out.

Anyway, it didn't take us long to get to our new apartment due to the fact that it was located inside the ghetto perimeters.

When Cecil stopped driving, we were at our uncle's old apartment building which sat right across the street from Range Funeral Home. I don't remember the name of the apartment building, but what's in a name anyway? I just know that it was like any other low-income housing complex I had seen. Whether it was the Pork-N-Beans Projects, Scott's Projects, The Graveyard, Victory Homes Project, The Match Box, or Roland Oats, they all looked the same.

You could change the name of the projects to Night Manner - The Village or Lincoln Field, which weren't the projects by definition, but they were all the same. Don't get me wrong the apartment was cool and all, at least at first. glance, especially if you were on the outside looking in. In terms of being on the inside looking out, let's just say it left much to be desired.

I thought I had enough strength inside of me to bear the raid, the drugs, and all the stumbling blocks that had been clandestinely laid in my path. Tonight, would be the night circumstances beyond my control would prove to me the strength I thought I had was nothing more than a grain of salt. It all seemingly happened right after we had finished unpacking our belongings.

Marvin and I dozed off to sleep. If I could measure the Z's I had put in before I was disturbed, I would have to say it was just enough to allow me a couple of snoozes and nothing heavy. That's before I heard muffled cries that woke me out of my stupor. I grunted a couple of times and rolled over onto my side before I realized what was going on. It wasn't hard to tell that Cecil was using my mother as his personal punching bag. In layman's terms, he was beating my mother like she stole something.

At first, my mother tried to conceal her agony and defeat, but after Cecil's assault grew more intense, she couldn't restrain herself anymore. I heard her screaming at the top of her lungs for Cecil to stop hitting her, and her screams were so fearsome that they sent an eerie chill down my spine. Strands of hair even stood up on my back.

I'm thinking to myself as I'm watching this madman punish my mother, "What the hell could've happened so bad to cause them to be fighting like cats and dogs?" It wasn't actually a fight, though. It was more like a good old-fashioned beat down. That really messed me up, especially when earlier things appeared to be so peaceful and loving. Then it dawned on me. I knew it couldn't be but one thing, drugs, or the lack thereof.

The more my mother screamed the more Cecil kept beating on her. I heard the grunts, and I could almost feel his punches as they went into her body. Something told me I had to do something. Without exactly knowing what was going on, I moved a little closer in an effort to get a better look. I was hoping I would wake up out of a bad dream. I was about to pick something up and bust his brains out. I was going to kill this dirt bag, and that's all I kept saying to myself! At least that's what I was thinking I was going to try to do until I saw Cecil putting in work. It was like the closer I got the more he started looking like a giant. It suddenly dawned on me that I was nothing but a youngster in a man's world, one who couldn't dare match up with a full-grown man like Cecil.

I had to be realistic. I mean, it wasn't like Cecil was a push over or a chump. For one thing dude was huge. I'd say he was about 6'2" and cut up like a razor blade, plus he had muscles that looked as though they were than my entire body. I thought to myself, "Not only is this guy going to kill my old girl, but he is going to kill my little butt too if I try anything stupid." I had to do something besides just stand there. That something was what I did every time trouble stared me in the eyes.

I took off running leaving my mother, Marvin, my sisters, and my pride behind me because right then and there I had to go! I was so messed up I didn't even have time to put my shoes on. It was like every minute was precious, so I just took off. There was one thing I did do just before I left, though, and that was peeking in on Marvin and my sisters to make sure they were alright. When I saw they were still asleep I crept out the back door undetected and swiftly ran a half mile in a matter of minutes to my grandmother's apartment.

The funny thing was I didn't know her street number, but I knew exactly how to get there. I would have gone to get my Aunt Jean, but Cecil didn't fear her at all. He would have jumped on her too.

I didn't stop until I was there banging on my grandma's door. "Grandma ... Grandma ... Grandma!" I yelled hysterically.

My feet were burning like they were on fire, so I kept dancing around to try and cool them off. When my grandmother opened the door, she looked at me like I was crazy and then looked back at her clock on the wall. It read 3: 31 a.m. As she wrapped her robe around her waist I noticed the confused look on her face, but it could've been a look of anger from me waking her out of her sleep. I don't know but I had to take that chance. "I'm sorry for waking you up, Grandma," I murmured with trembling lips. "Chil", what's da matter," she demanded to know. "He gone kill her, Grandma!" I shouted in somewhat of an awkward sound.

My English was broken but my words must've been enough to get my point across. I could see my grandmother tense up, and when she did, I didn't need to say anything else. Grandma knew exactly who and what I was talking about. Without even saying another word she rushed to put on her shoes, and we dashed out of her apartment. We walked as fast as we could to my mother's rescue. Both of us were tired while cutting through the dark streets under the glow of busted out streetlights, but we kept our pace.

By the time we made it back the beat down was over. Cecil was gone and an eerie feeling loomed around the apartment like a scary movie. What surprised me most of all was the fact that my mother was still alive. She was lying on the cold floor, in a fetal position, crying uncontrollably.

"Oh Lord... please, Queen," my grandmother murmured, sauntering over to her daughter. She kneeled down next to my mother and wrapped her arms securely around her shoulders. Then she rocked her back and forth all the while chanting unintelligible hymns and words of disgust. I couldn't understand what exactly it was that she was saying, but they weren't good for Cecil.

Nevertheless, I could see and feel the love, sorrow, and pain between the two mothers. If my eyes weren't deceiving me, I could have sworn I saw my grandma wipe away my mother's tears while she was giving her the consolation that she needed to assure her that everything would be just fine.

Perhaps Grandma was just wiping the sweat from my mother's swollen face. I really couldn't tell.

Out of nowhere Grandma started to pray for my mother. She started out with her most famous words, "I rebuke you Satan in the name of Jesus." She chanted while thunderously stomping her feet and raising her fist in the air. Her voice was so heavy it echoed off the base of the walls and right into my mother's spirit. Strangely enough, my mother commenced to react to my grandmother's prayer and began to shake. When grandma placed her hand on my mother's forehead, she got worse, well she was really getting better, but it looked as though my mother was still in pain.

I don't know if grandma was binding the devil up like she proclaimed, but by the time she would get finished doing whatever it was she was doing my mother would be throwing up all kinds of icky green goo. It was almost gross to watch. Marvin finally came out the room wiping the mist from his eyes. I didn't want him to see our mother in the condition she was in so I walked him back to the bedroom. I knew Grandma would make her better as she always did. That is until my mother decided to get high again.

Thank God Grandma decided it was best for her to stay all night. Being that Marvin and I was kids, the idea of leaving us to deal with a situation as complex as my mother and stepfather's love battle or their addiction to drugs didn't sit well with my grandmother. My mother was still going through the motions, but for the most part, she looked better than she did before grandma came over.

I know my grandmother meant well, and I wanted to tell her I could deal with my mother from here, but I didn't say anything. I just thought I'd leave well enough alone. I mean, with Cecil still on the loose there was just no telling when he was going to decide to come back and finish what he started. So, I for one was cool with the fact that Grandma was staying. With her here Cecil wouldn't dare step foot back in our apartment, not after what he had done to my mother anyway. Don't get me wrong, it wasn't like he was scared of my grandma. I mean, what could a little old lady like her do to him?

In the religious sense, Grandma was powerful because she had the faith of that mustard seed the preachers always talked about that could move mountains. I often prayed to have that kind of faith because with it I could pray for the mountain of addiction, the one that had me thinking that mommy wasn't going to be walking with me much longer, to disappear.

It seemed as though Cecil was the vampire and grandma held the wooden cross, a veil of holy water, and the word of God. She could use them to drive through Cecil's heart, soul, and understanding. It wasn't any secret that most people who were strung out on drugs had a very low tolerance when it came to reasoning, but most cases when God was brought into the equation they would surrender.

Take Cecil for example, he did everything he could do not to hear Grandma preach the word of God to him. It was like her words broke him down like a double barrel shotgun. I'm not saying I didn't want him to come back. No way, I'm not saying that at all. After all, Cecil was all we knew as a daddy after our real daddy left. My mom never explained to us why our father decided to leave, and the question never crossed my mind to ask her. As far as I was concerned Cecil was my daddy, and in my own unique way, I loved him. I just thought he could use a couple of days away if nothing more than to just cool off. Then maybe he could ease his way back in good favor with Grandma, my mother, and me.

That's normally how things worked around here anyway. One moment they were fighting like cats and dogs and the next moment they were all lovey dovey like love birds. I know the relationship seemed strange but so did everything else around here, even after all the drama. I felt deep down in my heart that Cecil loved all of us. I mean how could he not when he raised us?

The next time Marvin and I opened our eyes it was a brand-new day, a new day of hopes, a new day of struggle. My grandmother had already left. and from the looks of things Cecil hadn't come back, or at least not to my knowledge.

My mom was still lying in the same position she was in last night, untouched and unmoved, and looked so peaceful. I just wanted to kiss her and ask her if she was alright, but my better sense told me to let her rest. I assumed she was going to need all the rest she could get when she faced Cecil again.

It took us a few days, perhaps even a week, for things to get back to normal, but after a while, all seemed well in love and in struggle. Ironically, my mom was back on her feet and moving around the apartment like it was all good. We hadn't heard a word from Cecil and as far as anyone could tell it was like his presence wasn't missed. We just went on about life like it was the normal thing to do or like it was normal not having him around.

For the first time in a long time, my mom was smiling, singing, and doing all kinds of other motherly gesticulations that would make any child me and Marvin's age feel loved. I had been instinctively watching my mom ever since that night and she was acting kind of strange.

I couldn't put my finger on it but I think she was trying to hide something from us. She was acting too nice and the whole place had this sweet, homely feel to it. I don't know maybe it was me or my self-conscious looking for the norm, or what had become the norm. Maybe she had finally gotten tired of Cecil's crap and decided to leave him alone altogether. I didn't know what it was but after I noticed her doing all the things, he used to do like walk us to and from school. I knew something was up.

The days and nights seemed pleasant in our new apartment and there wasn't that much drug activity going on. To add grace to our new start as we climbed the ghetto ladder, Marvin and I met some new friends. Marvin started hanging out with some kid named Bean who live downstairs in the same apartment building with his mom, Francis. She and my mom got kind of tight, too.

I had a couple of friends, but we seldom did anything in the fashion of playing. Who had the time to play with so much real life going on in the hood?

My mom tried as best she could to hide the fact that she was struggling to pay her bills. That was one good thing about Cecil. He was a mean hustler, one who piggy-backed on the streets day and night until he came up with something, and he made sure the bills were paid. I think because he made things happen was one of the reasons why my mother cared so much about him.

One morning we found out where Cecil had disappeared to. It was a school morning and Marvin and I had gotten up to prepare ourselves.

Sometime during the night, I think God and his wife started fighting and rain pounded the earth relentlessly with Mrs. God's tears. That's what I was told anyway, that when it rains God is beating up his wife. Maybe it was the devil beating up his wife and her tears were actually the rain that we saw. Whichever tall tale was correct it was another story altogether. It was a fact whoever was fighting must've decided to go at it all night because it rained nonstop.

Ordinarily, Marvin and I wouldn't have a problem with the rain, but we had to go to school and with it pouring down like cats and dogs. We were bound to get soaked and wet before we made it there. Who wanted to be sitting in a classroom all wet trying to pay attention to a teacher pounding your head with the chronology of American history?

We would be doing more sneezing and coughing than paying attention to what was being taught. So, we had to grab our raincoats, which in actuality were plastic bags. They worked fine because of the way my mom used to do them. She would simply poke holes in the top of the plastic bags so we could slip our heads through and that was our shield from the rain.

She also had remedies to keep our feet dry. All she did was tie some plastic bags around our shoes to keep our feet inside and that was it. We had on full homemade rain gear! Mind you it wasn't the best, but for the most part, it kept us from getting wet. On this particular day, she was nowhere to be found. I was thinking maybe she wanted us to stay home which wasn't a problem with me or Marvin, but that wasn't it. I finally found my mom sitting in the kitchen sobbing.

"Mommy, what's da matter?" I asked cautiously. She looked at me and then buried her face in my chest. Still crying she sobbed, "Cecil, ... he in jail!"

A HUSTLER'S MIND MADE UP

I kissed my mom on the jaw before we parted ways. Marvin and I walked to our classes to learn our lessons and my mom left the school in a hurry. I already knew why she was trying to get back home. She didn't mention it to us but I know she wanted to make it there so she could be home when Cecil called from the county jail.

I had to walk Marvin to his class first or else my mom would beat my butt. She would always give us safety precautions for everything from how to escape a fire, to how to protect ourselves. from strangers, and everything else in between. After I was sure Marvin was safe and sound, I went on about my business.

I thought I heard his teacher say something to me like, "Why is Marvin late?" I wasn't sure what she was saying and to be totally frank I really didn't care. Whatever she was saying just went in one ear and out the other. Man, I didn't have time to be trying to explain what already was self-explanatory. "Why do she think we're late?" I thought. "We don't have a freakin car!"

We were poor and on top of that it was raining cats and dogs. I was hoping she would let us chill out! Perhaps she would have if it had not been for the fact that Cecil was in jail and now, she had to make moves on her own to make ends meet. She already had enough to deal with and she didn't want to be bothered with kids pulling on her shirt tail every five minutes for this and for that.

I walked through the halls and headed to my class. I was taking my own sweet time to get there because I had to think about some things. The halls of Orchard Villa Elementary School were empty, with the exception of the rain that blew in the hallways from the strong wind as well as the water dripping down from the old roof, but other than that it was empty.

Within minutes I was standing at my classroom door ripping the plastic bag off my body. I could tell the class had already started because my teacher was calling roll. I walked in any way and headed for my seat, but before I could sit down the teacher called me. I saw her pointing her finger at me.

"May I have a word with you, Mr. Campbell?" she said, holding her index finger up to her face and twirling it for me to come to her.

I already knew what she wanted. It was time for her to quiz me again and give me the success and failure speech. I had heard the same speech a million times. What I didn't know was what I was going to tell her. I walked over to her desk with rainwater dripping from my head and nose. I could feel the other students watching me and I could hear them snickering, "Mrs. Tate, get 'em!"

Mrs. Tate was a tall, white woman with blonde hair. She acted like she grew up around blacks, or maybe she just had really good teaching skills in the area of dealing with her black students. Mrs. Tate was a no-nonsense woman when it came to teaching her students. Most people believed she really wanted to do all she could to make sure we learned something each and every day.

"Mr. Campbell," she said sternly, looking me dead in the center of my face, "... do we have a problem with you getting to school on time?" she asked with an attitude. I nodded my head no.

"Well, why don't you tell me why it is that since you've started coming to school you've been late two out of five days a week?"

I shrugged my shoulders saying I don't know. In my head I said to myself when I get up in the morning, I have to make sure my brother and I are groomed, pick out our clothes, iron them, if need be, make a mental observation of the frame of mind my mother is in before I head off to school, and don't you see it's raining today?

"Well, I'm going to have a talk with your mom and see what the problem is, you can have a seat for now," she said sarcastically. I was about to walk away when Mrs. Tate realized she had one more question to ask me. She called me back to her desk.

"And by the way, Mr. Campbell, I would like to know what you are planning to be when you grow up?" she asked in a tone of voice like she was demanding an answer.

I was so thrown off balance. I thought that it was a trick question, by the way, her eyes were glued to me. If she was expecting an answer right, then and there she had another thing coming because I didn't have an answer for that question either. In fact, up until she asked me, I had never even given it any serious thought. It was a good question, though. I thought ... "What in the world am I going to be? A junky, a notorious jack-boy, or this high-class drug dealer all the youngsters in the hood would love to try to be like?" The thought of a doctor, lawyer, or some other prestigious professional never crossed my mind.

Mrs. Tate grabbed me by the face and irritably said, "Well, you better get it together, buster! Now go have a seat."

My mother would usually be waiting at the door right after school, but when the bell rang, and I didn't see her I knew right then Marvin and I were going to have to walk home by ourselves. My mother knew we could walk home alone. I guess when she came that was her way of spending some quality time with us.

All the other children burst out the classroom to meet their parents or guardians and I walked out to grab Marvin. When I got to Marvin's class he was sitting outside the door, and when he didn't see our mom with me his face balled up in a knot.

"Where is mommy?" he asked, confused, and disappointed. "I
don't know, let's go," I said sternly, picking up his book bag.

For a minute I thought it was going to rain forever but no sooner than we stepped outside the schoolhouse the rain stopped. There wasn't even a drizzle. The skies cleared up in a matter of seconds and just like magic the day turned from ugly to beautiful. The only thing that was left behind to show Mother Nature had been in the hood were big holes everywhere with inches of water in them and a rainbow that stretched from here to the other side of the world. Its colors were beautiful and Immaculate.

As Marvin and I walked home I could remember thinking to myself how I wish I could follow that rainbow away from my lowly conditions and away from my lowly state of mind, but I knew that was merely a dream. Much like the idea of me someday escaping the hardship I was forced to endure day in and day out in the ghetto. It wasn't a military secret, I still had Cecil's image replaying over and over in my mind of how he stood over my mother almost punching her to death. I wondered if one day he would do just that and kill her.

By the time we approached our apartment we noticed a lot of people standing out in front of the building. People were everywhere. At first, it looked like someone was fighting, but as we got closer, we noticed a number of people picking over our clothing and furniture. My heart dropped and to make it worse some of them were people we knew very well. I thought, "What the heck is goin' on?"

The front door of our apartment was wide open, and I could see two men toting stuff out and throwing it on the ground. We didn't have very much but what little we did have we cherished. Right, then I knew we were being evicted. I wondered where my mother or her friend Francis were.

When we didn't see them, we stayed across the street and watched our belongings disappear right before our teary eyes. We were too embarrassed to go and tell people to leave our stuff alone. We just wanted to wait until our mother returned.

Besides being embarrassed, I was mad as well. Tears started rolling down my face as I thought of my teacher's question of what I wanted to be when I grew up. I wished she was here to see what was happening to me while she was somewhere living a perfect life. One thing was for certain, I told myself with sincerity as tears continued rolling down my face that when I get older this was never going to happen again.

Whatever it took, whatever I had to do, and whenever I got old enough to have a family on my own, they would never have to go through this. My family will have the best life has to offer because I am going to provide for them to the best of my ability. If I have to sell drugs, rob, or kill then so be it. Well maybe not kill. It's just that my tears blurred my vision and my reasoning to the point where I was forced to think crazy. I could no longer see the people attacking our belongings like a hungry pack of wolves attacking bloody meat. I visualized Cecil getting his hustle on as what caused the Miami SWAT team to raid our house. Then out of nowhere a song started playing in my head that confused me.

"I'm yo mama, I'm yo daddy, I'm that nigga in the alley, I'm yo doctor when you need, want some coke, have some weed, you know me, I'm your friend, yo main boy thick and thin, I'm yo pusher man." I used to always hear Cecil play that tape and he sang it all the time like it was his.

Okay, my teacher also asked me about college, but from that point, I knew I wasn't going to any darn college. I had other pressing matters to tend to. I started thinking I could sit back and let the currents of the ghetto life sweep me away or I could grab ghetto life up and fashion it to work for me and my family.

I was a kid wrapped up in this lifestyle just like any other kid who was a product of his environment, and I wasn't about to sit around any longer and let this condition handcuff me. Okay, teacher, now you do the math. "Come on Marvin let's bail," I said, wiping the tears from my eyes. My eyes burned with anger but now my heart was crying. I bit my lips so hard blood started oozing out. That's just how mad I was.

We were just about to walk off to go to our grandmother's house, but before we could get started my mom's friend Francis pulled to the curve where we were standing. She was driving this dull, red Chevrolet. I think it was a Caprice Classic. She was acting like it was all good. It was like as soon as I saw her, she made me feel better. I even squeezed Marvin's hand with excitement when I realized we were going to be riding in the car with her.

"Come on y' all. Get in. Queen told me to pick y' all up from school. I was just about to head that way."

"Where is our mama," Marvin asked. He was still crying but that didn't stop us from moving in the direction of the car.

"Sonny, I know you ain't been crying," Francis asked in her old upbeat voice that seemed to never be broken or down.

I looked over at her thinking, "Nah, I ain't been crying." I had other thoughts, too. They got derailed at times, but it wasn't like I couldn't ever get back to them. I was thinking that one thing I could say about Francis was that she had character and spunk. Or did I mention that already? Well, it's worth mentioning again. She was always smiling, and she kept something to say, even if it was with a slick tongue. She had the words to somehow make you feel better even in the worst of situations.

"No, I ain't been crying," I said, lying through my teeth.

"Yes, you were," Marvin Interjected, trying to bust me out.

I couldn't let him put me out there like that, so I spoke up and said, "Bro stop lyin'!" I looked at him as seriously as I could. I was like, "Damn, Marvin, chill out. You know I can't be exposed like that." I think I had a crush on Francis and that was the whole deal.

"Now, Sonny, I done told you baby, no crying. Things gonna be alright you just gotta be tough, strong, and bold. Don't take it personal. One day everything is all jacked up and the next thing you know, you sittin' on top of the world," she said.

Right, then I broke down. I confessed to her like I was sitting in the back of the police car trying to cop a plea.

"Yes, Francis... I was crying because I love my mother. I know she is a good person, and she does everything that she could for us. It just hurts me to know that a person can have a mother that loves them so much... and have an addiction so bad that it has us living in such hard times. But I love my mother because no matter how hard times get, she has never given up on us or ever abandoned us," I said between sobs. My words were broken but Francis understood exactly what I was saying.

"I know that baby that's why I try as best as I can to help my friend."

The little pep talks Francis had with me and Marvin as she drove us to our grandfather Ira's house seemed to rejuvenate us a little, but it wasn't like we had totally forgotten about everything. Being kicked out wasn't one of those things you could erase just like that. That's something that will stick with you for the rest of your life. Seeing all of your family's worldly possessions thrown in a big pile into the street and all types of people picking over it like it's a part of a free rummage sale was traumatic.

I noticed that she was taking another route to my grandparents' house. I wasn't familiar with the way she was going but I wasn't about to ask. I figured wherever she was taking us it would be like child's play compared to what my grandma had in store for us.

My Uncle Marvin stayed in a condo on One-Hundred Thirty-Fifth Street and Twenty-Seventh Avenue. It was a nice three-story building with a pool downstairs. The inside was wall to wall carpet. There were two large bedrooms, a microwave, central air conditioning, and some types of furniture our eyes hadn't seen before. He had a girlfriend named Brenda.

Brenda was beyond beautiful. She was a gorgeous shade of pecan tan with long, wavy hair that made her look as if she had Indian in her blood. She was what they called a brick house. She was so fine that she would make your face frown when you saw her beauty. I said to myself while I fantasized, "One day I'm going to take Brenda from my Uncle." Damn, she was the bomb!

HOPING IN ONE HAND WHILE SH***ING IN THE OTHER

Other than being in a new home and a new environment, Marvin and I couldn't help but feel like we were in paradise while living at our Uncle Marvin's house. I mean everything was super flawless and complimentary.

There was a remote control for the TV and one for the Sony entertainment center that was surrounded by a cherry oak unit. There was even a phone for every part of the house, including the bathroom. Let's just kick the boo-boo here, my Uncle Marvin had it going on. Compared to how we were living I'd say he was living in paradise.

My uncle gave us the royal treatment and everything that was within reach was ours for the taking. If we wanted it, we could grab it.

My Uncle Marvin laid down his rules. There was no staying up after two a. m. in the morning, eat only in the dining room, no crying about things you can't do anything about, and if you try that mess you pulled on Ira, I'm going to beat your little behind. My Uncle Marvin warned us, and if you abide by those rules you could swim in the pool for as long as you liked. When he said something about the pool a big smile came across our faces. "Uncle Marvin, can we get in the pool now?" I exclaimed.

"Oh Yeah!" he responded.

Marvin and I couldn't wait to get out the door. Before we got outside, we didn't have on anything but our underwear, Superman and Batman trousers to be exact. I got to the pool first and hit the prettiest swan dive that you ever saw. It was like I was floating in the air. Marvin hit the pool next, well he jumped in the pool and clung onto the side from there, and then to our surprise, my Uncle Marvin hit that thang.

He dove in with all his clothes on. That was the funniest thing in the world to us and Brenda was laughing her side off, too. We had so much fun that I wished I could put the entire event in a bottle and save it for rough times.

We still hadn't seen our mom, but we knew wherever she was she was trying to get things back together. She had her hands full, too, because she had to get our home back and plus get Cecil out of jail. I thought about Cecil and how he was making out, but it wasn't like it was something I dwelled on. In one way I was saying that's good for him and the other I was just numb. The very next day we were woken up by the sounds of our mother's voice.

"Sonny... Marvin... y'all get up and come see ya momma," my mom shouted like a lioness calling her cubs.

My eyes popped open to see Marvin hot tailing into the front room. He didn't even hit me to let me know he was gone. I was a little drowsy, but I was aware of what was going on. The first thing that came to my mind was she was coming to pick us up and take us to our grandmother's house. I couldn't think of why she changed her mind in the first place. The only thing I could think of was my Uncle Marvin must've told her he didn't want us staying at his house and for her to come and pick us up.

Man, that dumb crap I did by stealing those twenty dollars from my Uncle Ira really caused a lot of problems! Anyway, I almost burst out crying when I thought my mom was there to pick us up but remembering what my Uncle Marvin said I tried to keep my composure. Rubbing my eyes, I hopped out of bed with a breach of disappointment in my heart and headed to the front room.

"Sonny," I heard my mother scream again before I made it where she was.

Marvin was already sitting in my mother's lap just laughing and giggling like it was all good. From the looks of it, he had no idea Uncle Marvin had sold us out.

"Come on in here, baby boy," my Uncle Marvin said with a devilish grin on his face.

"Hey baby, you alright?" my mother asked with a funny smile on her face.

I nodded my head that I was alright as I waited for her to drop the bomb on us.

"Look, babe, y'all momma gotta lot of things to take care of so Marvin gone let y'all stay here for the summer ... unless y'all wanna stay at your grandma's," my mom said.

"No Ma... I wanna stay with you," Marvin yelled, clinging to my mother's neck.

"I know, babe, but I gotta get some things together first. Okay?" I shook my head yeah.

"So, when you gonna be finished, Ma?" Marvin asked.

"It won't take me long. And I left some money with Marvin for y'all to buy some stuff."

"And I gave it right back to her, believe dat," my uncle interrupted all proud like.

"Cause dese are my little nephews and dey uncle gone make sure they're straight. Ai,n't dat right, Sonny Boy?" Uncle Marvin said, shooting me a look as if he knew that I was thinking he sold us out.

I had this askew look on my face like I was saying my bad. He still had that devilish grin on his face. Only this time it melted me like a piece of chocolate. All I could do was smile from ear to ear.

"So that's it?" I thought. We were going to be chillin' like villains up in the condo for the summer. It's on and popping now!

"If y'all need me, I'mma be staying at Jean's house. And Sonny, you look out for your lil brother. Don't let him get in no trouble."

"Trouble, what trouble? Girl, these are my nephews and I keep telling you as long as dey wit me dey straight! Cause I'll kill anybody if the put their hands on anyone of 'em, especially Marvin," Uncle Marvin said, pointing at Marvin.

"Chill", please boy," Brenda murmured, getting up and walking back into the bedroom.

Marvin kept holding on to my mother's coat tail. When he found out he wasn't going with her for real he burst out crying.

With summer coming to an end, I couldn't believe that time could slip by us so quickly, but it did. When we looked around not only had two months come and gone but school was right around the corner, and just like that, all our fun was over. All the swimming in my Uncle Marvin's pool, all the fancy eating at Burger King and McDonald's, all the watching cable TV and the late-night shows... was over just like that. I couldn't believe it!

What blew my mind the most was when our mother showed up at our uncle's house with Cecil wrapped around her arm like a piece of paper wrapped around like a lollipop.

IT MUST'VE BEEN AN ANGEL

The first thing I noticed when we got downstairs was that Cecil had a new car. I believe it was a Delta '88, blue with light blue bucket seats. When we got in the car, Marvin was sitting in between them asking them both all kinds of questions.

"Dis yo car, Cecil?" he asked. Cecil smiled nodding his head yes. Marvin kept firing questions at him.

"When did you get *out* of jail, Cecil? Are we going to yo house, Cecil?" Marvin asked all excited. Before Cecil could get his groove back my mom intervened.

"Boy, stop asking all these questions," she barked. Cecil and my mom were laughing at him like crazy and telling him to sit back. He would listen to them for a minute and then the next minute he'd be right back at it.

"Dis yo car, Cecil? You gone take us to da dive in?" he stammered.

"Man, that's drive in," I corrected him.

Like I was saying, everybody was happy so what in the world was my problem? Cecil was home with a new car, new clothes, and it looked to me like he even had a new attitude. Right? Yeah, right. Well, it's like this, I knew Cecil was a tiger and I knew a tiger never changed his stripes.

In fact, the whole problem I had with him was I kept seeing this image in my mind of him with blood in his eyes and death in his face that night he was beating on my mom. I just knew he was trying to kill her, and the fact that he hadn't succeeded was what made me think he'd do it again. The only difference being that the next time he might accomplish his goal. I believe he knew how I felt, and the way he kept avoiding making eye contact with me was all the proof I needed. What made it so bad was when he did say something to me his words seemed coaxed, forced, or reluctant.

"Isn't She Lovely," by Stevie Wonder was playing on the radio and Cecil was singing the words to my mother like she was the best thing that ever happened to him in his life. He was just popping his fingers, bobbing his head from side to side, and grinning like a Cheshire Cat. I thought to myself, "He got the con game on lock."

Marvin was clapping and rocking to the beat like he was a part of the Commodores and there I was sitting looking like I had rocks in my jaws. What tripped me *out* the most was the fact that Cecil stuttered badly, but as long as he was singing, he never once did. I tried to hold it in, but I couldn't do anything but burst *out* laughing. I don't know what it was, but it must've been an angel. To be truthful, it really felt good to laugh in the thick of all the love, hate, good, bad and ugly.

Cecil drove us to our new neighbourhood. He was talking all about the new place we had, and I couldn't wait to see how it looked. The way he was talking was like it had something on Uncle Marvin's house, and I just wanted to see what it was going to be like.

Who were going to be our friends, how were our new neighbours, and would we after a while get kicked out like we did before? Those were the questions in the back of my mind that I didn't have the slightest answer to, and I had a feeling neither did Cecil or my mother. When I saw all the brick houses, I thought, "Okay, Cecil might have something."

At least we were moving in a house this time and not some shady projects, but right in the middle of my thought Cecil hooked a right turn onto Fifty-

Third Street and pulled into the driveway of a set of beige duplexes, right across the street from Grandway Supermarket.

Marvin and I had our own room and my mother and Cecil had theirs. The other room was for my sisters. I don't know about anybody else, but I was impressed. I thought Cecil really out did himself this time.

"Sonny, is you going to help us bring the stuff in the house or stand there gazing all day?" my mom asked me, waking me out of my daze. "Sonny, here... take dis lamp and put it in my room," she said, pointing in the direction of her room. I took the lamp out of her hand and before I could walk the lamp to the bedroom and absorb my new home, I heard Cecil's voice call out, "Sonny, come ride up here on Fifteenth Avenue with me!"

"What, me?" I thought, pointing to myself asking him with a mere gesture. Was he actually talking to me? I was hoping he wasn't because he was the last person I wanted to be riding alone with. I was thinking he was gonna take me somewhere and kill me.

"Yeah, come ride witcha stepdaddy. We gone go hang out on the Ave for a minute."

Sweat broke out on my forehead and I wiped it away with the back of my hand. I was so nervous I had to catch myself from outright saying no to him.

There's no going fast or going slow here about my nerves because they were doing their own thing. Every breath I took, as Cecil and I took the back roads to Fifteenth, was a calculated one.

I didn't know when it was going to come but I was just waiting for him to mention something about me going to get my grandmother on him that night. I already knew what I was going to say, "you were trying to kill my momma. What you think, I'mma just stand there?" The mood seemed subtle between us, sometimes shifting and other times standing still. At most, I watched him out of the corner of my eyes singing blissfully and popping his fingers to the radio like it was all good, but I never let my guard down.

"Woo super fly, you gonna make your money bye and bye, Bu if you lose don't ask no question why, cause the game you know is to survive," he sang in his own broken melody.

It became more confusing. I started thinking that maybe he had forgotten about the whole incident and wasn't sweating it. I wasn't certain what his angle was but I'm telling you I still wasn't about to let my guard down. I had already made my mind up that if he tried something I was going to jump out the car and take off running. I hope he didn't think I didn't know the route because I knew the area we were in and knew it wouldn't take me but a hot second to find my Aunt Jean's house.

Cecil brought his car to a smooth halt in front of a store called Mr. Wonderful. There was an older cat sitting on a stack of milk crates just outside the door of the store with a cool cap on. There were black faces, seemingly from all walks of ghetto life, hustling and bustling to the ghetto's simplistic pace.

There were light and dark-complexioned brothers and sisters, some short, others tall, and some in between. They were everywhere, convicts, beauties, and beasts all doing their own thing. It took me a minute to find out what the lick was, but it hit me when I saw dudes running to their stash spots and coming back to serve their customers. I knew then that we were in a dope hole, and not just any drug hole. This one was the infamous Fifteenth Avenue. No, wait, let me put that in a more diplomatic term, it was "THE FIFTEENTH AVE."

Fifteenth Avenue was the main strip in Miami. Everybody who was somebody walked the thin lines of love and hate on Fifteenth. Some of the unruliest women you ever wanted to see and some of the most ruthless killers you ever heard of hustled on this avenue. If anybody was somebody they were there and if anybody was trying to be somebody, they were somewhere around there, too. The thing about Fifteenth was it was like an old bottle of whiskey, never a dry moment.

"Wwwwaait, right heeere, Sonny," Cecil stuttered, hopping out the car. "I'mma holla, atttt Mr. Wonderful!"

As soon as Cecil got out of the car and walked to the man sitting on the crate, I started observing my surroundings with a more detailed interest. I had never actually been on Fifteenth before, but I heard about what went on up here. I had just never seen the place up close and personal like I was today. Since I was planning on being a hustler when I grew up, trying to learn as much as I could, was a prerequisite.

Things were moving fast, too. At first, I noticed Cecil and the older cat he described as Mr. Wonderful embrace each other warmly with their smiles, lightening up the block. The next thing I know they disappeared in the store and the hustler mode that was dwelling in me kicked into full gear. I thought I better watch Cecil's back, so I got out of the car and looked up and down the Ave for the police.

CHAPTER THREE

POETIC INJUSTICE

I wasn't out of the car a hot minute before Cecil came back out of the store with this urgent look on his face. He was walking briskly, so I assumed he had handled his business.

"Booooi, what chu doing out da car?" Cecil nervously stammered as soon as he got in. He ordered me to get inside the car, too. Both of us slammed the doors and locked the locks as well. Cecil always told us to lock our car doors.

"I was looking out for the police," I said, looking as serious as I could. All Cecil did was laugh.

"What's funny," I asked.

"What's funny is boi whatchu know 'bout watching somebody's back?"

"I know a lot," I said to him.

"Yeah, I know what you know a lot of," he said sarcastically, passing me the bomb and told me to stuff it down my pants until we got home.

I quickly did what he said and stuffed the package down my pants. I never questioned Cecil's authority or second-guessed his decision to have me ride with the drugs instead of him. All I thought was that his reason was primarily based on my presumption of innocence. If we were to get stopped by the police the last place, they would think to look for drugs was down the pants of a ten-year-old, and that's what tripped me out the most. In Cecil's logic, I was too young to watch his back but old enough to hide his drugs.

We pulled into the driveway and Cecil shut the car off. We were just about to exit the vehicle before Cecil remembered he had to get his drugs from me. The mission was complete and now it was time for him to cover his tracks. He couldn't let my mother know he had used me for his personal mule, at least that's what he murmured under his breath. I had thought as well, and I wasn't exactly ashamed to say it.

"Cecil, I can help you sell yo drugs if you let me," I said out the clear blue sky as we got out of the car. Cecil just looked at me crazily and shook his head. He had this look on his face like boy be for real. He just didn't know I was more serious than a heart attack.

The next day when Marvin and I awoke, Cecil and my mother were nowhere to be found. The first thing we did was raid the kitchen area. There were all kinds of cereal on top of the refrigerator and a brand-new box of Hungry Jack pancake mix in the cabinet. Marvin was dying to get his mouth around a bowl of Frosted Flakes, and I couldn't wait to smash some flapjacks. I went off I cooked five golden flapjacks for myself, stewed them down with syrup, and went to work. Marvin hooked up a giant bowl of cereal. It didn't take him long to eat a half a box of cereal and it didn't take me long to eat all of those pancakes by myself. The next step for us was to tour our new neighborhood, find out if there were any children around our age we could play with.

As soon as we finished eating, we put on our clothes. Marvin put on a pair of dungarees and a t-shirt, and I threw on a pair of cut off shorts with a tank top. We walked up and down our street, down the back street, and on up to the Grandway Supermarket. The first thing we realized as we made our way inside the store was it had toys. Lots of toys. Big toys, small toys, and toys we had never ever seen or heard of in our lives. Neither one of us had one nickel to our name but that didn't stop us from shopping in that good ole negro spirit we knew as window shopping, which sometimes turned out to be shoplifting. It was our first day in the store, but it didn't matter because Marvin and I stuffed all kinds of things down our pants. In a matter of days, we must've had every Hot wheel's car they had. We stole so much out of the store that it became a hobby, especially around Christmas time. Man, we racked up.

For some reason or another, the nights were long and the days longer in our new home, but there wasn't any sleeping for me. I was steadily growing, or should I say evolving, into a product of my environment. Each incident turned into a lesson more than anything else, and each lesson I used to help further my understanding about what I had to face one day in life. Like the SWAT incident, I learned to be more observant of my surroundings.

I took notice of everything, even the late-night traffic coming and going in and out of our house. This activity stuck to me the most not only because it told me my mom and Cecil were back up to their old ways again, but because I knew it was directly related to the reason SWAT raided our house in the first place, and I wasn't trying to relive that event again.

I had a trick this time, though. I made it my business to learn getaway routes. I knew whose house I could run to in case of emergencies and the ones to stay away from. There was this old man who lived behind us who acted like he had a crush on my mom. I could go to him anytime, and then there was a lady down the street named Ms. Elaine who stopped us one day when we were leaving Grandway and talked to us about her whole life.

I don't think she was wrapped too tight. Perhaps, but crazy or not she made sure we understood if we ever needed anything we could come to her house. So, I put her on the "to go" list as well. I also knew Grandway had police officers that were ready and willing to take anyone to jail who broke the law. Marvin and I had to find that out the hard way one day because we got caught stealing.

Months passed and our lives were back in full swing. Yes, there was the drug abuse and the fear of the Insurance Man coming to collect whatever was his due, but all I knew was that it was a good thing that we weren't out in the open where people could see us because they would gather from miles around to see the greatest show on earth. There was dope feigns, black queens pushing mad poison into their body parts, and junkies laughing at others gagging yet waiting on their turn to tear their lives apart. That's some poetic injustice for you.

I was sitting in the front yard one day when I noticed two men hanging around our house. I knew I hadn't seen them before and ordinarily, it wouldn't have bothered me except for the fact that even though they weren't wearing the army fatigues like the SWAT men had on that dreadful day, I believed they were up to no good.

Nevertheless, I studied their actions and the expressions they had on their faces closely as I was trying to figure out exactly what they were up to. They looked suspicious, and when I finally realized whatever, it was, they were doing or were about to do was probably bad I decided to make my move. By that time, it was too late as I watched them quickly pull out two guns and run right past me into our house.

All I heard was, "Get down suckas! You know what time it is. It's a jack and don't make it no homicide."

That's all I needed to hear, and I was out, running full speed to Grandway to get the police. When I explained to the black officer, the same one who had caught Marvin and I stealing, what was going on he put me in his patrol car and took me home. This time, I sat in the front seat. It was an experience I'll never forget.

For a fleeting moment or so I felt like a crime fighter on a desperate hunt to arrest the bad guys. We arrived just in time enough to see the two men coming out. When they spotted us, they took off in the opposite direction through the back yard. The police pursued them, but they got away because he didn't have any backup. He radioed in for them, but they hadn't arrived, so he was unable to put on a real chase. Being in a police car chasing someone was kind of fun, though, but all the excitement only lasted a hot minute.

When we got back everyone was standing out on the sidewalk. We cruised up and both of us hopped out. I ran up to my mother to let the officer do his civic duty and he questioned everyone there. He asked everyone there if they knew the two robbers.

Of course, in a black neighbourhood, nobody said anything to him. They didn't care if he was black or not and I never understood that. Someone could rob or kill you and even if they knew who it was, they wouldn't say anything. They waited until he was gone and then went to telling everything amongst themselves. All I heard them say was a short, black man named Happy Tat, was the one who did it. Cecil even vowed to find him and kill him.

Things were crazy that day. In my opinion, I had done my mom and Cecil a favor, but it turned out to work against them. When the policeman started looking around the house, he found small pieces of drugs. He wanted to take my mom and her friend to jail but I pleaded with him not to. Even with all the evidence lying around the officer cut my family a break and didn't arrest any of them.

That night I fell into a deep sleep and all of a sudden, I saw a bright light flash before my eyes. It was more like a flame, one that looked like it was coming out the end of one of those M-16 assault rifles being fired by one of those guys from the SWAT Task Force. I knew it was strange, but even though my eyes were closed I witnessed the light. Not only that but seconds later I heard a boom like sound and something crackling. It was so loud I woke in a cold sweat scared to death. Talk about paranoid? I was that and shell-shocked, too. I thought whatever it was that was going on outside was coming to get me. Moments later I looked out of the window of my bedroom and saw the large tree in the backyard split in half. I was relieved to know that the light I saw was lightning and the noise was the thunder.

After that, it was back to living from one day to the next. I admit the days still seemed long and the nights longer, but I was making the best of everything. I kept remembering my uncle's words whenever something happened that I didn't have control over, "No crying about things you can't do anything about."

That rule helped me overcome a lot of stuff in my life like Cecil and my mother's drug addiction and all the high and low points that came along with it.

IN THE REAL WORLD YOU HAVE TO BE YOUR OWN MAGICIAN

Christmas was right around the corner, but instead of wrapping gifts and singing Christmas carols we were packing our belongings and trying to figure out where in the world we were going to sleep. The landlord wanted us out of his place and off his property ASAP, no ifs, ands, or buts about it.

"Y'all get y'all junk and go!" he bellowed, before walking out the front door and slamming it in our faces.

Dude was so hot at my mom and Cecil that he refused to change his mind even after they tried to sweet talk him out of it. He wasn't buying it! He wasn't about to listen to any sob stories about how it's cold outside, hear my mom tell him about her having children and needing a home and he definitely didn't want to hear anything about it was Christmas time especially when he was a Sunni Muslim. In fact, Cecil was a Sunni Muslim, too, but even their religious bonds weren't enough to change his mind.

All he kept saying was how many chances he had given us and how the robbery was the last straw. The funny part about it was he and Cecil used to kick it when we first moved around here. Cecil even used to talk behind the man's back about how stupid he was! At one point I thought he was getting high too, by the way, he used to come to see Cecil late at night, but apparently, that wasn't the case and tonight he was showing Cecil that there was a thin line between friendship and business.

With it being so sudden we didn't have any place to go. Cecil was talking about staying at a hotel for a couple of days, but my mom was against it. She kept telling him that she didn't want her children staying in a room like they were thrown away.

"Well, where else we gone go?" Cecil asked impatiently.

"We can go stay at my father's house."

"Yo ... yo ... dad, daddy's house?" Cecil questioned as his voice rose.

"Yeah," my mom replied.

"Girl whatchu tryna do get me cursed out? Ya... ya know yo momma don't like me." Cecil sternly stated.

"Boi, my momma, and daddy ain't thinkin' about you. Besides, dey don't even stay dere," she snapped back as Cecil just shook his head.

My mom made a phone call to let whoever was at the house know we were on our way. I don't know who it was she was talking to, but whoever it was made clear that they didn't want us anywhere near there. They were arguing back and forth, and Cecil had his ear to the receiver trying as best he could to listen to what was being said, but my mom kept pushing him away. I didn't know what was going on, but I could tell whoever it was my mom was talking to was telling her things she didn't want to hear.

Until today I never heard my mom curse the way she was cursing. She was cursing up a storm and telling somebody she was going to kick their butt when she got there. Then all of a sudden, she just hung up the phone and told us to bring our little butts on. It was evident that she was hot and for the next few minutes nobody, not even Cecil, uttered a word to her.

He even knew when my mom was mad about something it was always best to let her cool down before you said something to her because when she got mad, she just started throwing everything. We didn't even talk amongst ourselves. Everybody was just silent and looked stupid until my little sisters went off. They must've sensed that something was wrong, and they started screaming and crying as loud as they could.

For a minute everything was chaotic. The landlord kept yelling to make sure we were leaving. At the same time, Cecil was hollering at me and Marvin talking about how we needed to get ourselves together like we were the ones on drugs and the cause of this mess. I could've told him a thing or two, but I just kept sucking my teeth instead. My mom kept making these strange faces like she was auditioning for a gangster movie.

The drive there was the worst. The smoke from Cecil's cigarette was choking us half to death and not to mention how we were crammed inside his car like sardines. My two sisters, Tiffany, and Cecelia were sitting in the front seat and me and Marvin were jammed up against the right door next to all kinds of other stuff like lamps, clothes, and whatever else could fit in the back seat with us.

"Man, ya squashing me," Marvin complained.

"Sonny, scoot ova some, it's enough room back dere," my mom said.

"Ma, I'm ova as far as I can go," I whined, looking at Marvin. He was acting comical, so I had to laugh at him.

So, here we were again, on our way to a new residence. Everyone called my mom's family's house The Green House because it was the only greenhouse in the neighborhood. Cecil wasn't the only one who didn't want to go there. Marvin and I didn't want to go either but we didn't say anything. We let Cecil do all the complaining. I mean, since he could get away with saying whatever it was, he wanted to say to my mother, why not let him stick his neck out there? That's if you could understand what he was trying to say in the first place.

You really had to get used to Cecil's speech impediment. My mother surely was used to it. She could understand everything he said no matter how bad he said it. I don't know what his real reason was for not wanting to go to The Green House, but I know what mine was. I was just sick and tired of seeing everybody live to get high. I even wondered what reason I had to keep waking up every day only to watch misery spin around like a DJ mixing up a hit on his turntable.

THE GREEN HOUSE

When we got to The Green House my Aunt Sheryl was sitting on the porch looking crazy at us.

"I don't know why y'all come round here," she barked at the top of her lungs. She was waving her arms frantically and making all kinds of crazy gesticulations with her body.

"Sheryl, ya don't run nothin' round here," my mom yelled, hopping out the car and running towards the porch where my aunt was standing. By the time she got there my aunt ran inside and slammed the door behind her and right in my mom's face.

"Sheryl! Open dis door! I'mma beat you down when I get in dere! Ya betta not come out," my mom screamed and shouted.

My mom continued to scream as she banged on the door and windows. We watched her bang on the door for a minute, arguing back and forth with my aunt until she decided she wasn't getting anywhere. That's when she ran off the porch and headed to the side of the house. I didn't know what she was going to do, but I knew once she got her hands on my aunt it was on and popping because my mom didn't play. Cecil might be able to beat her down, but another female didn't have anything coming.

None of us knew exactly what she was going to do once she got inside, but the one who needed to be concerned about that was my aunt.

"Man, I don't even know why Queen just don't go to a hotel," Cecil murmured unenthusiastically.

He was just about to say something else until we heard my mother screaming and shouting again. It sounded like they were tearing up the whole house. I heard all kinds of stuff being thrown around and curse words I'd never heard before coming out my mom and aunt's mouths. My mom could cuss like a sailor when she wanted to. She had that kind of voice that would make you cringe if she cursed you out.

Cecil hit the horn for her to come out when all of a sudden, all the commotion stopped. We were wondering what was going on, but suddenly my mother appeared in the doorway like a magician waving for us to come in. Her shirt was barely on as it had been ripped pretty badly. She was trying to fix herself up and as soon as she twisted her blouse back around, she was good to go. She attempted to fix her hair, too, as she disappeared back into the house.

To me, the house was immaculate in its own right. It was nothing like the glamorous homes in Beverly Hills, but when you compared it to the low-income housing projects or any other place, we lived it was the most spacious piece of property out of them all.

My grandfather was a preacher; a prominent preacher I might add. The Reverend Ira. T. McCall was his name, and he had a reputation for doing big things like having one of the fattest cribs in the neighborhood. As far as I knew there wasn't a house around in the vicinity of the ghetto that could touch his. It wasn't my first time at the house, I had been there plenty of times. Every time I went there, I was just awed by its size and beauty.

When you entered through the front door, like we did, you would walk directly into the front room. This was the sitting quarters where everybody would mostly sit around doing whatever came to mind like watching television, talking, or doing drugs. Yeah, they did drugs here too, at least that's what I was told. I would find out for myself in due time.

It was the perfect spot since my grandmother had her own apartment and granddaddy stayed in the back. They had plenty of time and space to do their thing. I hadn't seen them do any drugs there, but since we were staying there now, I was pretty sure I would. I couldn't wait either. I was particularly dying to see my Uncle Marvin. Marvin and I hadn't seen him since we were at his apartment, and I were especially dying to see if what my mom said about him was true. She told me one day when I asked to go stay with him that my Uncle Marvin was shooting the lights out, meaning he was on drugs too. She told us he had even lost his apartment and Brenda as well.

I just knew my mother was lying on my Uncle Marvin and just trying to keep me from asking her could we go stay with him. I mean, I respected. my mom's call, but perhaps she didn't know him the way me and Marvin did. He was a trooper, one who was smooth as silk and cool as ice.

I felt the front room was the most charming part of the house. Itseemed to be filled with lots of memories and love. Everywhere you looked you saw portraits of my mom and her sisters and brothers when they were young smiling or laughing into the camera and decked out in all kinds of old-fashioned clothes.

What intrigued me the most about The Green House, though, was how it sat on the corner of Eighth Avenue and Sixty-Eighth Street, right dead smack in the middle of the ghetto, in front of a dirt road.

Well, actually it was a path that led from the village. That's "THE VILLAGE", not your everyday living quarters but a complex better known for housing some of the most notorious African Americans that ever walked the ghetto. Those included killers, gangsters, bandits, and even more killers, bandits, and gangsters.

At the time, my Aunt Sheryl and my Uncle Walter lived in the front part of The Green House. We took the Florida room because it was the only place that was big enough for us. There were six of us altogether, but we fit in there comfortably. It was already furnished, including wall to wall carpet, and except for a few haves and have nots it was perfect.

We just laid all the stuff we had out in various places, and all the other stuff we had that couldn't fit we stashed in the utility closet. It wasn't until after eleven p.m. before we got settled in and ready for bed. Marvin and I stretched a blanket across us, my mom fixed up a little bed right next to us for my sisters, and the last time I saw my mom and Cecil before I dozedoff, they were cuddled up on the couch together whispering in each other's ear. The next day we woke up to my Aunt Sheryl's voice.

"Y'all getcha lil' tails up," she bellowed forcefully.

It was hard to ignore her voice. When I opened my eyes the first thing, I noticed was that my mom, Cecil, and my sisters were gone. Then I noticed my aunt standing over Marvin and me with all kinds of cleaning stuff in her hand. She had a broom, mop, some towels, and other stuff.

"This is for y'all. Ya momma gone to work and since y'all ain't in school y'all could clean up!" At first, I looked at my aunt stupid like, "Man, l ain't gonna clean-up nothin'." I was thinking we had only been there one night and here she wanted us to clean up already.

"Here, boy! Don't look at me stupid cause I'll whip ya lil tail", she threatened," ... and wake Marvin up too," my Aunt Sheryl said, walking away and twitching her butt like she was the finest thing in the world.

It took everything inside of me not to tell her I wasn't cleaning up nothing, but before I could say anything I heard one of my mother's golden rules echoing in the back of my mind: "Respect your elders, Sonny." That's all I needed to hear. I took the stuff she had and started cleaning up. I was so mad that I didn't wake Marvin up or go brush my teeth. I just went to work all by myself. I swept the front room, mopped, and cleaned the kitchen, cleaned the bathroom, and raked up two trash bags of leaves in the front yard.

Actually, I had only intended to rake the front yard but trying to be nosy and get a look at my grandfather's place, I inadvertently kind of made my way to the back yard. My mom had already told me before we came over here not to bother my grandfather, but I convinced myself that I wasn't bothering him. Technically, I wasn't. I was just raking the yard like I was told to do.

Beads of sweat were protruding off my forehead like crazy. All I was doing was raking and scooping up everything. When I came from around the side of the house, pulling just enough leaves in my rake to fill the rest of the bag up, I noticed a giant standing in the doorway looking at me.

At first, I got a little nervous, even after I realized that the giant was my grandfather. He was staring at me and curiously eyeing me with this smirk on his face looking like what in God's graces is this kid doing back here. I got kind of nervous. The first thing I thought of was my mother's warning, but it was already too late. I had already violated her rule.

"Sonny, is dat you?" My grandfather asked hoarsely. At first, I froze then I nodded my head yes. "Well, come over here son and say hey to ya granddaddy. I ain't seen y'all in a while. I didn't even know y'all was here. Where ya brother? What's his name?"

"Marvin. "

"Yea, Marvin. Where is he?" My grandfather asked, giving me a big hug and kiss on the jaw.

"He in da house sleep," I said, squeaming at the same time, from his loving grip.

"Sleep?" my grandfather asked confused. "Where ya momma at?" he questioned.

"Auntie Sheryl said she went to work."

My grandfather had some yard chairs sitting around so we sat in them and started talking about everything a granddad and grandson could talk about. He drilled me about school, how me and my brother and sisters were getting along, and if Cecil and my mother was still doing drugs. When I told him they were he just shook his head in frustration.

"I done told that girl she gone kill herself one of these days," he said.

He had this shallow look on his face. If his look wasn't enough to make me feel troubled about my mother, his deep, guttural voice that had a sense of urgency in it was. The first thing I thought about was that how I wasn't alone in feeling that my mom was going to kill herself one day. The problem was getting her to see it. I stared into my grandfather's eyes as he talked and talked and talked like I was looking for some kind of gift to come out of his mouth.

It seemed as though sometimes his words registered to me, but I think during most of the conversation we were having I was in my own world. I was thinking about my mother and what exactly would happen to us if something happened to her like death, when all of a sudden, some words came out of my mouth unannounced. "I love you, granddaddy," I said sincerely. My eyes were watery, and I was just short of tears rolling down my face.

When I finished talking to my grandfather, I felt a million pounds lighter, and I ran back to the house to tell Marvin all we had talked about. I was so excited I even forgot to pick up the pile of leaves I raked up. But my elation didn't last long because as soon as I made my way back to the front door I was met by my aunt, the wicked witch of the ghetto.

She was standing in the doorway with this look on her face like she was the evil stepmother here to make life for me and my brother more miserable than it already was. She had her hands propped on her hips, looking, staring, and talking. She barked:

"I don't know where ya been, but you ain't comin' in dis house until you finish raking them leaves up!"

"Granddaddy said I could come in," I pleaded.

"I don't care what he said. You gonna finish!" she snapped back.

Okay, so my aunt was an evil person to treat me like I was her personal slave, but I still had to respect my elders. I figured I wasn't going to let her steal my joy and peace of mind I had gotten from talking to my granddaddy. I just wasn't about to let her do it. I figured she was going to be a problem, but the best way I decided to handle her was to avoid her altogether and act like whatever she said or didn't say didn't faze me. That did little good because it seemed the more, I tried to ignore her the more she bothered me and Marvin. She had even gotten so bad that she started whipping us. One day she was beating us down so bad I broke out and ran. I was trying to run to my other grandfather's house (my father's dad), but she caught me with a few strides and punched me in the face with a combination that knocked me to the ground. She called herself being mad because Marvin and I stopped by the school across the street from where we lived to play some basketball before coming home to clean up. While she was beating me, I was screaming up a storm trying to get her to stop, but she kept on hitting me. I didn't know what her problem was, and I wasn't about to make excuses for her. What I did do was as soon as my mother came home from work, I told her everything she was doing to us. I told her she whipped us, cursed us, made us clean up their mess and punched me in the face.

My mom was hot when I told her that. She was already beefing with her for the way she acted when we came to live there and was just waiting for her to breathe wrong so she could beat her down. Well, she breathed the wrong way by abusing us. I think my aunt was in the bedroom asleep or she would have heard my mom shouting she was going to beat her up.

"Where Sheryl at?" she screamed as I pointed towards the bedroom.

She snatched the telephone receiver out the wall while my aunt was asleep and busted her upside her head with it. Then she beat her down like she stole something.

IF A PICTURE IS WORTH A THOUSAND WORDS…

It was a rainy night in Florida when I saw my whole world flash before my eyes. The rain pounded the Earth's floor unmercifully, and Marvin and I were sitting on the porch with one of our mother's older friends named Alvin, kicking the boo-boo. I'd say Alvin was perhaps in his mid-twenties at the time, but since he hung out at The Green House, he came to do drugs with my family on a regular.

Marvin and I got to know him well. In fact, he was about the only one we talked to. It wasn't that many children in our neighborhood to kick it with so Alvin became our human outlet to our social circle. He used to spend time priming us up for the streets, teaching us the game, and the pros and cons of everyday ghetto life. For the most part, Marvin and I appreciated Alvin. You might even say we had a great admiration for him, a love, or a special bond. He was like our big brother and even though he didn't have much to offer as far as material bliss, he was very valuable to us. He just had one shortcoming; I'm talking about the one that stuck out to us the most. He was a stone cold junkie in every sense of the word. You talk about somebody that liked to get high? Alvin loved it.

Marvin was helping Alvin find a vein when a black Monte Carlo eased up to the curb and someone started calling him from the back seat.

"Hey, Alvin! Come here."

At first, none of us heard him. It was raining so hard, but then the driver blew the horn to get our attention. All of us looked in the car's direction for a split second and then Alvin threw his forearm up, signaling that he was coming. "I'll be right dere," he murmured in a sluggish tone.

I'm thinking, "Man, let them come to you." I wanted to tell Alvin not to go, but I just remained silent. I couldn't say anything. I was too busy watching him stick a needle in his neck, and I'm thinking, "This fool is gonna kill himself one day!"

Alvin started fidgeting for a moment but as soon as he stuck the needle in his neck it was like his whole body laid still. Marvin was still holding his arms so he wouldn't move, and looking at Alvin he was absent minded in the face. He was out of it. At least for a short moment anyway, until he heard the same voice holler out his name for him to come.

Alvin woke out of his daze and looked towards the car. We all looked at the same time. There were four dudes in the car, which was strange because none of them bothered to get out. Alvin started to walk towards the car.

"I'll be right back," he snickered, sniffing his nose. Before he left, he gave Marvin his needle to hold with a stern warning not to let anything happen to it.

I had my eyes on him the whole time. He walked awkwardly, staggering from side to side. He wasn't studying the rain either. He was just moving on about his business as if to ease between the raindrops. As soon as he got to the left back door of the car it happened. It was like as soon as he bent down and peeked his head in the window Marvin and I heard a series of gunshots go off.

At first, they sounded like firecrackers... pop... pop... pop ... pop ..., and then they went simultaneously. There was something about the sound that told me they were more than that. I heard Alvinscreaming, "No! No, G-Boi. Noooo, G-Boi! Don't kill me!"

I was so scared it was crazy. My heart started racing ninety miles an hour, but it still couldn't outrun the car that sped away. It seemed like it just vanished into thin air. It happened so fast that I didn't know what happened to me. I couldn't move and it was like I could barely breathe! I guess I was in shock. That was more than I could say for Marvin because when I looked around for him, he had taken off running.

I heard him screaming inside to somebody, "They shooting Alvin," but I was so out of it I didn't know what else he said. I still had my eyes on Alvin, not knowing what to think or what to do.

The first thing that came to mind was that Alvin was dying by the way he was screaming and crying for mercy. I watched him stagger back to the porch, and he was holding his stomach at the same time. When he got back to the porch, I saw blood spurting out. It was coming out from different holes in his stomach and was pouring down like the rain drops.

Alvin was screaming at the top of his lungs for me to help him, but not only was I stuck on stupid I didn't know what to do other than cry and beg for him not to die.

"Ohhhh help me God," Alvin screamed in agony. "Please don't let me die," he pleaded.

"Queen!" he shouted out my mother's name.

The first face I saw was my mother's when she and Cecil came running to see what was going on. Marvin was running right behind them, but I hardly noticed him. I was too busy trying to deal with the look on my mom's face. She had an immediate sense of panic in her facial expression coupled with the look of horror. I swore after knowing her all my life that I had never seen her look the way she did that night.

"Somebody call 9-1-1," Cecil wailed, holding Alvin's head in his lap. "Ya ... ya ... gone make it... b ... b ... brotha ... Jusss ... jusss… han ... hang in da... da... dere," he stuttered frantically. I kept screaming at the top of my lungs to Cecil not to let Alvin die.

What seemed like forever, but was only a few minutes later, the paramedics came and ushered Alvin away on a stretcher.

I'm telling you it's a lonely game we're playing in this life, hanging on to bliss. When the same faces you see, and love paint a picture of death it gets even lonelier. To watch a mother, uncle, aunt, or friend fight for dear life because they've consumed too much of a drug searching for that ultimate high is mind-blowing. To see death staring right at you and saying to you, in some weird way, "you are next" is extremely scary. I saw myself in Alvin and I saw Alvin in myself.

They say the first high you experience creates an ultimate state of bliss, and every high after that falls short of the state of bliss that one desires to feel. Again, that is why you have to consume so much of the drugs on a second or third time around. What was so appealing about the use of drugs wasn't that it had the power to snuff life out of you in the blink of an eye, but the fact that when other drug users found out that someone overdosed or almost overdosed on them, they wanted to know where the person got the drugs from so they could get some too. If someone overdosed on the drugs that meant the drugs were good, and everybody who did drugs wanted good drugs.

It meant so much to them that if they didn't have money to buy it, they would throw fits, throwing up, and doing just about anything they could do to get their hands on it. I watched my mother walk one of her friends around in the front room in a panic trying to make him drink milk and doing everything in her power to keep them awake. She used to say that if they went to sleep, they would never wake up. They would be on their way to the bye and bye, to that sweet place in the sky. Watching things like that did something to me!

You overdosed if you either used too much drugs or weren't being cautious of the drugs' potency. The thing was if you overdosed you did so because you wanted to. Alvin told us that you had too really be careful. "Don't take it for granted when you go to buy drugs," he would say. Then he would explain to us that the drug dealer would always tell you if the drugs were stronger stuff than his competition, but sometimes you had to use your own judgment.

I think that probably was the situation with my mother and father. Sometimes they had to test the drugs they brought from certain drug dealers to make sure it was good dope. I don't know, maybe or maybe not. I'm just grateful to God because I never saw my mother overdose or do some of the other things, I witnessed dope feigns do to satisfy their addictions.

I learned something else from Alvin and my mother that stuck with me all my life. That was when you thought of dope feigns and junkies you had no other choice but to think of all the other underhanded things that went along with it like prostitution, theft, and doing just about anything you possibly could think of to get high. All junkies weren't bad people and participated in underhanded things to get high.

Consider this contrast if you will. You may have a junkie who can work, or you may have one that has to hustle and just spends every dime they get on drugs, of course, there is a thin line between the two, but the line could be seen from far enough away to differentiate one from the other. I'm speaking in relation to my mother and the good I saw in her.

Granted, my mother was an addict by normal standards, however, she didn't have numerous boyfriends taking their turn on her and she was not doing whatever sexual favor they desired for a fix. She had a decent job, she kept food on the table, and clothes on the backs of her children.

****

To see a friend, get gunned down right in front of you like a dog was demoralizing. I knew I was young and wasn't righteously supposed to be seeing what life was showing me. I was not expected to understand certain things in life, but I used to see images of life and death steadfastly dissolving and evolving like it was nothing. I damn sure understood that something wasn't right. You talking about a picture painted a thousand words, but it may only take two words, black, and ghetto, to paint a thousand pictures.

The next day came ever so proudly as if not to be ashamed of the things it revealed to me just the day before. There was no more rain or a dark cloudy sky to suggest rain was ever around, and the Florida sun was bringing heat waves hot enough to make a spa out of any residence that didn't have the luxury of a fan or an air conditioner. Good thing The Green House had them both.

I tossed and turned in my sleep and for very obvious reasons. I woke up with a sense of grievance severe enough to dishearten the entire Earth. All I was thinking about was Alvin. I kept asking myself all kinds of questions like was he alright, was he still alive, etcetera, etcetera. What could he have done so bad to make someone want to kill him, and who were those guys?

Was he one of those so-called Insurance Men that were brazen enough to disrespect one of God's Ten Commandments, Thou Shalt Not Kill? I didn't have the faintest idea one way or the other and that's what made me feel like

I was facing the world alone, but I wasn't alone by a long shot. I mean the ghetto was so crowded its cup runneth over.

Later that afternoon all of us, well, me, my sisters, Marvin, and Cecil, were sitting around in the living room eating. Someone knocked on the door with three swift knocks like that were in a hurry for someone to open it. At first, it sounded like the police. The way Cecil jumped up looking crazy neither he nor my mom wanted to answer it. Then my Aunt Sheryl came from the back room mumbling talking about, "Damn, y'all don't hear someone at the door knocking," under her breath and answered it.

Everybody just stared at her like, "Hell Nah we ain't gonna answer it.

"That sound like the police!" I thought it was them too.

It wasn't the police, but Marvin and I were just as shocked when we learned who it was. It was our Uncle Marvin. Man, when we saw our uncle walk through the door for the first time in months both of our mouths dropped to the floor. He looked awful and even was acting differently in the way he moved like he had nerve problems. All I could do was wonder what happened to him.

"Wassup, Queen," my Uncle Marvin asked, walking towards the front room where Marvin and I were sitting. The loud knocking must've woken my mom because she was wide awake now and stretching with a good morning yawn. At first, she was still half asleep, but not anymore. She returned Marvin's greeting before she walked to the bathroom to tidy herself up. I was looking at her walk away, but I was watching my Uncle Marvin too. The funny thing about him was even though he was sitting right in the same room we were in he acted like he didn't even notice us. He kept addressing everyone else, but he left us out, and it wasn't like he didn't see us. He had to notice us because as soon as he sat down, he started talking in pig talk, "Yees-all is-ain't gis-at nis-o chis-ianna wisite," he said, cutting his eyes back and forth.

He called himself talking over our heads, but he just didn't know I understood every word he said. He asked my mom and Cecil did they have any China White, better known as heroin. I was sitting there trying as best I could to hold fast to my right to be free of ghetto vices, but all the effort in the world couldn't do me any good because the night came with a vengeance. My Uncle Marvin had a crew of people with him: two girls and three dudes who all looked as bad as he did. I was sitting there trying to see if one of the girls was Brenda.

All I could think of was what happened to Uncle Marvin that was so bad that could cause him to fall off his saddle. Once upon a time in life, he looked so comfortable and so in control, and I just couldn't believe he let himself go out like that. So, my mom was telling the truth! Then the needles, capsules of boy (heroin) mixed with capsules of girl (cocaine), plastic syringes, and other mundane utensils that he used to shoot drugs, came out of the woodworks and interrupted my thought pattern. Marvin kept nudging me telling me to look but I kept nudging him back telling I saw it.

Like I said, all of my uncles and aunts used drugs. Well, almost all of them. My Aunt Jean and my Uncle Ira were the only two that didn't get high, at least not to my knowledge anyway. I never saw either of them use drugs, but over the years I caught the rest of them in the act. God knows how many times to be exact. Most of the times they would act as if I wasn't even there, and I guess mentally I wasn't because they would just do their thing.

I still remember that after my mother and her friends got high off whatever drugs they took they would give the drugs enough time to dissolve into their system. Then their personalities would split, and the birth of Dr. Jekyll and Mr. Hyde would come out of nowhere. I remember seeing how their facial expressions changed, and how their attitudes shifted.

Some of them would suddenly fall asleep sometimes in mid-sentence, wake back up, and continue talking as if they'd never passed out. Others would see things, feel things, and hear things. I used to be consuming these images like they were my nutrients and asking myself at the same time what the hell is going on.

It took about a good ten minutes or so for the drugs to take effect, then an itch would occur being pursued by a scratch and then another one and another one, and pretty soon the itching and scratching would get out of hand. The men would be scratching their balls and body like crazy, and the women would scratch themselves everywhere they could think of. Since seeing my Uncle Marvin like that was new to me, he was the one I paid the most attention to. When I saw him doing all that stuff, I knew right then how crucial drugs were. I would have never thought in a million years he would be on drugs, but he was a dope feign too.

He would take the drugs and dump the capsules into a tablespoon and then take a lighter and heat the bottom of the spoon until the drug turned into a liquid form. As the drugs were cooling off, he would take an elastic string, or whatever he could find, and tie it around his arm tightly until a vein became visible.

Next, he would draw the drugs into the needle, thump the side of the syringe to get the air bubbles out, and push the needle into his vein. Slowly, his entire expression would change from exasperation from trying to get it right to liberation. That was crazy because I remembered Alvin shooting drugs into his neck and how some of the women who had burned out all of their veins would even find a vein in their vaginas to shoot the drugs in. He drew blood from his vein into the syringe, pulled the needle out, thumped the side of the syringe once more to mix the drugs with his blood, and then inserted it back into his bloodstream.

You could tell when the drugs entered his bloodstream because he would act as though he had climaxed by the way he would sigh, tilt his head back and slide his hand down his pants. I knew then that he reached his destination, a place where it was all good, a place where he didn't have a care in the world, and a place where he was free. But then he would start talking to himself.

"I see you... I see you," he'd say before he started brushing bugs off his legs and all over his body really slowly. Then the brushing would get sort of violent. He would start to shake the bugs off of him by stomping his foot hard on the floor and then start jumping around like he had ants in his pants, while trying to peek out of the window paranoid thinking the police were looking inside. The strangest thing about this wasn't the fact that he was the only one who saw the bugs on him, but the fact that he forced other people to say they saw them too.

He used to call me to pick bugs off him, and like a fool I used to be picking invisible bugs off him. I didn't have any choice! He was my uncle and I had to do what he asked. Hell, sometimes the way he acted made me think bugs were on him for real until I started refusing to help him. Boy, he would get so mad at me he would start cursing me out like I was a grown man.

"Bring ya lil punk a** in here and come help me get dis s**t off me," he barked. After a while he would get butt, booty naked, run outside, and try to stomp the critters off. If that didn't work, he'd break out running down the streets. My uncle was buck wild. He was the one who made me promise myself I would never get high on cocaine.

I felt sorry for him. I mean, I wanted to help him, but I just didn't know how out of all the people who shot drugs and displayed their side effects he seemed to be the worst. If he wasn't getting bugs off him that weren't there, he was seeing people staring at him that weren't there either. My mom asked him one time who was it and he told her it was the invisible man.

"Well if he is invisible, how ya see em?" she asked. He never bothered to answer her question.

I guess the way he was ignoring us was burning him up inside that he had to say something. That may have been his reasoning, but I don't know. My guess was he just got tired of trying to project to his nephews that he was still the man. I mean, he tried as best he could to project that image, but he just couldn't do it when he was looking how he was looking. So, he finally said it is what it is. He burst out and said one day, "I'm a junkie and so what'! "Just like that.

I CAN ONLY BE ME

Alvin stayed in the hospital for five days. He was scheduled to stay longer but he must've gotten tired of being there because one night he just up and left. I guess he decided he was well enough and that's why he snuck out. When I saw him, I kept telling him he should not have done that, especially after he told me the doctor said he was lucky to be alive and that he had cheated death. He wouldn't listen to anything I was saying, though. It went in one ear and out the other. He was right too, the doctor that was.

It wasn't every day that someone would get shot in the hood and live to talk about it, especially not the way he had been shot. Alvin told me two of the bullets that were pumped into him were destined to do more than bodily harm. They were destined to snuff the life out of him on the spot. Only something went wrong in the process because one of the bullets missed his heart by an inch and the other one missed his lung by the size of a needle head. Not to mention the four bullets that were pumped into his stomach.

Miraculously, they didn't do the kind of damage one would have expected them to do either. I'd argue on everything I love that he cheated death too. What tripped me out the most was that he still didn't regard life with the same respect as life regarded him. For one thing, he thought the whole thing was funny now and he kept on laughing about it like it was some kind of joke. He was laughing now but when that hot lead hit him, he was screaming like a little girl.

So now he was on joke time. I could tell you one thing; he wasn't fooling me. I knew he was scared to death. Up until then, I had never seen a man cry like that. I wanted to tell him about the "men don't cry rule" but I let him slide. I had to because it didn't even seem like it was worth it. He wasn't the only one who broke the "men don't cry rule." One day, I caught my Uncle Marvin breaking the rule too, and he was the one who put me up on it. He didn't know I knew about him because I never said anything.

One day I didn't know he was in the house, and when I came home from school, I had to use the bathroom really bad. As I was walking down the hallway, I heard somebody sniffling. At first, I thought it was my mom, but I knew it couldn't have been her because she was at work. As I got closer to the bathroom, I could see a man's shadow in the mirror. I didn't know who it was at first and in an effort not to startle him I eased up behind him. That's when I got the shock of my life. When I saw who it was, I was like, "Oh hell nah... I know this ain't my Uncle Marvin crying." I was like, "How could he tell me men don't cry in the dark and here he was boo-hoo crying?"

What hurt me the most was I felt like my uncle lied to me. It was like he was instilling something inside me that he didn't even practice. If I had never seen him cry, not crying would have been sort of like a man code for me that I wouldn't dare break. The other reason I was hurt was because I never thought Moo-Moo would ever lie to me, but he did.

Marvin wanted to say something, but I stopped him, and we eased back to the front room. I still had to pee really bad, so I went outside. I kept thinking all he had to do was tell me the truth that it was alright to cry sometimes because sometimes things get so bad that crying was the only remedy left. So, what Alvin cried! Who wouldn't have after seeing your whole life fade away before your eyes? But crying wasn't a pressing issue. The issue was Alvin and why he snuck out the hospital. It was obvious that he still needed to be there. He had bandages everywhere all over his body. Like I said, he didn't regard life with the same kind of passion life regarded him. And I soon found out why he couldn't stay at the hospital, too. He was craving for a fix. That's all he kept asking for and repeating to me while looking all pitiful. "Sonny, I can only be me... and I'm a junkie to the best of my understanding," he said just before he squeezed the heroin into his veins.

I told him straight up, "Alvin, you gone kill yo self-one of dese days."

Cecil and my mom came home at about four o'clock that evening. Marvin and I already knew not to mess with them. They had a "don't mess with me" look on their faces so I didn't bother them. I wanted to be the first one to tell them about Alvin sneaking out of the hospital, but they saw him for themselves.

He was sprawled out across the floor knocked out. It was a surprise to me that they acted as if he wasn't even there. Cecil stepped over his body and kept going on about his business and so did my mom. When I saw that, I knew something was up with them.

We met with many forces while living in The Green House. Some of those forces we could combat with, straight up and beat down, and then there were those more stringent situations that combatted with us and beat us down. In all, I can honestly say there was never a dull moment. It was like if somebody wasn't getting beat down somebody was getting shot.

If they weren't getting shot at, they were getting high, and if they weren't getting high they were getting robbed. We got robbed by the same person so much that it wasn't even funny. It was this dude called Happy Tat that liked to rob people and used our house as his personal come up. What was funny was how this same dude managed to find us wherever we went and rob us at his leisure.

I don't know why he always robbed us. It wasn't like we had anything of value that would cause him to keep coming back time and time again, but he did. He kept coming back and he kept getting away. Well, I actually do know why he kept coming back. He was a junkie too, a stone cold one who knew we- had a house full of his kind. That was his niche, just getting in to see if he could get his hands on a capsule full of boy or girl. Thays all he wanted because half the time he didn't ask for any money. It was like he was robbing for his own death.

I left Alvin's limp body lying in the middle of the floor. I would've stayed around to finish our conversation until he woke up, but I had my mom and Cecil's nonchalant attitude on my mind. Something was up with them. I could tell. Just for my mom's sake, I wanted to be in their presence to make sure nothing crazy happened to her. I knew how Cecil was. All three of us were sitting in the Florida room, and since that was our portion of the house that's where we often lounged at. I sat across from Cecil and my mom trying to watch and hear whatever I could. I was trying to play it off like I wasn't paying them any attention, but I had both of them in perfect view. I was checking out how neither one of them said anything to each other, and that surprised me a little.

It was getting late. I think the last thing I saw before I drifted off to sleep was Marvin planting a plaintive kiss on my mom's face and the next thing, I knew I was counting sheep and watching cows jump over the moon. I must've been in a deep sleep because that's the only time I dreamed, and it was a scary one too. I had a dream that we were staying back at the apartment across from Range Funeral Home.

Marvin and I were walking home from school when all of a sudden, we found ourselves inside of the funeral home looking at the dead bodies. It was cold, creepy, and extremely quiet. The scary part was when I approached one of the caskets and saw my mother laying inside looking like she was asleep. She was asleep but it seemed as if I could hear her say, "Ya see Sonny? Dis is what happens to ya when ya abuse drugs". I was so scared seeing my mother like that; I started screaming and yelling for her to get up, but she wouldn't move for anything in the world.

It took a turbulent wiggle and a violent scream of my name to wake me out my dream. When I opened my eyes, I noticed Marvin standing over me telling me to wake up.

"Boy, ya talking in yo sleep," he said jokingly before he went back and laid down in his spot. I immediately noticed it was the next morning and I was kind of glad yesterday was over with.

Beads of sweat popped off my forehead and strands of nervousness ran through my body. I was truly thankful that I was only dreaming, but at that precise moment I realized, albeit a dream or not, that I had to talk to my mother before it came true.

I looked over towards the couch where I last saw her and Cecil lying, but neither one of them were there. I remembered my mom liked to wash on Sundays, so I had one more place to search for her. There 'was a small shed in the back of The Green House and that's where she had to be!

I hadn't even made it to the sidewalk that led to the shed before I heard muffled cries coming from the direction I was heading. At first, I froze in my tracks. I didn't know what it was. I was about to turn around and head in the other direction, but something told me to keep on walking. So, I did, and that's when I got the surprise of my life. Again!

The first thing I saw when I looked around the corner was Cecil hovered over my mom like a hawk hovering over his prey. Seeing him standing there wasn't the only thing that caught my eyes, though. The other thing was the way he was talking crazy to my mom as he pounded her in the face.

"Queen ... I... I... will be ... be ... beat ya to death," he stammered. The speech impediment was in full effect, "Kiss my butt sucka!" my mom responded. She was breathing hard, and even though Cecil was pouncing on her she wasn't backing down. She kept running her mouth.

I didn't know what they were fighting for this time but whatever it was I knew my mom didn't deserve being beaten down like that! I froze for a moment. My heart started beating so fast I thought it was going to jump out of my chest. I was so hot that I could feel the blood boiling in my veins. My eyes got watery as I clenched my fist, bit my bottom lip, and watched Cecil punch my mom wherever he could get his fist to land. It was the last punch that he threw that struck my mom in the face and made me realize I was going to kill him if it was the last thing I did.

I heard my mom scream from his fierce blows right before I crept back in the house. I don't think they noticed me standing there, and as far as I was concerned that was the good part. Now I could creep his butt.

I ran right past Marvin and hopped over Alvin's body heading for the kitchen. As soon as I got there, I searched through the drawers looking for the biggest knife I could find. When I found it, I took off back to where they were. I was like a cat stalking Cecil from behind. When I got close enough to him, I drew my arm back as far as I could. I didn't know exactly where I was going to hit him at, but I was determined to drive the knife through him, even if it meant killing him dead. "His head... his head ... "I kept thinking.
Stab him right in the head.

I had his head and back in perfect view. At the last minute, I was thinking that maybe I should hit him in the back. Cecil must've felt me behind him because before I could make my move he turned around and stopped me in my tracks.

Our eyes immediately locked on each other. I don't know who was more scared him or me, but I stopped in my tracks. I was still holding the knife in the air and still willing to finish the job I set out to do.

"Boooi, ... iiif... yaaa... stt... sttabb me wi... with da... da... dat knife ... I ... I 'mmma b ... beat yo ... yo, butt like a ... a ... man ... "Cecil said stuttering, pointing at me and shaking his finger in my face.

I can't lie, he made me freeze up and then he snatched the knife right out my hand.

I still felt like I made my point to him that I wasn't going to keep letting him beat up on my mom. I knew that from the way he helped her up from the ground and started brushing her off. When my mom snatched away from him and told him he better leave before my Uncle Walter came home, I knew then that she was tired of taking those beatings from him.

CHAPTER FOUR

CONVICTS

Before I noticed anything, time had flown right by. The next two months came and went so fast it wasn't funny. So much happened in that window of time that altered our lives a little. For one thing, Cecil and my mom had broken up, seemingly for good. We hadn't seen or heard from him in months, particularly ever since they had that fight, and my mom hadn't so much as even mentioned his name. She had a new boyfriend named Phillip.

Actually, she had another friend named Derrick, but Phillip was the one who stole her heart. I knew why, too, because she was able to have her way with him. Everything she told Phillip to do he did. If she said jump, he would jump before he even asked her how high. Phillip was a cold sucker for love.

If you ask me, I guess she loved the dude, and to add to his admired qualities he didn't do drugs.

It was about a few months after Phillip and my mom hooked up when he decided that we should all have our own place. He didn't like the idea of my mother staying at The Green House. So, Phillip, my mother, my two sisters, and Marvin and I moved into a house in the back of The Green House.

The house had three bedrooms, one bathroom, a large Florida room, wall to wall carpeting, big mango, and coconut trees, and a very large yard.

Soon after we moved in, I was about to turn twelve years old. It was about eleven in the morning when I woke to the sound of my mom's voice singing "Happy Birthday."

"Happy Birthday to you, happy birthday to you, happy birthday dear Albert, I mean Sonny, happy birthday to you," she sang playfully as she planted a big kiss on my jaw.

It was so early in the morning, and I was cranky, so I pushed her face away. I mean, birthdays were for girls and people who had the luxury of providing gifts to the birthday person. We didn't exactly fit that description. The only thing I was probably going to get was another whipped up cake and a couple of pictures that would only prove for me to never forget the embarrassment all birthdays in this house brought.

I remember the picture Marvin and I took one year when I was about four or five years old. That birthday we did get a couple of cap guns and that was cool, but the picture my mom made us take holding them looking like two outlaws who had a bad clothing day was too much.

My mom loved that picture to death, though! She practically showed it to everyone she could, and she wrote "Convicts" on the bottom of it. I guess it was to express a mixed symbol of blacks inside a racist society destined to gun their way out.

Phillip was standing over my mom's shoulders with this big smile on his face. If I didn't know any better, I would have thought it was his birthday the way he was cheesing. "So how old is ya today, Sonny?" he asked me with his smile enlarging and his words never faltering.

"Twelve. "

"So that mean I get twelve licks then," Phillip said, drawing closer to where I was laying.

I was thinking to myself, "Now he can't be serious because he knows good and well, we don't get down like that." You see, unlike my mom, I had a problem with Phillip whipping me and Marvin every time something of his was missing. He always blamed us, especially whenever money went missing. He never bothered to find out who was taking it. He always just assumed it had to be us.

I remember one day he burst through the door with hell on his mind. He had this ashen look on his face of which and I read as a sign of trouble. I just knew he was coming to whip our butts, but little did he know I was sick and tired of him hitting us. I didn't know what his problem was and for once I didn't give a damn.

"I done told yall, 'bout stealing my money," Phillip barked, taking off his belt.

"Man, you not gonna beat us dis time. I swear to God we didn't take ya money," I retorted, huffing and puffing.

I was scared. I just knew he was going to slap my little musty butt down. It surprised me when he didn't budge.

While my mother worked for long hours busting her butt trying to make ends meet or whenever she felt shy and started slipping into darkness, I was there making sure my brother and sisters were straight. It was up to me to do the cooking, cleaning, and whatever else had to be done. If it was hair to do for my sisters, I was on top of that like white on rice. In fact, doing hair was one of my specialties. I had braiding down to a science. Over one finger, under the other, and between another and another was easy as one, two, three. I could braid and do ponytails or plaits as if it was a natural thing, but it didn't come so natural after all. In fact, I learned to do hair the hard way.

The night before a school day my mom used to sit me in between her thighs and braid my hair. My hair was long. My mom could twist my hair into whatever style she wanted. I loved sitting in between her thighs because it felt like we were bonding. She always braided my hair around the sides and the back of my head. The only problem was sometimes; she'd leave the top undone. I don't know why she wouldn't finish it, but she would just stop.
Then she would start nodding and fall asleep with hair in the middle of her fingers.

My hair used to be nappy and looked crazy, but I still had to go to school. I got into a lot of fights because of my hair too! Sometimes my classmates would poke fun at me, and I would get so mad I would fight whoever said something slick about me that I didn't like. Eventually, I got tired of fighting, so I started studying the way my mom used to do my hair until I learned to do it myself.

Whenever my brother or sisters would get out of line, I would put them in check. Check one would be a warning to stop whatever it was they were doing wrong, check two would be a sterner warning to stop or else, and check three, would be a spanking at the expense of tough love. Nine times out of ten it never came to check three because my brother and sisters got along well.

When I say I learned leadership responsibilities like how to be a bookkeeper, how to import and export, how to distribute, and more importantly how to count within the privacy of my own home believe me because it was true. I didn't lead the same life that most twelve-year-olds led. While other kids my age were worrying about the latest movie or their report card, I was worrying about feeding my brother and sisters and if we would be safe.

I was being groomed by the ghetto from a very young age.

The ghetto was teaching lessons that I would need to learn if I was to survive as an adult. Think of it on a smaller level. If I could be responsible enough to lead my brother and sisters, cook for them, clothes them, then surely on a larger scale I could lead a couple of knuckleheads, including myself, out of the belly of the beast. The ghetto!

Phillip caught me one day by myself. He just came home from work, and before he could even get to his room, he kicked his shoes off and sat beside me, and said:

"Sonny, wassup my main man? How was school today?" he asked, trying a little small talk.

"Don't know, didn't go," I said with unabashed interest.

"Oh yeah? Why not?"

"Didn't feel like it," I responded.

"Aye, ya know I'm doin' da very best with y'all and yo mom. It ain't easy, Sonny. I mean, I love yo mother. I really do, but somehow, I don't think she feels the same way." Phillip sighed in his frustrations and in choosing his next words carefully he asked me. "Whatcha think, Sonny? Ya, thank she loves me?"

"Man, my mom crazy 'bout ya;" I said, lying through my teeth.

Realistically, I didn't know how my mom felt about him or anybody else. I knew how she felt about me, my brothers and sisters. and on a selfish level that was all that mattered to me.

However, after I told him that, he was happier than a sissy in boy's camp. He pushed my body back on the floor where I was sitting and started trying to tickle me. Phillip and I rolled across the bed like we were wrestling with him trying to reach my funny bone and me trying to keep him away from my stomach. At first, I tried to hold my laughter in, but after a while, I just burst out into heartfelt laughter.

Laughter was the joy of life and for that moment I enjoyed indulging in its Godly like rites. I think I even peed in my pants from laughing so hard. We had a lot of fun in that small time, but Phillip still had some things he wanted to discuss with my mom that I couldn't do her or him any justice in.

A HUSTLER'S BABY

"So, tell me something, Queen. Why do ya have to keep running backward and forward to The Green House?" Phillip asked. "Ya gotcha own house now and ya ain't gotta keep running back dere! Everything ya need is right here unless you still messin round with dat dope or meeting that busta Cecil dere ... where did you go last night?"

"Boy, watchu talkin' 'bout? Dat's my family and ain't nobody doin nothing," my mother said.

"It's just, something tells me you lying!"

I was listening outside their bedroom door. It was early in the morning, and I was still a little sleepy from staying up past my bedtime, but when I heard Phillip slap my mom I was wide awake. I heard my mother grunting and tussling trying to fight back, but I could tell the more she tried to protect herself the more Phillip took his rage out on her. All I could do was think about the talk Phillip and I had yesterday, and now they were fighting like cats and dogs. The messed-up part was that Phillip had my mom dead right. A lot of times she did go to The Green House to get high or meet Cecil. I couldn't figure out how in the hell Phillip knew it, but he did.

Right or wrong she was my mother, and I wasn't about to stand there and do nothing. I kicked and banged on the door for them to let me in.

"Leave my momma alone!" I shouted hoarsely. When no one opened the door, I ran to the kitchen and grabbed a knife. I tried desperately to pick the lock, but I couldn't. I heard my mother's constant screams, and I heard Phillip viciously beating her, but there wasn't a damn thing I could do about it.

What could happen in just six months that could cause things to go from bad to worse? A lot! My mom and Phillip's relationship was rocky, but she had learned a lot from Cecil and wasn't with the butt whippings. It's true they constantly argued and fought but my mother just up and decided she was leaving.

A week or two later we ended up at The Green House. It didn't surprise me when I saw Cecil was there too. Deep in my heart I always knew my mom would end up back with him because she always did. Cecil was a part of her, and she was a part of him, so no matter how much they tried to distance themselves, in regards to their mischievous courtship, their hearts were somewhat inextricably intertwined. They fell in and out of love more than Romeo and Juliet. The only difference was that their story was real.

Up until then I never noticed or had known Cecil to ever have a job, but he wore so many hats it was hard to tell what he had going on. You just had to watch his movement and make your judgment.

Every morning Marvin and I got up to go to school Cecil would get up right along with us like he had a job to report to. He put on khaki pants and a shirt with his name stitched on it. We went to school and Cecil went to work. That afternoon me, Marvin and Alvin were standing in the yard when a white van pulled up in front of the house. Two guys were sitting in the front and one of them had on this baseball cap. I didn't know who they were at first and neither one of us was going to walk over to them to find out. After what happened to Alvin that day, we were all nervous and somewhat self-conscious. I was ready to take off in a minute if I saw anything that looked crazy until we spotted Cecil. He hopped out of the back of the van wearing a smile and talking jive at the same time.

We released all our anxieties. At first, I thought the two guys were going to pull off after they dropped Cecil off, but as soon as Cecil got out, they commenced to back the van up in the yard with him instructing them. When the van parked, Cecil slid the door open and all three of them started unloading these huge boxes, one at a time. We just sat there until Cecil said something that made us aiders and abettors to whatever he was doing.

"Sonny, O... O... open... da-da-door," Cecil told me as he and the other guys struggled to hold a box steady. As soon as I opened the door they slid in and stacked all the boxes in the Florida room.

I didn't know what was in them but whatever it was it had Cecil and his friends happy. He was so happy that when he saw how Marvin and I looked he broke us off with a few dollars. "Now that's what I'm talking 'bout," I thought.

That's why I liked Cecil. He was a money getter, and he didn't mind breaking a shorty off. That was all we needed to get us going. Soon as he gave us our share, we jetted to the corner store and bought a foot-long hot dog, a pack of Lance Cookies, and a Jungle Juice. Then we sat right there in the store and devoured our stuff as quickly as we bought it. After we munched out, we hung around and played a couple of video games.

We were on the pinball machine, and I kicked Marvin's butt three games in a row. I don't know how long we stayed there, but we would've stayed longer if we hadn't run out of money. This was one of those enjoyable times in our life. Whenever games or money were involved we had the luxury of escaping all those other things that somehow made life difficult to live or understand. I had to boast to Marvin how I kicked his behind on the machines and how he was a sore loser. He acted like he wanted to fight me, but I didn't feed into his sickness.

When we got back home Cecil, and my mother were sitting around laughing and joking like it was all good. I looked at them with a wary eye because that was something we weren't used to seeing. It wasn't like they didn't have those moments where they enjoyed themselves because they did, but it wasn't made so obvious as it was today. Honestly, I was happy to see them getting along. I mean, as long as they were smiling that meant they weren't fighting. I just didn't have any idea how long it would last.

Perhaps until whatever it was in those boxes ran out, and that's all I had on my mind. I wanted to know what was in them really bad. All types of things came to my mind like money, money, and maybe even some more money. Really, that was all I could think of since I knew money was the only thing that could make everyone happy like they were. What else could it be I asked myself? Drugs?

I wanted to go in the Florida room where Cecil and my mom were and see what was going on. The only thing was I didn't wanna just pop up out of the clear blue sky. They'd know right off the bat that I was trying to be nosy. So, I had to be slicker about it and use my wits. The suspense was driving me crazy, so I had to make my move. My plan was to walk through like I was going to the bathroom and try to see and hear whatever I could. I needed to find out what was up. I mean, if we had all of a sudden inherited some form of wealth, I needed to know so I could be happy too.

I slid the glass door open and started to walk in. I noticed that. Cecil looked back to see who it was that was coming in, but I just played It off and kept walking. They were hiding something. I just knew it by the way my mom got up and walked out as soon as she saw me. It was suspect.

"Ca-Ca-, Sonny. Ca-ca-come ova here," Cecil said to me, waving his hand. I went to see what he wanted. "Ya ... ya ... re-remember ya-ya ... ask ta-ta-ta help me se-se sel-sell drugs?" Cecil stuttered. I shook my head yea. "Well, I'mma pu-pu-putttt ya... ya down on... on dis lick... ya gone be ... be my account. An' howwww ya .... ya like dat?".,

I still was looking crazy and not knowing what was going on. That is when Cecil hit me with what he wanted me to do. I was shocked.

"I wan ... want ya ... ya ta ... ta think of dis pro-product as dope. Only it's, it's not. Dis is ... is betta dan dope." Cecil dug in the box as he was talking and pulled out stacks of food stamps. His smile grew large as he kept pulling out more and more food stamps. I was like, "Oh snap!" I had never seen so many food stamps in my life.

I knew my mother got them but that was nothing compared to what Cecil had. When I saw all of those food stamps, I started talking like I had some sense. I didn't know what the hell an accountant was, but whatever it was I knew I could do it if Cecil was asking me to. I'd learn it if I had to. All I had to do was put stamps in five-hundred-dollar bundles, put a rubber band around them, and put each bundle in a paper bag.

"Ya ... ya think you ca-ca-can ha ... han ... dle dat without messin' up?" Cecil asked with a crisp smile on his face.

"Hell yeah, playa!" I blurted out like I was one of the boys. Cecil and my mom laughed at me. That was a good thing, too. It let me know they were gradually accepting what I was evolving into a hustler baby.

Cecil took four bundles and gave them to me. Then he left the house again like he was going to work. I don't know how long he was gone, but by the time he got back Marvin and I had done all of it. As soon as he walked in and saw Marvin and I sitting there chillin' and the stamps sitting on the floor in five-hundred-dollar bundles like he said his face glowed.

"Damn ya... y'all wa ... was ... wasn't playin'," Cecil said, checking a few of the bundles to see if I was on point. They were and he loved it. He broke me off with twenty dollars and he gave Marvin ten.

We did the same thing I don't know how many times. Every time Cecil left, he left me with bundles of food stamps to put in five hundred dollar stacks. He would come back with real money. He was selling them so fast he started giving me more to get ready for him. As quickly as he left and came back, I had stacks waiting on him. I knew he was probably thinking I would lose my count, but since I was separating the ones, fives, tens, and writing everything down my count was straight.

Every morning Cecil got up and took to the streets hustling stamps like he had a real job. I guess he did have a job to do being as though we still had boxes of stamps to get rid of. The only difference with his job in contrast to someone else's was that he was breaking the law.

I didn't know it and it never crossed my mind until one day Cecil finally told us where the stamps came from. He said one of his friends worked at the food stamp office and she left the vault door open for them to come in and rob the place. The only thing they had to do was get in, and that wasn't a problem. One day they went to the food stamp office, dressed up like they were janitors, and knocked a big hole in the back. Then they cleaned the vault out. They got away with several cases of stamps and then divided the boxes up between them.

Things were running smoothly. I had a real job and money was flowing through the house like it was nothing. My mother even got a little sassy about things, staying in and out of Northside Shopping Plaza and buying everything she could think of like she had it like that. A few days passed and Marvin and I were playing hooky from school. It was one of those days I didn't feel like going and we decided since my mom was at work and Cecil was gone, we'd chill.

We had the best excuse to tell them in case they came home early. It was simple, "No one woke us up." Marvin and I were chillin' outside playing like we were big dope dealers. I had a wad of one dollar bills Cecil had given me in my pocket and a box of food stamps in five hundred dollars stacks in a bag. I was playing like I was coming to cop two bricks of heroin from Marvin so I could put them out in my spot.

Marvin had a bag of flour, and he was talking about he wanted ten thousand dollars for it. I looked at him crazily like, "That's all?" Then I flipped through my one dollar bills all sporty like and said, "Brotha, dats all you want? Here, I'll just give ya twenty and ya can keep da change." Marvin started laughing like he was digging my gangster accent. I had that thing down packed.

He didn't know I was cool like that, but I had to show him I had a little Hollywood in me too. I had watched enough of that gangster stuff on TV like JD's revenge, The Mac, and Super Fly just to name a few. I was just about to flash my cop money to Marvin when I saw two plainclothes white men walking in our direction. The first thing Marvin did was run in the house. I wanted to run too, but he was so scared that when he ran in the house, he locked the front door.

I was like, "I know my brotha didn't just lock the stupid door on me!"

I tried to play it off, but for real for real I was spooked. I kept pulling on the door and looking at the men drawing closer at the same time. The first thing that hit my mind was that it was those truant officers coming to take us to school. I mean, it wasn't like it was our first-time playing hooky and it wouldn't have been the truant officers' first time coming to our house. The only thing was, this time, they looked more official. I knew all the truant officers and these two looked new. They even talked differently.

"Come here, son," one of them said, pointing his finger at me. I shook my head no. "Is your momma and daddy here?" I shook my head again no. "Well, do you know when they'll be back?" The other one asked. I shook my head no one more time but this time, it must've pissed them off. "Well, can you talk, or are you a dummy?" One of them said angrily.

That's when I found out who they were and what they wanted. Not by their choice of words, but by their badges they flashed and the message they left me to give to Cecil whenever he got home.

"You tell yo daddy, Cecil Brown, his butt is going to jail for good this time for robbing the food stamp office. Just make sure you tell him we'll be back!" I still had the bag of stamps in my hand. Luckily, they didn't ask me to see what was inside the bag or I probably would have been going to jail too.

Once they left, I went to the door and banged on it. "Marvin, open dis door," I screamed, "wit yo scary self!"

"I ain't scared, Sonny."

"You is!"

"I ain't ' I "

"Just open da door."

"I ain't doin' nothin", Now! Chillin' me scary I ain't doin nothin"!"

"Man, come on and open the door. That was the police!"

Man, Marvin had me so mad I wanted to swing on his butt. First, he locked me outside. He didn't even care what happened to me, and now he was playing around because I called him scary. Damn, all I did was call a spade a spade. I thought, "How in the hell are you going to run in the house and leave me outside with the police?"

***

Later that afternoon, both my mom and Cecil came home. As soon as they walked through the door, I told them about the two men that came around asking questions about them. At first, they thought I was lying until they asked Marvin.

My words sent them into a panic, especially my mom who was acting scarier than Cecil. I guess when I told her that the police asked about her whereabouts too, she was in just as much trouble as Cecil. I couldn't tell if she was or wasn't. All I knew was that they asked me were my mom and dad home. Cecil kept asking me over and over what they said, what they looked like, and how many times they came. I could've sworn he asked me the same questions a million times, but I knew for certain I kept giving him the same answers.

"It was two white men in suits that said they'll be back," I said. Cecil and my mom went into a frenzy. They started scrambling around and running back and forth to the window like they were crazy.

"Ya ... ya ... y'all getcha ya ... yall stuff," Cecil stammered nervously.

***

The first couple of days and nights we stayed in the Stardust Hotel on Biscayne Boulevard. After a couple of weeks passed, Cecil had gotten the word that the feds were on his trail. Someone told him that they even had a picture of him, and they were showing it around to everybody. When Cecil heard that, he got even more scared. He decided it was time to lighten his load, so he dumped us and decided to go on the run alone. He and my mother tried to figure out ways they could remain together, but in the end, Cecil insisted that he was out.

The next day around noon, check out time, a maid was knocking on our door asking us their most favorite words, "Are you staying over or are you checking out?" It wasn't a secret that we had to dip. The messed-up part about it was that Cecil didn't even have the decency to leave us with any money.

The days seemed long and sort of chasing as we and our mother wandered about the streets trying to find us a place to rest our head and a bite to eat. I would guess that was no problem. I mean, all we had to do was go back to The Green House and get on with our lives, but that was the last place on my mom's mind. My mom was spooked to death, and she wasn't going anywhere near The Green House. That was out of the question! She would rather walk the streets with us all night chanting, "Mommy gone take care of her babies."

By the time night fell mommy and her babies were still on the streets with no permanent place to go. It was a good thing we were in Florida where the temperature stayed warm or else, we would've been through dealing.

All of us had an indecent look about ourselves. We had a look of desperation on our faces, but no one bothered to stop and give us a hand. Even though it was past midnight, cars were just passing us by like it was normal for a lady to be out in the streets this time of night by herself with four young children.

Marvin had a stoic look on his face, my sisters had an absent look on their faces, my mother always kept a confident look on her face as if to say let me do all the worrying, and my damn feet were killing me. I couldn't tell you how long we walked but it felt like we had been walking for hours. Then my mom finally came up. We ended up at the Emergency Housing across the street from the Joseph Caleb building on Fifty- Fourth Street and Twenty-Second Avenue.

There was this pretty, light-skinned lady at the desk and she was asking my mom all kinds of questions like how long we been on the streets, did she have any place to go, was she married, etc. ..., etc, etc. Whatever she told the lady, my mom eventually persuaded her to let us chill.

The Emergency Housing had a three-day grace period. After that, if you didn't at least attempt to find somewhere else to go your company was no longer welcomed. Then you had to take to the streets and make room for someone else. By that time though my mom found out about another shelter home that would welcome us to their safe haven. The name of it was Women in Distress. It was located on Eighteenth Street right off of Biscayne Boulevard near Over Town. What I was wondering was how long we would be able to stay there. It wasn't like we could stay forever.

One day while we were eating dinner, the director of the shelter called my mother into her office to talk. When my mom returned, I noticed she had completely lost her appetite. I could tell by the way she was twirling her food around with her fork. She wasn't eating anything. Plus, she had this sad look on her face that told me it was time to hit it. I think we stayed there for as long as it took Marvin, my sisters and me to finish our food: Then all of a sudden, my mom jumped up from the table and said, "Let's go."

She didn't even bother to clean up the area we were just eating in. As we were walking down the street, she told us the lady told her that the Women in Distress shelter was for women only, and that meant no children or pets were allowed. She said she asked the lady could we stay there one more night, but the lady told her we had to leave. So, we were back at it again, trying to find somewhere else to lay our head.

My mom took us to the neighborhood youth center called the Harry Belafonte Tacolcy Center located on Sixty-Second Street and Tenth Avenue, right in the heart of the ghetto. When we got there, she told us to go play on the playground while she went inside to talk to the people about us. My sisters, Marvin and I would've liked to tear the playground up, but we sat on the swings staring at the door my mom entered and hoping she returned with good news. We didn't know what to expect.

We might have stayed outside for about thirty minutes or so before my mom returned, and we were glad to see her face. All of us hopped off the swings and ran over to her when she walked out of the building. She came out flashing a door key and said they told her we can stay in the center at night after the place closed, but by sunrise, we had to be gone.

MIAMI TIMES
- 1973 -

Make no mistake about it, we had many grievances about sleeping inside the Tacolcy Center, but who were we going to petition, the governor? I don't think so. He had other matters that perhaps he and his constituents found more pressing than a family living in a bottle. We certainly couldn't go to the police because they were the very ones who had us in this predicament. So, we learned to live with our circumstances, taking it one day at a time.

We stayed at the Tacolcy Center a few nights until someone thought they had a duty to bring our stay to an end. No, they didn't do the humane thing like offer us a place to stay or perhaps the next best thing and call somebody who eventually called somebody else who could offer us some kind of assistance. We just had to go. I don't know how it went down. All I knew was one morning we woke up thinking we were about to do our normal routine and found news reporters and police everywhere.

They started taking our pictures and asking us all kinds of questions like how long we'd been staying on the streets. There was a lot of commotion going on. My mother was trying to answer every question they asked her as best she could, but I don't think she was fully aware of what was going on herself. It was early in the morning and like I said there was a lot of commotion going on. She had this stupid look on her face like she was just as surprised seeing all of those people standing around looking at us, the homeless family as if we were the main attraction in a circus.

All of a sudden, I spotted my granddaddy running briskly through the crowd, and he was heading straight towards us. At the time I couldn't explain how he knew we were there although I was glad to see him because I knew our street life was over.

I later found out they had put us on the news and my grandmother on my father's side of the family happened to be watching TV that day. She said when she saw her grandchildren, she phoned my grandfather to go pick us up immediately. That night we stayed at my grandfather Ira's house. I remember the night was chilly, but it was all good, at least we were home. We appreciated it because for the first time in days Marvin and I hammered a good night's sleep. When we woke up the next morning, we noticed our mom was gone. We looked everywhere for her, but she was nowhere to be found. Apparently, she had other things to do so she left us behind with the impression that since we were with our grandfather, we would be alright.

My grandfather had the Miami Times newspaper in his hands. When I saw him, he was flipping through the pages trying to find what article he wanted to read. He always read the newspaper to keep himself abreast with what was going on in our community. The Miami Times discussed black issues from deaths to current events. In the hood, the Miami Times was the paper of choice over the more suburban Miami Herald.

When we walked into the living room, I couldn't help but notice that my grandfather Ira had an absent look on his face and his expression never changed as he peered over the paper's contents. He didn't even say anything to us. He just got up from the table where he was sitting and walked into the kitchen. I noticed the newspaper still lying on the table and what it had on its front page explained the look my grandfather had.

There was a picture of us right on the front page looking dirty, hungry, and completely thrown away. The picture itself was enough to make me cringe. I didn't even have to read the words, although my eyes scanned over them. The heading stuck out in my mind the most. Surely, he had taken us in, bathed, clothed, and fed us, but he loathed the fact and idea that he had inherited someone else's responsibility. The matter may have seemed subtle on the outside, but it was discomforting if not degrading to him on the inside.

I couldn't tell you what his problem was. Being that we were his grandchildren you would think he would accept us with open arms. Not! Like I said, my grandfather loathed the idea of having to take care of us. He had a major flaw. He was one of Miami's biggest preachers and felt his accepting us meant giving up his illusion of perfection. His pride couldn't handle our cries. His fear of being judged, disliked, excluded, or even rejected by his faithful congregation and pew members who looked up to him like he was a god was more than he wanted to deal with.

Recalling the status quo of my grandfather's preaching lifestyle put my understanding of the situation in perspective. "The black priest, "respectfully, was like a "black God." The blacks in our community who had somehow inherited conditions of turmoil, mischief, and discontent without sanctuary came Sunday after Sunday to listen to my grandfather belt out his sermon. He had a rousing baritone voice that some say was hypnotizing them almost to a point of making them feel like they had taken a dose of morphine. That was his problem.

If preaching a thunderous sermon about the equality of raising our children versus raising bastard children was enough to get his congregation up on their feet screaming "hallelujah," then him inheriting and raising two bad kids on his own would certainly be enough to blemish his angelic reputation, and he wasn't about to let that happen. My grandfather sought to reconcile his situation. There was a simple solution to his problem that had our grandmother Louise's name written all over it. After a few days, he packed our things and herded us off to yet another place we would commonly call our home.

We moved in with my grandmother on my father's side of the family. It wasn't like we had a say in the matter because our opinion was nothing more than a meaningless gesture. We just had to suck it up and go. That day my grandfather went to my grandmother's house begging her to please take us in. He agreed to help take care of us just so long as it was from an arm's length away. That meant he would be at his lot across Miami's city limits, and we would be at ours, which was out of the periphery of his sanctuary. In actuality, we landed right back in the vicinity of The Green House.

My Grandmother Louise's house was right around the corner. As we drove down the road, I kept thinking about the way we were being shuffled around from one extreme to another like cattle, and the fact that our mother was MIA clearly showed intimidation that she didn't want us. I thought along the lines that somehow if my mother didn't want to have anything to do with us then who's to say my grandmother wouldn't refuse to care for us as well. Boy was I wrong! My grandmother was ecstatic when she saw us. In talking about us staying with her there was no arguing about the matter, and she took us in without giving it a second thought.

"Chil', my babies know dey welcomed in grandma's house. Y'all just come right on in here and make yourselves at home," my grandma said, all happy go lucky like.

My grandmother was a short, sweet, God-fearing woman. She worked at a nursing home on the beach. I don't know the name of the place, but I knew a lot of rich white people took their moms and dads there to be cared for once they got too old for them to look after.

Ironically, my granddaddy had a job too. He worked at a steel factory making big steel plates and stuff. Boy, that joker had some big hands too. I used to get scared if he just pointed them at me. I'd be like, "Man, if he hit me with one of those joints, I'm dead!" They were big and rough; I guess from handling all kinds of raw materials for years. He used to tell us how strong you had to be even to carry some of the metal plates from one place to another.

Between his going around the corner to the bootleg liquor house like it was his obligation, he found time to break bread with Whitey. My granddaddy drank a lot too, but even in his drunkenness, you knew he was the man of his house. He just had that aura of total command about himself. When he wasn't drunk, he would sit in his rocking chair, all majestic like, overseeing his kingdom.

Everything was in respectful order when he was sober... the dog, the fish, and even the chickens and ducks he raised in the backyard. He even had a garden where he grew collard greens, corn, peppers, and some things I didn't know the name of. Like I said, even his garden submitted to him along with my grandmother and everybody else. One day, my granddaddy decided he was going to retire. It wasn't all his decision, though. He was diagnosed with Emphysema. Emphysema is a local or generalized condition of the lungs by distention, accompanied by labored breathing, a husky cough, and frequently by impairment of vision.

The doctor said if he didn't give up smoking and drinking, he wasn't going to be around much longer, but my granddaddy wasn't only stubborn he was a die hard. He told the doctor he'd give up smoking, but he was going to drink liquor as long as they made it. I fixed many drinks for him, and in doing so I wondered what it was about the stuff that had him hooked.

I turned thirteen years old while at my grandmother's house. Marvin was eleven. In no fancy pattern, we lived, grew up, and became young men in our own right. I think, with the exception of the everyday craziness that came along with the ghetto, living with our grandmother was the first-time life seemed normal or to slow down to a simpler pace. Things were lovely at my grandmother's house.

My grandmother had rules, strict rules and they weren't just given to us to be marveled upon but to be abided by at all times. Of course, you could break them if that's what you chose to do, but your rebellion was met with the ghetto's penalty and that was a good butt whipping. In the days that came and passed, while living with my grandparents, I would sustain my share of butt whippings. I broke rules on a regular basis from skipping school to hanging out way past grandma's curfew.

That was the thing that got me in trouble the most. Hanging out. I hung out like an older person, never stopping for a minute to smell the roses and never caring if roses were ever around. Who had a rose bed in the ghetto anyway? All we saw as far as the eyes could see were weeds and sprouts.

At thirteen years old. I was one of the coolest young cats around. That was a part of my growing up experience. Making a simple walk look as though it was a stroll or making simple words more attractive by dragging them out at the end of the last syllable. All the older guys in the hood were attracted to young cats that had the gift of gab about themselves and a suave attitude to go with it.

Fortunately for me. I had both qualities and a motivated spirit to do more, that's one reason the older cats liked me to hang around them twenty-four seven. It was simple, they felt like I needed to be exposed to some things I would need to know coming up in the ghetto. That was their rationale anyway. What they didn't know was that at thirteen years old I had already been exposed to enough crap to make a septic tank run over, time after time. Hell, I even thought at one time or another that I could've enlightened them on some things. To attempt to do so would have been ludicrous because they would have just said that I didn't know what I was talking about. If they knew what I had experienced first-hand, and had I have said so, it would only have resulted in a heated argument and possibly a fist fight. All my friends were older than me, but that was only by age. Age, as I said, was just a number and my knowledge came from my experiences.

To say that since I walked and talked like a man that I took on manly attributes would be an understatement. I started smoking reefer and drinking. My choice of liquor stemmed mostly from the influence that my Uncle Marvin had on me back in the day when he used to down a quart of Colt .45 like it was nothing. That used to look so cool to me and I pictured myself drinking them.

Drinking wasn't just something I picked up from my Uncle Marvin, it also came from my granddaddy. When I think of it, I would have to tell him even more since it was my granddaddy that was the one who actually had me fix drinks for him. I couldn't tell you how many times the aroma of liquor swept across my nose, enticing me to take a sip. I never did back then, but I was just waiting until I got a chance to get my drink on. Now at sweet thirteen I was drinking hard liquor. My personal favorites were Golden Champagne and Schlitz Malt Liquor Bull. Those drinks just tasted good to me. I always turned the bottle up making sure I gulped down every drop.

"Aaahhh," I'd say, wiping the residue from around my mouth.

Every time I drank or smoked, I liked to listen to the sounds of Sister Sledge, Parliament Funkadelic, Teddy Pendergrass, or some Barry White. Man, Boozilla had a booming sound system in his room with fluorescent lights that glowed in the dark. He had pictures on his wall that glowed too. The music seemed to set the mood and the liquor, and the weed set my mind at ease. What could I say? As a man thinketh so is he, and as a man believeth so shall it come to pass.

As a young boy, there were numerous ways I could make money. I could throw newspapers, or I could hustle at supermarkets toting old ladies' bags for cents on the dollar. That's what I could've done, but how would a cool brotha like me look doing something like that? I was a hustler's baby from the cradle and that's what I had to represent. I mean, through the pain and the agony was the truth, and the only truth that I knew was drugs. The pain was the fact that I knew drugs were harmful to me and to others but that didn't matter. The agony was that I believed that they were my ticket out of the ghetto. However, the truth was that was the furthers thing from the truth. I started off selling dollar joints. I had a homeboy named Mugbone who stayed around my way. Mugbone was a short, red skinned brother with pop eyes and long, nappy hair. He loved to crack jokes but to be real he wasn't just funny. He was funny looking. Just to look at Mugbone was like listening to a joke.

Mugbone had this job working at Brahman Cadillac and every week he used to buy an ounce of weed for us to smoke out. There was Boozilla, Rick Browne, Dollar J, Poushead and Joetux. We all waited for Mugbone to come home to smoke out on Fridays like it was some sort of a ritual, but pretty soon all that smoking played out. I remember it was on a Friday.

Mugbone had just come back from copping an ounce of weed. Back then you could get some real powerful weed for twenty dollars an ounce. Instead of smoking it all up, we came up with the idea of me selling dollar joints at my school because I had a little clientele there. Me and a few cats would go to Jerry's pool room and cop a few dollar joints from the House Man on lunch break.

There weren't many, but the students used to wait to get them from me. I had girl and boy customers, black and white. By having such a big social base, it allowed me to get rid of at least ten joints a day. That's ten dollars a day and at least fifty dollars a week. The number always came out to be fifty because I didn't take any shorts or promissory notes. My motto was "money in sight and it won't be any fight". With the odds and ends I made, I brought food and drinks.

After school, I sold joints too, usually to the neighboring folk wandering aimlessly around with no specific destination in mind. They were the ones who allowed me to sell as many as fifty joints a day and sometimes more at night. During the week Mugbone would cop a few more ounces than usual, but by the end of the week I finished selling all of it and was sitting pretty. Then Mugbone and I tallied up our work. Both of us started keeping Haitian banks (a few dollars) in our pockets and we started feeling more and more like we were hot stuff.

My grandmother never knew what I was doing. For the most part, I was able to keep her in the dark. She did the best she could do to provide for us under the Star-Spangled Banner that governed the ghetto, but I had to do more. As she constantly marched for dimes from the white man trying to make ends meet most, if not all, of my mischievous deeds, went unnoticed.

That's not to say that we didn't clash like a lion and a hyena brawling in the wild from time to time, though. Sometimes I would come home late, and my grandmother would be waiting on me to whip my behind. "If it's one thang I don't play is comin in my house at all times of the night," she said, and then, slash! My grandfather's belt would go across my back and boy it used to hurt like hell. As soon as she used to hit me, I would just take off running like a bat out of hell only to have her on my tail slashing away. Whop, whop, whop!

I used to have to go through that every night because I couldn't shake her. She used to be in the same spot waiting on me. Whop, whop. I'm just lucky that my granddaddy was knocked out by his drunkenness because he would have beaten the black off my butt with them big, huge hands he had. Man, my grandmother didn't play, though! She would beat you wherever the belt landed, on the neck, face, and every which way but loose. I got tired of that, though. I realized that the more I cried the more she beat me. So, I decided the next time she caught me coming in and whipped me I wasn't going to cry, no matter how much it hurt. I was just going to take it like a man.

<u>I MET A BAD GIRL NAMED PASSION</u>
- 1978 -

Mugbone and I had a great relationship. We didn't do all that fussing and fighting about crazy stuff like money and girls. No, for the most part, there was no need to. There was no need for us to beef about anything when both of us were making our little bread and doing whatever the hell we wanted to. Things were going so smoothly that Mugbone was thinking about quitting his job at Brahman Cadillac.

It wasn't like he was attached to it anyway, especially not when all he did was wash cars. For all the work he did busting his butt for those uppity white people, they wasn't paying him jack. It wasn't like our little weed scam was jumping on a regular basis, though, but the drug game, even in that small sense, seemed more lucrative for us when it came to getting money. There was no hassle, and nobody was telling us what and what not to do.

Everything was gravy. I even ran into my mom a couple of times. She and Cecil had hooked back up and they were staying in The Village. Phillip still stayed in the back of The Green House. The only difference was he moved his whole family in with him. I used to go by his crib every now and then to check him out. That was my way of trying to get my shine on for all the times he whipped me. I wanted to show him up.

Every time he let me in his house, I would make it my business to pull out a fat stack of money and then stuff it back down in my pocket. I must've done that about ten times in front of him making sure he saw it. I'm surprised he didn't just say, "Sonny, I see ya lil bankroll ... ya ain't gotta keep flashing it." I kept flashing it, though! I liked the expression he used to have on his face every time I did it. Man, that joker's eyes used to get as big as hubcaps when he looked at my wad of cash, but he didn't know they were all ones. All he saw was a couple of the twenties and tens on the top, but that was it. The rest was all ones.

I used to do the same thing to Cecil and my mom. Well, truth be told I couldn't try my mom like that. She still had the power to tell me what and what not to do. At least that's what she thought! I think most of what she said to me did well as long as she was around, but as soon as I was gone it went out the other ear. She used to tell me that I shouldn't show off and tote money on me like that. People will kill you for a dollar these days, she'd warn me. I used to listen to every word she said, but as soon as I got out of her sight, I pretty much did the opposite.

There's a flip side to this part of the story. As good as I testified things were going between me and Mugbone, that didn't mean we didn't have our run-ins with other fools in the neighborhood. You have to remember we stayed in the heart of the city. My grandmother stayed on Sixty-Sixth Street and Ninth Avenue, The Green House was right around the corner, and The Village apartments were right in front.

There were other little ghetto knocks around too, but The Village was supposedly known for having the hardest shorties around. Every shorty in The Village was supposed to have a knuck (fight) game out of this world. They could see you anywhere, and if you weren't from The Village you had to go to Knuckle City, throw your set up right then and there, and get it on. I even had it out with one of those brothers from The Village. His name was Ray-Ray, and Ray-Ray tried me over some petty stuff. We were playing sandlot football and he got mad because I tackled him. It was a clean tackle, but he didn't like it. What he didn't like was how everybody was laughing at the way I knocked him on his butt. He started talking crazy, calling me all kinds of names and I took it to him.

I was greasing him too. I was putting those dummies on his butt good, but when I saw all of Ray-Ray's sisters, brothers, cousins, and friends coming, I broke out running. You would've run too if you saw all of them coming at you. I didn't even know he had that many family members in the first place or else I would've had second thoughts about fighting him. It seemed like the whole village was chasing my black butt. Boy, I was so scared. I ran past my house to the Pork & Bean project without stopping.

The field where we were playing football sat right on the corner and just across the street from Phillip's house. Right beside his house sat The Green House. I was so scared; I didn't think about those residences. The messed-up part was none of my homeboys I was with tried to help me, not even Mugbone. I know one thing, though. I told all of them that I was never going to play football with them ever again, and I didn't care how much they begged me.

I woke up the next morning in a hellish state. I was still pissed off by the way my homeboys stood around and let Ray-Ray and his peeps try me. It wasn't like I was alone. I had homies there that could've done something, but they didn't even move. Apparently, they talked a good game as long as we were by ourselves, but when it came down to putting your money where your mouth was of course you know everybody started crying broke.

I put on a pair of my best jeans. They were starched down to a tee, and I had on my green Converse tennis shoes. I wanted to go see those cats and get some things straightened out about why they didn't help me. I promised myself that the first one I saw I was just going to swing on, and my mind was made up already. I especially wanted to straighten Mugbone's yellow butt because out of all people he should've at least said something. I knew he couldn't do anything by himself, but I wasn't trying to hear that either.

That's just how we rolled in the hood. When you down with a brother you are down with them to the end. If it was me, I would've come clean for anyone of my homies. On second thought, I might have done the same thing they did, seeing all those grown-ups. Damn school!

I was going up to the pool room to hang out and wait until I saw one of the homies so I could get things straightened out. The pool room was the hangout spot for the adults at night, but in the early hours of the day, it was mostly used for young adults and teens that chose to shoot hooky. Perhaps the owner would've made some noise about us being there, but the ghetto had rules that prohibited him from saying or doing anything. One of them was simple enough to encompass them all. Mind your own damn business!

I knew around lunch break the place would be crowded with teens trying to get a game or two of pool in before they headed back to school. That's the time Mugbone showed up too. He usually took his lunch break at that time, and I had every intention of straightening his butt out. Little did I know, no straightening was about to happen, Unbeknownst to me, I had a different date with destiny that was yet to come. They say you could plan, but God was the best planner. Now I'm a living witness to that philosophy. Good thing I was looking good that day. That may have been the thing that made all the difference.

"Yo, Sonny, ya want a sausage sandwich?" one of the pool room attendants asked.

"Naw, um straight," I replied, while thinking about what I was going to do and how a sandwich could hinder my performance. I didn't need to catch cramps and have to dookie once I started kicking one of them brothers' butts. I was talking strong too. I had forgotten all my friends were bigger and stronger than me, but all the pool sticks lying around made things fairer and I had one standing right by me.

I was sitting on the stool way in the back that faced the door just waiting for one of them to show up. Not only that, but it sat in a blind spot where people coming in couldn't see you. If anything, you saw them first. So, if you had any dirt to do you could creep them before they knew anything. I sat back there for a while listening to the jukebox play some of my favorite hits, but no one I knew showed up.

I decided to walk down the street to Family Affair, a chicken joint known for serving the young ghetto populace fried chicken wings and fries. For a moment I had forgotten during lunch break a lot of people went there to eat too. In fact, mostly everybody stopped there first before they went to the pool room. Some hot wings and fried covered with some ketchup and mustard definitely outweighed a dried-up sausage sandwich. If the line wasn't too long, I was thinking about getting some when I got there.

Usually, the place was packed, but by the time I showed up there weren't that many people there. There were only two fat girls in line and two people approaching, a red skin girl and a dude. I thought the dude was the girl's boyfriend. I didn't know one way or the other, but I knew one thing I was sweating the girl hard. She was fine to death with a young Janet Jackson look. I think she was a little shorter than me, or at least she looked shorter than me. It was close. She may have been the same size or taller being as though I was so short myself.

I had my back leaned up against the wall and arms folded up to my chest. Oh yeah, my legs were kind of arched in this military posture, just not as straight and accurate, but with my feet pointed at a forty-five-degree angle. In the hood, people called this look the gangster lean or city boy bop. For the most part only dudes who called themselves "real brothers" posted up like this, and I thought I was about as real a brother as they came. Nevertheless, this posture gave brothers like me plenty of play. I was just getting it down packed, but looking at me you would've sworn that it was natural. It was the telltale sign that spoke, "Ya don't wanna mess with me."

In the city, everyone knew when they saw young black dudes posted up anywhere gritting and bobbing their heads as if to say, "stay away", that they were trouble. I had a grin on my face to intimidate the green dude the girl was with, but I had the gangster lean in full swing to impress the young lady. I had to mix it up like that. I didn't want to look like a fool and at the same time run the girl away from me. For the most part, I was a bonafide novice when it came to women, never having experienced the yoke of passion but desiring it at them same time. Never having my popsicle inside a girl's ... well, you know the rest, but desiring it at the same time.

It was hot as hell; I will say that much. My armpits and green silk t-shirt were drenched with sweat, but that wasn't fazing me. I was still posted up by the window like I was Family Affair's security guard. When I cut my eyes at dude, I noticed he wouldn't even look my way. I knew I had him in check from there. Now all I had to do was work on his girl.

She was already sweating a playa's gangsta. She even smiled at me where I could see her gold tooth. Man, I was impressed. She was all that and a bag of chips. I even dug how she spoke all slow like. That sounded sexy to me, stimulating my mind and causing me to think or believe I should be the one holding her hand instead of that el-seven (square dude) she was with.

I had totally forgotten about Mugbone and the rest of those cowards for leaving me to fight the whole village crew by myself. The only thing that was important to me now was getting Red's name and her seven digits. Seemed like she was sweating me so hard I was about to crack for it in the brother's face. It wasn't like his coward butt was going to do something about it anyway. I already could tell he was soft, but I wasn't that type, so I decided to put my stalk game down first. I wasn't going to try the man like that because I wouldn't want anyone to do it to me.

I knew how I was going to get at her. I was going to follow them all the way back to school and then try to holla at her whenever he wasn't around. That was my plan, but by the time we got in front of Edison Sr. High School the guy she was with broke off and walked into the projects across the street. I didn't know if he was leaving because of me. What messed me up was that I was thinking of how I was a long way from my stomping grounds.

That dude could've been going to get his boys to come back and try to dust me off, or it could have been that he just wasn't going to walk his girlfriend any further. She looked like she was going to the middle school which was still a long way off. That's where I was going to school too, whenever I went. All my other homeboys went to the high school, whenever they did. It didn't matter to me one way or the other because I was going to holla at her.

As soon as the dude was gone, I went at the girl. First, I sipped at her trying to get her attention. "Pssssss ... Pssssss," I went like a snake. Sweat was still streaming off my head, but it didn't matter. I was trying to get this young honey. When she looked back smiling, I trotted up to her and put my rap game into full effect. "Yo, lady, whatcha name?" I asked all cool like, wiping a drizzle of sweat off my forehead.

"Passion," she said, blushing and smiling like a Cheshire Cat.

"Day was yo boyfriend?" I asked. I thought I had her from there, but I decided to press on.

"No, boy! I don't even know that boy. Every day he sees me walking to Family Affair and just follows me," she said.

"He was toting yo' books."

"So., He asked to tote 'em, so I let 'em."

"Well, I'll tote 'em now."

I walked Passion all the way to school, but I kept looking back to make sure the dude wasn't coming. When we made it to school, we commenced walking to her class. All the while I was still mackin because I wasn'tabout to let her get away. Things were going too smooth for me, so I had to keep the press down.

I even walked in the class she was in and sat by her. Good thing they had a substitute teacher that day because I even stayed with her until class was over and watched her in her studies. I thought about me for a minute but quickly dismissed any ideas of going to class. School wasn't for me it was for people like Passion. I just wasn't one of those people. She looked so pretty sitting there all attentive. I just wondered why I couldn't do that. I already knew why, though. I had issues.

I was about to sit with her in her next class too, but she didn't want me to get in trouble. So, we left after that. Passion stayed in the Pork & Bean projects, and I didn't live too far from there, so that made it sweet. On our way home, we laughed, joked and talked about everything two teenagers could talk about. As one adolescent to another, I think we were crazy about each other. I had to be crazy about her to do all that walking, and she had to be crazy about me to skip all the rest of her classes. At least I knew I was crazy about her. I might even say I was in love. In fact, I was so crazy about Passion that I was willing to stay out late at night and endure all those butt whippings my grandmother used to put on me for violating her house rules.

Now as an adult looking in retrospect, being that Passion was the first girl who let me get in her pants, all the butt whippings were worth it. Imagine that, if you will. From child to boy. from boy to teen, and from teen to quasi-young adult I never experienced the sensation of having sex. I knew right then how much power it had having one day experienced it for the first time. Wow! I couldn't even explain the transformation to you. All I could say then and now is that, in so many words, she had me sprung.

That same night we had sex for the first time. The next night, we did it again and again. We hit it off well, but the only problem was Passion's mother didn't care a lot for me. I don't know why and don't think her dislike came from anything grounded. I just came up short one day and she held that against me. One day Passion, her mother and I were sitting on the porch. Her momma asked me to buy her a soda and I told her I didn't have any money. Boy, why did I say that? Her momma went off.

"Ya see Passion. Whatchu want with him? His butt can't even buy you a soda." Boy, that taught me a valuable lesson. Every time I went around there from then on out, I made sure I had soda money in my pocket.

"Sonny, didn't I tell you about coming in my house dis time of night!" My grandmother screamed as she jumped from behind the door. I looked at her like a deer caught in headlights. I hadn't forgotten about what she said. It was just that having sex had me sprung so I had to pay the cost to be the boss. Whop!

HA! HA! HA! THAT JOINT WAS FUNNY

The very next day Mugbone, a couple of other hard heads from around the way, and I was sitting around tripping. Actually, we were gossiping like old women, but our masculinity chose to define it on other terms such as kicking it, tripping out, or simply bugging off the weed we had been smoking. Mugbone was talking about how many girls he splacked (had sex with) on a regular basis and everybody else was talking about how he was laying on his johnson.

"Man, I ain't kidding. I got so many hoes I can plow the whole world," Mugbone said jokingly. "Mug, you ain't got nothing!" one of my homeboys replied. "Now, me? I get more coochie than a pack of panties," he said.

Everybody burst out laughing at him. I thought he was funny, but we were laughing more so at him than with him. He had the nerve to be talking about how much he was getting. It wasn't like he couldn't get any, but we just knew he wasn't getting as much as he was professing to get. His name was Junebug, and he was the fattest, blackest brother on the block. Plus, he had really bad breath.

"Now Bug, ya know ya laying on yo pole," one of my other home boys retorted. "Who gone let yo big butt get on top of them?" Junebug got mad when he said that. If it was one thing, he didn't like it was when someone was making fun of things he felt, he couldn't change. Of course, he was fat, he couldn't help it. Everybody in his family had big bones and of course, his breath was a little bad, but so what. Yeah, he was black as hell too. So, what else was new?

There wasn't anything he could do about that. He always blamed that attribute of God. He stated that he couldn't help it if God made black beautiful and everything else outside of that mundane. He didn't care though and he argued repetitively that he was doing it on a regular basis. I kept thinking otherwise self-consciously, but who were we to argue. If he said he was getting some like that, there was only one way to prove him wrong, and that was to ask the girl he said he was getting it from. If she said, he was lying he would forever be scared and labeled as someone who lied on his johnson. The thing about it was that no one wanted that label.

That's why when one of my homeboys asked Junebug to tell us her name he shut up. In fact, he got so mad he wanted to fight, so he and Gobag started arguing. I could tell Gobag didn't really want to fight so I jumped in it and told both of them to stop tripping. We were homeboys so there wasn't any sense in us fighting with each other, especially when it came time to fight that day and they left me. None of them showed up and now all of a sudden, they wanted to fight each other. "All these guys claiming the fame were actually unpopular to themselves and all of the other guys: They were faking the funk and making themselves enigmas inside bodies of lies". But for me, when it came to having sex, I was quiet as kept, I was so deep inside of Passion on a regular basis, it behooved me to think I didn't t have the elements of a hood emperor king, sex czar, or a monarch let me tell It. Ha! Ha! Ha! That joint was funny.

I wasn't laughing so much at what I knew, but I was laughing at what they didn't. Ya feel me? I mean, I could've told those old heads that I was getting more butts than ashtrays. I could've given them specific names in place to back me up. I couldn't even enlighten them on some things about the birds and the bees. Passion and I got busy everywhere, including her back porch, living room, and even in her mom's queen-sized bed. Ha! Ha! Ha! That joint was funny, but I wasn't laughing. I was simply enjoying the luxury of privacy, I mean, I wasn't any damn fool by a long shot.

I wasn't about to tell them my pleasure and have them running back dry snitching on me by telling Passion what I said and getting me knocked out the box. Besides, I didn't feel like going through that with them brothers anyway. They thought they knew every damn thing and they really didn't know jack.

I had other pressing matters on my mind anyway like my brother Marvin, my lil' sisters, and my mother and her addiction to drugs. I couldn't explain it, but I was suddenly taken aback by all the hardships we had been through and how we were separated like the tribe of Shabazz. I think it was seeing how Passion and her family were all closely knit that made me envy her and her situation. I just wondered how we could be of the same world, have so much in common, and yet our circumstances were so dissimilar.

What bothered me the most was lately I hadn't really been spending a lot of time with Marvin. It was like ever since we moved in with our grandmother, we kind of drifted apart. I think what happened was our real dad started coming around more and more and Marvin kind of gravitated towards his better half. Me? I was more so rebellious and believed all the jargon my mother instilled in me about him like how he didn't do much for us and how he wasn't our dad. She said that Cecil was. Yeah, I knew the difference, but I didn't think I needed him for anything, not this late in the game anyway. So, I lashed out at him trying to be a father, or a father figure, every chance I got when the only father I had ever known was the one that had the word "step" as a prefix.

My little sisters Tiffany and Cecelia, still stayed with their grandmother. My mom and Cecil went to see them once in a while, but those visits didn't include us. Marvin and I couldn't go unless we got permission first from our grandmother. I guess since we stayed with her, we were under her dominion and control and we only moved at her worship. You know what I mean?

Every time we asked her will she let us go. She never even gave a second thought. I think she just wanted us to know she was running things. The thing was every time we went to see Cecelia and Tiffany, I was filled with trepidation. Not so much to see them, but to leave the perimeters of the ghetto. It was good to just leave every once in a while. Leaving the ghetto was like a breath of fresh air you wanted to just keep inhaling.

Tiffany and Cecelia lived in Hollywood, somewhere, up north of Liberty City away from all the confusion that came With the City life. To me, they had it made in the shade even though they didn't think so. Let them tell it they thought their grandmother was too strict with them. They constantly complained about how she used to tell them they didn't need any friends to play with because they were their own companions.

Perhaps they didn't know, but their grandma was right. With friends came consequences, mostly at a detrimental expense, and I had to learn that lesson the hard way. You couldn't tell them that, though. They wanted to get out. They wanted to see the town and perhaps smell the roses. They just didn't know how good they had it and how I would've changed places with them anytime. I would've changed the city life and the hole in the bucket style living I was imprisoned to for theirs at the drop of a hat.

My sisters' grandmother' house was immaculate. The first thing we used to see when we drove up was the expensive looking trucks and cars. To them, those cars may not have been all that, but not to us. They were all that and some more. The other thing that stuck out to me was the huge picture window that was on the front of their house with a well-manicured garden that sat right beneath it. I made it my business to smell the flowers every time I passed by. They just had a sweet fragrance to them. On the inside all of the furniture looked new, and the refrigerator used to stay stacked. You telling me they wanted to give all that up? They had to be insane!

My mother? Well, she was a different set of facts altogether. It has been said that a boy loves his mother more so than a girl. All I could say to that was I knew my sister loved my mom with a gazillion brushes, but I loved her to death too. What hurt me so bad was that she was still up to her bad habits, especially getting high. Something told me it was just a matter of time before she killed herself. I mean, so many people had died in the hood from overdosing. I just knew she would someday too. It just wasn't any other way around it. Drugs killed and destroyed everything that got in their way. I had to talk to her and let her know she had to stop getting high before something bad happened to her. Then what would happen to us if something happened to her? It was time for me to get going.

"Hey y' all Imma holla at y'all later," I said.

"Wussup, dog? Alright, we gone stop arguing," Junebug said. "Hang out with ya boys."

"Naw, it ain't y'all my brother. I just gotta go holla at my mom. I'm comin' back, though," I said then slowly walked away.

I looked everywhere I could possibly think of for my mom, and I couldn't find her anywhere. I checked the Gr House and Mugbone even drove me around the set to look for her, but she was nowhere to be found. I wanted to go by Phillip's house but there were too many police over there. I didn't know what happened and I never even gave it a second thought. I just kept looking for my ole girl, but that night something was going on because The Village Apartments were swamped with all kinds of ambulances. Somebody must've gotten hurt. It was getting so late, so I decided to take it to the house. I would've stayed out a little longer, but this was one night I didn't want to be bothered with my grandmother's trash. I didn't know how I would feel getting a beating in the middle of my sympathy, so I just told Mugbone to drop me off.

"Ya straight, dog?" Mugbone asked me as we crept at a slow speed to my grandmother's house.

"I'm straight, dog," I said dryly. We pulled up to my grandmother's house a few minutes later. Then I exited the car wondering where my mom was. "Man, if ya see my mom, tell her I need to holla at her."

"Alright, my brother."

Before I left Mugbone, and I divided our spoils from the weed. When I walked in the house, I instantly knew something was terribly wrong. My grandmother was sitting on the couch with her head in her hands, sobbing hysterically. She was also mumbling something, but I couldn't tell what the hell, she was saying.

"Grandma, what's wrong?" I asked, panicking, but she didn't respond.

My granddaddy was there too, so I started on him. "Granddaddy, what's wrong with grandma?" I asked with a concerned temper, but my granddaddy didn't respond either.

I looked around the house for clues of Marvin. When I didn't see any,

I ran to the back room where he and I slept. I was thinking something happened to him, but I found him lying in the bed, dead asleep. "What in the world is going on?" I thought. "Why is my grandma crying like that?" I had to find out what was the matter with her. I didn't know what it was, but I was thinking if anyone had messed with my grandma I was going to see them bastards. No matter how big or small they were, their butts were going to get dealt with! I had Mugbone's 22 pistol in my pocket and had murder on my mind.

I ran back into the living room where my grandma and grandfather were. By the time I got there, I saw all my mother's sisters and brothers in there with them. I even saw Cecil. The strange thing about him standing there was the fact that my mother was nowhere around. Something definitely was up. Everybody was looking crazy, but nobody was saying anything.

"Grandma ... grandma, what's wrong? "I cried, pulling on my grandma's shoulder. Man, my grandma still didn't say anything, but this time, Cecil did. I heard him in the background loud and clear.

"Queen got shot in the head," he said. I don't know what happened after that I think I blanked out.

CHAPTER FIVE

HER BRUSH WITH LIFE AND DEATH

Two weeks had passed since my mom got shot and was hospitalized, and Marvin and I hadn't heard a word as to her condition. No one told us anything. Zilch, zero! The last thing we heard was that she was still in the hospital, and that was it. Not a single word on how she was doing and no information as to when she was coming home. I figured two things; One, certainly, there was more behind this sage than we were being told, and two, whatever that was or was not my grandmother and family thought we were too young to know.

That was the thing that bothered me the most. She was our mother, so we had an inherent right to know what was going on with her or anyone else in our family. That's true but try telling that to a bunch of grown-up people who were under the sole impression that they knew everything.

Let them tell it, I was even too young to pry, so in other words, I left it at that. Whenever my grandma said something, whether it was or wasn't what I wanted to hear, in her mind she thought it was good enough for us to know. So, Marvin and I accepted that and the fact that whatever she was telling us was all she thought we needed to know. Her last words would always be, "That's all I'mma say."

For the most part, I figured whatever the situation was she wasn't dead. I would've known that much no matter how young and stupid everybody thought I was. For one thing, I didn't see any flowers or sympathy cards around and that would've suggested to me that someone was dead and there was a funeral in the making to bury them. So, what was the deal, though? I begged the question so many times.

In the two weeks, that passed our weed empire collapsed. I couldn't help that though, because I was under strict orders from my grandmother to come directly home after school. That meant no hanging out either. My grandmother didn't want to catch me with Mugbone or Cupbone either. I mean, she stressed that in no uncertain terms.

To make sure I heeded to her orders she would have one of her neighbors drive us to school every morning and she would personally pick Marvin and me up after school. Man, I used to be so embarrassed. Big and bad as I was or thought I was my grandmother picked me up from school.

Her tough love for me even fractured my relationship with Passion. One day when she finally drove up, I didn't even see her until she jumped out the car and was going off.

"Boy, I done told ya about yo no good friends. That includes piss tail girls too!" she screamed, pulling me by my shoulder and urging me inside the waiting car.

Before we left Passion standing there alone, she pointed her index finger at her signaling a stern warning for her to stay as far away from me as she could. She just went off on the girl for no reason! I couldn't believe how she was acting. She was acting possessed. I thought she should've been telling me to stay away from her. I was more so the aggressor in our relationship.

Since Passion and I weren't allowed to see each other, we did most, if not all, of our courting during school. I skipped class every day to be with her and sometimes she skipped class to be with me. We had a systematic thing going on. Sometimes we would chill in her class, we would walk to and from lunch together, and sometimes we would even have sex behind the stairs or in the bathroom when most students were in their classes getting their study on. That was the most beautiful part of our relationship, all the sex that belied our young hungry nature reaching out to be fed.

I remember one-day Passion's class had a substitute teacher sitting in, who from the looks of it didn't; seem to care about what was going on in the class. The reason why I said that was because she didn't take roll and for the most part, she never lifted her head out of the magazine she was reading. She let students in the class do pretty much what they wanted to do. Everybody walked in and out of class at their leisure, talked crap, and a couple of hard heads even had a dice game going on in the back. They were some rowdy shorties.

They were making all types of noise and cursing but the teacher never said a word. Passion and I were chilling when all of a sudden, she brought the subject up about my mother. Since I didn't have much information to go on as to my mother's whereabouts or condition, I basically played the conversation by ear. I didn't have to pick her because she just said whatever was on her mind.

"I heard yo momma got shot," she asked as she stood over me playing in my hair. She asked like she already knew the answer to her question. I knew she knew by the way news spread around, but that wasn't the issue. I had really long hair and Passion used to like to braid it every chance she got. "Boy, hold yo head still!" she demanded.

"Ouch girl ... " I squinted. "Dat hurts," I kept telling her as she was pulling my hair too tight, but she kept arguing otherwise.

"So yo momma ... "

"Ah girl," I screamed, interrupting her before she could finish asking me what she wanted. I was twisting and turning so much that Passion got sick and tired and just quit. She wasn't about to stop there, though, she was grooming me like I was a pet poodle or something.

"Okay then. Since you won't let me do, your hair let me sit down," she said, putting her leg over my lower torso and squatting down in my lap. She was facing me, and I was facing her with my legs on the bottom and her legs on the top. That was cool but she was making me real horny. I had to get her mind on something else.

"My mom got shot. She's in the hospital now," I said answering Passion's question.

As soon as I said that she stopped doing what she was doing. She stood up off me, looked me straight in the face, sucked her teeth and said, "Boy, please. Dat lady ain't in no hospital. I be seeing dat same lady walking around da projects with her head wrapped up. Shoot, dey say she got out da hospital da same night. My momma says she ain't even get shot. She says da bullet jus scraped her." She demonstrated with her hands the direction of which the bullet traveled. If her calculations were indeed correct then that would mean only one thing, my mom cheated death. The funny thing about the whole thing was that after Passion finished telling me what I hadn't been told, she just sat right back on my lap like it was all good. I was like, "Damn." That's how it was though when you were younger. You said whatever was on your mind. Your feelings were raw, no empathy, and no remorse, just somewhat cold as a freezer.

For a moment there was an awkward silence between us. That's until she started popping her gum and humming between her murmurs one of her favorite tunes. I couldn't remember what she was singing for the life of me. It was like for that fraction of a minute I was completely out of it. My mind was processing that information so fast I couldn't even keep up with it.

I kept seeing my mother walk up and down the streets as if her life was functioning normally when in fact her everyday living was more like playing Russian Roulette. That's one thing that tripped me out. The other thing was the fact that the streets knew more about my mom than Marvin and I did. I had to find her and talk to her.

It was on a Wednesday and at two forty-five p. m. the bell rang. School let out for the day at that time. Usually, school let out at three, but for some reason, unbeknownst to my better senses, someone above the normal minions decided to cut the children some slack by letting us leave fifteen minutes early. The good part about it was my grandma didn't know the difference. At least I thought she didn't. I was thinking she thought we got out of school at three every day until I saw her, and the lady next door parked in front of the school waiting on me and Marvin. I guess grandma wasn't as stupid as I thought she was.

It was a good thing Marvin, and I spotted her first. Actually, Passion was the one who saw her. We were just about to head home when Passion hollered, "Boy, there go yo grandma right dere."

As soon as she said that Passion and I struck out in the opposite direction. I wasn't trying to hear that Grandma Louise crap. I heard enough, and much of what I heard was either lies or not the whole truth. I was going to find my mom and see what was going on for myself. To me, at the time, nothing else made sense and I wasn't trying to hear crap from nobody. Now if seeing my mom meant disobeying my grandma, then so be it.

Passion was laughing the whole time that we raced down the street to freedom. The ghetto was depressing but if you just ran through it like we were doing, you could act like it wasn't there. We cut through the distant shadows of the ghetto Normandy, the crowded streets, the rundown projects, and the back alleyways. I couldn't help but feel exhilarated as if to be free from bondage, from servitude, and from Grandma Louise's strict golden rules and regulations. I was also thinking in the back of my mind that my grandma was going to tear my black butt up when she got her hands on me. Passion and I were out of breath, but our relationship was full of love.

We spotted our neighborhood approaching. We had lost my grandmother, but every once in a while, we trotted just to make our journey home a little quicker. It wasn't like our neighborhood was right around the corner from our school. To be honest, I wouldn't be surprised if someone said it was three miles, it seemed to be a long distance, but being young and energetic we didn't know the difference and didn't care. To us, the walk to and from school seemed terse, and today since we were running it seemed terser.

Passion stopped running first and then I followed suit. We walked briskly down the back road looking back periodically, joking, and still enjoying each other's company. For the most part, I loved being in Passion's presence. To me, she brightened up the serious side in me. When I was in her company, the world seemed as though it was my foot stool.

As we made our way through the Balkanize Housing Units, I couldn't help but think the first person I was going to see was my mother. For a minute my mind even started playing tricks on me. Everyone I saw in the distance looked as though they were wearing a bandage around their head and looked exactly like Passion described her.

Since Passion stayed in the Pork & Bean Projects, I thought it was best that I hung around to see if I could find my mother. I decided I'd leave before it got dark so I could at least have a fighting chance with my grandma. I was figuring if I got home early, I wouldn't have a curfew to deal with and as far as me leaving school, I would simply attempt to reverse my error in disobeying her rules with her error in not telling me the truth about my mom. Perhaps that wouldn't be a full attempt, but it was better than no attempt at all, but little did I know my grandma had plans for me.

I stayed at Passion's house for hours and still didn't see my mother. It was going on eight o'clock and besides, it was getting late, and Passion's bedtime was approaching. Passion's mom was starting to look at me crazy. She already was bending her rules by having me around her house when she didn't care that much for me in the first place, and here I was taking advantage of her hospitality. It wasn't my fault, though, I was just trying to see my mother and get a handle on things. I mean, as if it mattered, I believed Passion's mother understood.

I was just about to get back to that butt whipping I knew was waiting for me at my grandma's house when I saw a woman walking from a distance. Unlike the couple of women, I saw when my mind was playing tricks on me, this time, I had a feeling in the pit of my stomach that gave me confirmation that it was her this time. I ran toward her, and when I was a few feet in front of her, I dove in her arms and said ...

"Ma ... ma... what happened to ya?" I said barely. "What happened ma? What happened?"

My mom kept hugging and spinning me around like I was her prize. Then she finally said, "Ain't nothin' happen, babe. Momma fell and hit her head on the edge of the bed."

When she told me that I was shocked. I looked at her like she had nine heads. I was like, "Man, I can't believe my mother would lie to me, right to my face. Didn't she know I knew Phillip had tried to kill her?" Did she even know all the things that Marvin and I had been through, not knowing and thinking we would never see her again? Did she even care, not so much about us, but about her own welfare?

It was painful for me to think she did, especially after her brush with death. She was still spitting in the wind and playing fiddle faddle with life. I mean, you would think she'd say she quit by now, but from the looks of it, she was just getting started. I had to at least tell her how I felt about her inordinate behavior.

As soon as she finished hugging and squeezing me like she hadn't seen me in years I told her what I desired to tell her for a long time. She held my fat cheeks in her hand, squeezing them together. It looked like she was about to give me another fat kiss before my words stopped her in her tracks. I just said it.

I grabbed her by the arms and with tears rolling down my face I said, "Mommy please stop using drugs, ya gone kill yourself. If that happens, I don't know what I'mma do without chu," I said sincerely. I squeezed her arms like it was going to be my last time holding her. Her radiant eyes pierced through me, almost like a laser. Then all of a sudden something happened, something that I never expected. My mom burst into tears, and I followed suit. Passion was watching us from her porch.

When I got back, she saw how I looked and made sure not to say anything that would further upset me. She just laid my head in her lap and stroked me back and forth across the head. Her touch was lulling. I watched my mother disappear into the ghetto shadows. She walked slowly as if she had the world on her shoulders. Then she was gone. It didn't take me long to realize I still had a mountain to climb. That mountain had a name, and it was called "Grandma." It was after ten o'clock p.m. in the Magic City and the city was still alive. Ghetto inhabitants galloped atop the ground looking for something to get into.

I was making it through the paths and broken-down sidewalks to grandma's house. On my way there I carried a basket full of thoughts, a bouquet full of possibilities, and a pocket full of stones. The thoughts stemmed from me explaining to my grandma why I broke her rules and the pocket full of stones were just little odds and ends I had in my pocket. I was wondering if it would be enough to support me while I lived on the streets. There was a strong possibility my grandma would lock me out of her house. She often threatened to do it.

Even though my mind was working overtime, I had Passion to thank for the little exhilaration I was feeling. She had given me a little sex adventure in an effort to make me feel better. We did it right on the porch while her mom slept in the front room. We were taking a risk she'd catch us in the act, but we risked it anyway. In fact, doing it in a crunch like that gave us a kind of rush. For the most part, her Love Potion Number 9 did the trick.

Talking about Love Potion Number 9, she had me feeling like I was on cloud nine. Passion told me sex was a potion and it had the right antidote in it to make you feel free from whatever it was you were imprisoned by. She said each orgasm was the gift of life and it released oneself from the mental or physical restraints. She also said each bump and grind, no matter how quick or long, was a deep expression of our teenage love.

Whatever that meant! All I knew was that that girl was super smart, super spiritual, and a "Super Freak!" Rick James didn't have anything on her. That girl could really move her pelvis, twist and churn her buttocks. All I did was move with the flow of things. Whenever I would hear her chanting Love Potion Number 9 in her seductive tone, I just pulled my Jimmy out and went to work. Believe me, that was on a regular basis. Love Potion Number 9, Love Potion Number 9. Splack! Splack! Splack!

Sex with her was the bomb, and as I walked home, I suddenly started thinking about how I had Passion moaning and groaning and strumming my pain down my back with her fingernails. From that moment on nothing else mattered. Not that I could remember anything else more important to think about in my life other than my mom. I was just free from it. I just kept repeating to myself "no more pain," but more pain was coming whether I liked it or not, or whether I knew it or not. Grandma had my number.

When I walked in the door, the first thing I noticed was the pitch darkness gazing into my face. That's when it hit me. I had stayed out late once again and therefore I had to expect another butt whipping. I couldn't begin to tell you how it felt to be enthralled by darkness, the look and sound of it. There was no noise, but at the same time hearing raging horns and clocks screaming in your ears was something. They sounded like they were there, or at least something was. There was a voice, or voices, of evil lurking in the darkness exalting a sense of confusion and fear in me. I knew my grandmother always waited on me behind the door, but tonight she had company.

My grandfather with the big hands was waiting too. As soon as I walked in the door, but before I could get in good enough, both of them jumped out at me and started tearing my behind up. Whop! One was talking and the other one was putting the belt all across my body. The only thing about this time was that they didn't know Passion had already set me free and I wasn't about to be imprisoned by their beating. I just made up in my mind that no matter how thick the pain was I was going to take it like a man. Whop!

The next morning, I woke with a slight headache. I hadn't slept well during the night from being tormented by anxiety and apprehension. I still had my mother's welfare on my mind and the expression she had on her face when I told her how I felt. She looked imprisoned by her addiction, and I just wondered, for the sake of wondering, if she knew anything about Passion's remedy.

Of course, I got ready for school. This time I noticed my grandmother's friend didn't bother to take me. In fact, she even urged Marvin not to walk with me. "Marvin, babe... ya stay here witcha Granny. Grandma gone bake you a cake," she said. I didn't pay her any attention, but Marvin's smile blazed anew. I just walked on to school with the hopes and desire to see Passion. For the moment she was my only inspiration. For the most part, she was the shadow accompanying me as I walked beside the still water of the ghetto.

When I arrived at school Passion was nowhere to be found. She had taken leave that day. At least that's the conclusion I came up with after I searched the school grounds looking for her. Passion loved school and never missed days unless it was absolutely necessary, so I figured something had to be wrong. I left school as quickly as I came to go find out what was going on. With exception of the few brisk walks, I pretty much ran all the way to her house. Something in my heart told me something was wrong. My pulse quickened and my adrenaline raced as I ran the entire way.

I knocked on her door and my eyes danced around the projects. I was still expecting to see my mom, but she was nowhere to be found either. It didn't take Passion's mother long to answer the door, but it would take me years to get over what she said to me.

She just looked me straight in my eyes and said, "From now on ya stay away from my daughter! I had a bad dream last night... you and my daughter were having sex on my porch and before dat dream come true I'mma stop you and her from seeing each other!" Passion's mother shouted as she pointed her index finger in my face, "My babes a virgin and she gone stay dat way until she meets a lawyer or doctor!" Then she slammed the door in my face. My eyes caught a glimpse of Passion in the background and that was it.

The next thing I heard was her mother telling me to get my narrow black behind off her porch. I heeded her every word, although my heart was broken into a million pieces. I found refuge as soon as I made my way up to the pool room. It had been weeks since I visited the spot. By the time I got there it was around twelve in the afternoon, and I found out that nothing had changed.

Teens still packed the joint traversing the ills of life. Drugs, alcohol, and other blissful items to abuse were abundant, for the most part, I was looking for freedom and a release. That's when I spotted Mugbone and some of my other friends. I quickly joined them, and we started smoking a fat joint. When nine o'clock rolled around I found myself walking home, but still smoking on my joint. When I finally got home, I was very high. Of course, it was past my bedtime, but little did I know I wasn't going to be sleeping in the same bed as usual. My grandmother and grandfather were waiting on me to come home again but this time, they had all the lights on in the house. Not only that but as soon as I walked in, I noticed that all my clothes were sitting by the door. "Since you ain't wanna cry last night, you think ya grown. I called ya daddy to come getchu," my grandma said relentlessly.

"What! My daddy?"

TWO-TWO AVE PLAYERS
- 1980 -

My dad was the one who picked me up from my grandmother's house that night after given the notification to come get me. When he got there, we didn't t exchange, any words, I simply picked up my stuff and carried it to his car. No wassup," no "how are you doing," no nothing. My father was never the talkative type.

There wasn't a lot of history between my father and me. I never pictured him and my mother together. I do remember a pink duplex on Fifty-Third Street and Thirteenth Avenue which was supposed to be the first place my mother and father lived together. I was very young then, and if it wasn't for my mother recalling the event to me, I would never have known an instance when all of us shared the same space. To this day, I've never asked my mother or father why they broke up. For the most part not only did I figure the topic was off limits, but that it was none of my business. My mother never bothered to enlighten me, and my father hadn't sat me down to discuss my birth or why he breached his contract as a father. I just let the chips fall and stay where they laid.

Even though I was sad that my grandmother kicked me to the curb, I still felt an obligation to give her a big hug and kiss goodbye. Deep down inside I knew that it killed my grandmother to see me go but seeing that I was raised more righteously outweighed all the love in the world she had for me. My grandmother knew first-hand what lay ahead for a child who had a hard head like me, and all she wanted to do was try as best she could to keep me from meeting up with that dead end that lay at the end of the path. Something drastic had to be done if I had grown to the point where her discipline had become shallow, but my grandfather and she were crying up a storm when I left out the door. "Grandma love you, babe ... "I heard my grandmother say before the door closed and disconnected our physical bond.

"Granddaddy, too ... "my grandfather stammered tearfully.

It was an extremely emotional situation. Marvin was even having a hard time accepting the fact that his big brother was leaving. His sad face caused my father to ask my grandmother could he come too. As far as he was concerned, we were a duo, but one my grandmother would now stand between. She frantically told him no and with that being said not another word was spoken. My grandmother grabbed Marvin and clutched him between her arms. It was already enough that she hated to see me leave, but to watch both of us go after she had gotten so attached to us was worse than pulling the trigger.

When we left, my father traveled north down Twenty-Second Avenue and took a right turn on Eighty-Sixth Street. I made sure to watch the route he took since I was leaving all of my friends. I needed to know how to get back to them in case I missed them or in case they missed me. Once we pulled onto the street where my father lived, I couldn't help but feel a sense of elation. I don't know what caused this reaction and before I could try to figure it out, we were parked in his yard. My father's house was beige with a couple trees in the front yard. It was set in the middle of the block with two larger houses on each side. It didn't have a fence and judging from all the houses on the block it was the smallest, but my father told me as we made our way out of the car that he was in the process of building an extra room.

I always prided myself on my good manners in the presence of adults, so when my father's girlfriend Deloris met us at the door, I was polite.

"Hello, Lil' Sonny," Deloris said, moving to the said and letting us past. She grabbed some of the bags I had in my hand, walked towards the couch, and set them on the floor.

Since it was already late Deloris, my father, and I prepared for bed. The next day I woke up to a soul food breakfast of bacon, grits, eggs, and a glass of orange juice. Now you talking about a change in lifestyle? This was it! Breakfast in the morning? That was just something Deloris did on a regular basis. She prided herself in cooking good meals for her man, and since I was now a part of their family, she quickly did whatever it was she could do to please me.

She was super nice, and we clicked instantly, but I would later find out that my father did all that he could to make me feel at home too. Anything I asked him for he gave me, and if he felt like it was something he wanted me to have he made sure to give me that as well. At the moment I woke, all he could give me was some room so I could get busy in grubbing on the big breakfast Deloris had prepared for us!

When I moved in with my father it was the end of my tenth-grade year. Miami Edison Sr. High was outside of the district I had moved to, but luckily for me, there was a school a few blocks away from my father's home. It was called Miami Central Sr. High School, the home of the Rockets. Miami Central sat right on the corner of Ninety-fifth Street and Seventeenth Avenue. I learned in the days to come that the four-way intersection that sat in front of it was pretty popular with the students who went to the school.

They literally named the corner four-way, not because of its physical layout but because on each corner sat some business that catered to the student's needs. On one corner there was a plaza where inside was several different stores like a barber shop, beauty salon, a mom and pop's store, a game room, dry cleaners, and even headquarters of the downtown Jitney Service that ran from Central right through the heart of the city. I used the Jitney Service a couple of times to get back to the city, but that was before I bought a bicycle. From that point on I didn't see a Jitney or a bus. My bike took me pretty much everywhere I wanted to go. The only place I didn't ride to was school. Don't ask me why I just never did.

One of the first things I did after I enrolled in school was join the basketball team. Since I was the shortest guy on the team the coach let me play my favorite position, point guard. I liked the position because it allowed me to bring the ball down the court, set up the team, and shoot whenever I thought I could make the shot. Unfortunately, for my teammates, that happened more often than not. They used to get mad at me for not passing them the ball, but I had a jump shot that was out of this world. I could hit even if I was on the run.

For the first couple of months, things went pretty smooth for Deloris, my dad, and me. My dad made sure I had lunch money every day, and the fact that I played basketball and rode my bike over to Passion's house after basketball practice pretty much kept things in perspective for all of us. However, there was a flip side to that coin. Make no mistake about it, my father lived inside the ghetto perimeters. His house wasn't in the eye of the ghetto, but nevertheless well in the vicinity. You could still feel the strong winds traveling at high speeds, winds so powerful they had the tendency to knock down trees, lives, and even your hopes and dreams.

In the wee hours of the night or day when schools came to a close, what was commonly known as the four corners, turned into a haven for junkies and drug pushers. Most junkies made their residence right there in the different sections and some of the pushers turned the Jitney stand into a ghetto style Vegas strip joint. People used to be packed on the corner, especially on Friday nights and holidays. You could hear gun play like crazy.

You would think that you'd be a little past the hardest part of the ghetto life once you leave certain areas like Liberty City, but that wasn't the case. It didn't take me long to find out that things hadn't changed from where my grandmother laid her head and where I now laid mine.

I think my father's neighborhood was classified as an area where most middle-class blacks lived. The area was called "Little River". It was far from being little and there were no rivers. There were a few canals though that contained some of the neighborhood's waste and a lake or two that had danger, do not enter signs on them, but they didn't account for the name. In fact, nothing in the neighborhood did. There were, however metaphorically speaking, rivers of black folk running like streams of water.

"Lil' Sonny... Lil' Sonny!" Deloris yelled at the top of her lungs. "Boy, ya betta get up for ya be late for school," she cried.

I rolled over to the edge of the bed. My eyes hadn't opened yet, but my mind and ears were doing their jobs and trying to do the job of the other parts of my body that at the same time seemed inoperative. I could hear Deloris clearly and I thought about what she was saying. I even pictured in my mind what part of the house she was calling me from. I pictured her in the kitchen fixing me and my father a big breakfast. The thought of her catering to our needs put a blush on my face, but it didn't stay there for long and neither did the picture of Deloris standing there in the kitchen. That's because she was standing right over me.

"Boy, get yo behind up," Deloris demanded, snatching the 'pillow. My eyes popped open only to find her standing over me grinning and telling me to get up. "Ya gon be late for school, boy," she said, holding the newspaper under her arm and pulling the cover off me with her other hand.

My body shriveled up from the draft running across my legs. By now I was wide awake from my stupor. Deloris walked back out the door mumbling under her breath. I had to be to school by seven-thirty a.m. I wondered if Deloris had any idea of my school's schedule considering it was already eight-thirty. I figured it wouldn't do me any good to tell her that though, since she seemed so adamant about me going to school. I just crawled out of bed and headed to the bathroom to wash my face and brush my teeth.

I was thinking I needed to go to school anyway since I had a package Mugbone had given me to get rid of. Plus, today was Friday. I just knew I would get rid of them all on lunch break. Today I rode my bike. I knew I wasn't going to make it to homeroom class but I would definitely make second period. I pedaled non-stop down Seventeenth Avenue overlooking my neighborhood's dress code until I got to school. Young life stood against the walls of Arab stores trying to figure out what trouble they were going to get into today.

The first thing I noticed when I got there was that I didn't have a chain or lock to secure my bike, but I didn't sweat it. I just pushed it to my class and parked it outside of the door. I went to my homeroom class first just to get logged in for the day and then I went to second period. All of the students hadn't gotten to class yet, so I didn't feel bad that I was running a little late. I missed my first-period class, but it was only one day, and besides, if I failed the class I could always make up the credit by taking a night course. It wasn't any sweat. The desk I normally sat at was in the back. Whether in my classes, the back of the bus, the Jitney, or anywhere else I always found myself in the back.

Call it hereditary premised around the years and years of Subjugation that my people went through when they entered the country. I just thought I was doing something slick and being different. By my understanding, heading to the back of the class only meant I could watch everything and be out of the way when the teacher decided she wanted someone to read.

something to the class. In situations like that, she always picked the students in the front.

As soon as I took my seat, I noticed other students coming in to get their study on. Most of them I knew by name, including Dennis. I knew him especially because he was the class bully and the class clown all in one. For the most part, he thought he was the baddest thing walking on the face of the earth. Every time you looked around, he was jacking somebody up taking their money, jewelry, shoes, and sometimes even their pride. Dennis didn't; bar anyone. He treated girls with even less respect than he did boys. He would grab them all over their bodies and would actually fight them if they got slick out the mouth with him.

I hated his guts. I had already made a promise to myself that if he ever tried me, I was going to kick his butt. I knew the fool couldn't fight because he had a lot of mouth. I learned a valuable lesson from my Uncle Marvin at an early age about brothers like him. One, if he fought girls, he was soft-hiding behind the question of his own masculinity, and two if he did a lot of talking, nine times out of ten he didn't have a knuck game to back it up with.

The reality was even though I thought Dennis couldn't back up his mouth he did have plenty of back up. The question never crossed my mind as to why some of the students allowed him to take advantage of them when he was only ninety pounds soaking wet with a look that he would literally break in half if somebody screamed loud at him. This insight came clear to me one day as I saw Dennis hanging with one of Miami's own notorious gangs called "The Two-Two Ave Players".

The Two-Two Ave Players were some crucial dudes that lived by violence, what made them so dangerous was that in a group they couldn't think rationally if at all. They would do some of the dumbest stuff like fighting other students as the smallest expense. If you looked at them funny or if you talked to anyone of the girls out of their neighborhood, you stood a big chance of getting beat down.

I made it my business to stay out of their way. That was easier said than done being that there were so many of them. It looked like those brothers used to be everywhere. Everywhere you went you saw them in groups of fifties dressed in their lumberjack shirts and steel toe boots.

"Wassup, Sonny?" Dennis asked as he took the chair beside me.

He scooted his chair over an inch or two so he could see directly down the aisle. That was his favorite spot since from there he could look right up Ms. Kyles' dress. Ms. Kyles was the school teacher. She was a black female who looked strikingly young for her age and too beautiful to be wasting her time trying to teach a group of students who could care less.

"Chillin'," I said nonchalantly without averting my eyes from my test.

For once, second period ended on a good note since all of Dennis' attention was snared by a cat nap. Ms. Kyles was able to teach a healthy lesson on white history. In those forty-five minutes I could honestly say I learned about how the West was won and how the black man lost his pigmentation. Before I knew it, school was letting out for lunch.

I quickly jumped to my feet and headed towards the door. I had my bike parked right outside the classroom and I was trying to get to it as fast as I could. I needed to get to the four-way so I could set up shop. Four-way was jumping off the hook. Scores of students dressed out in summer attire had the block on fire. Some of the sexiest mommas I'd ever seen in my life stood in groups modeling, or should I say lobbying, for the dude who drove through in the hottest ride. The Two-Two Ave Players even had their corner blocked off where nobody dared to go.

For a minute I saw my future unfolding before my eyes. Candy apple paint jobs, armor oiled vogue tires, and booming sound systems were the norm. The next thing I knew I was awakened from my stupor by a young man wearing a multi-colored lumberjack shirt and black boots. "Hey Sonny," he called out to me, "you got any more of dem dollar joints?"

As soon as I heard the magic words, "dollar joints," I knelt down to my socks. "Yeah, how many ya want?"

"Brotha, give me a hundred if ya got 'em... all my boys smokin'". After I counted out a hundred joints and received my c-note I hopped on my bike and headed west towards the crib. From where I was standing that was straight down Ninety-Fifth Street heading towards Twenty-Second Avenue. The school was to my right and the sidewalk extended as far as the length of the school.

I was intending to pedal along it until it ran out. I had a heart full of butterflies jumping around inside me because I was proud of myself for having sold out so fast. I couldn't wait to get to Mugbone to tell him we needed to get more joints. The plan I had in my mind was to tell him to drive by the school around lunch break. I thought the bike game was playing out for me. I mean, if I was going to be the neighborhood pusher man then I need to represent. Whoever knew a dope peddler to be selling crazy weed and still ride a bike? When I got in front of the school, I noticed Dennis just making his way out the building. I wasn't paying him any attention. His foolish behavior flashed before my eyes.

"Hey, Sonny... let me hold your bike!" Dennis yelled out to me. I didn't respond at first, I just kept pedaling. "Well F you den coward!" Dennis yelled. His words struck a nerve. I didn't know if it was what he actually said that made me wince or the fact that I was just waiting for an excuse to whip his butt. For all the slimy stunts I had seen him do and all the animosity that grew in my heart for him as a result was about to come to a head. This brotha and I were about to get it on. I thought, "Now he done messed with the wrong one!"

I wasn't one of those soft brothers he made his reputation off of. As I hit the brakes on my bike, I spun it around and hopped off it at the same time. "I'm finna beat this chump up," I mumbled. That's what I had in mind, but Dennis had faded away in the summer's heat, lollygagging with one of his homeboys. The next morning it didn't take Deloris' voice to wake me. At the break of day, I was out of bed and heading to the bathroom to freshen up. Time was of the essence, and I didn't have time to be stalling. I thought about Dennis and how he disrespected me all night, and I couldn't wait to get to school so I could take it to him.

Wherever I went I promised a long time ago that it would not be me to cower down to any man. If his dookie stank like mine, no matter how big or bad he thought he was, or how big and bad his crew was if he disrespected me, I was going to take it to him. I couldn't lie, the Two-Two Ave Players crossed my mind a dozen times. I just knew there was no chance in hell I could win against them. Those cats had leverage and muscle. So how could I win when all I had was one homeboy who lived a couple houses down from me who was scared of the Two-Two Ave Players? He kept telling me to let it go but I wasn't trying to hear any of it. It was on and popping!

I quickly threw on my jeans and shirt and laced up my tennis shoes. By seven o'clock I was heading out the door to get some things straightened out. I stuffed my loot under my clothes before closing my drawer for safe keeping and then headed out the door. I saw my father and Deloris' door closed so I didn't even bother to let them know I was gone. I'd figure they'd find out for themselves when they got up.

My homeboy and I arrived at school none too soon. Apparently, Dennis had made it there early too. Evidently, his earliness was centered on the same motive as mine. I wouldn't be surprised if he had stayed up all night strategizing on how he was going to kick my butt. I mean, obviously, he knew in using those exclamations that he had enticed a fight. His words were fighting words. The halls were considerably crowded with students walking to their individual destinations.

As I watched Dennis walk towards the class, I decided not to approach him until he got into the classroom. There wasn't any way I was going to start nothing with him in the hallway and give all his boys a chance to jump in on it. I had already told my homeboy to watch my back, but he was already scared to death.

Talking about scared, he didn't even want to walk to school with me. I had to make him. My plan was that I was going to whip Dennis' butt in front of the whole class and show him up so the class could see that he wasn't anything but a bunch of mouth. In the distance I watched Dennis disappear into the classroom.

Silently, I walked in my first-period class and took the seat awaiting me in the back. I heard several desks being scooted across the floor to a more suitable position for learning. The sound of metal rubbing against the floor had an eerie sound to it but I was unmoved. I didn't even notice the sun had filtered in and rested on my face.

"Albert Campbell," the teacher said, doing roll call. Silently again, I responded by waving my hand. I had only one thing on my mind, and it wasn't education.

Second period couldn't come quick enough. When the bell rang, I was on my feet and heading out the door. My second period class was upstairs, room two hundred and twenty-two, a few yards from the culinary arts class that had been discontinued a couple of years previously. I wasn't attending the school when they had that class but from what I heard about it, it would've been nice to attend. People say all they did was cook, bake cakes, and make all kinds of stews and dishes. On Fridays, they say the teacher gave them free time to cook fried chicken and macaroni and cheese.

I ascended the stairs with giant footsteps, ducking and dodging other students along the way. When I reached the top, I didn't waste any time getting to class. Although I didn't have the faintest idea what the end result was going to be, what made me dangerous was the fact that I didn't care. Dennis was standing in front of the class talking to Ms. Kyles when I walked in. It seemed like both of their eyes met mine at the same time. I couldn't read Ms. Kyles' mind, but it seemed like she was saying don't do it, but I couldn't stop what had already been put in motion.

"Den, what dat waz ya asid ta me yestaday?" I barked with mad attitude. I had my fist clenched together and my adrenaline was pumping while Dennis stood motionless.

"Man, I ain't say not-" he tried to say before I sparked him right in the face. I could hear the class go into an uproar as Dennis and I fell over a desk.

"Kick his butt, Sonny! Sonny, kick his butt!" someone out of the crowd bellowed. That's all I needed to hear. From there I just kept wailing on him in the face.

"Kick his butt, Sonny!" Students were screaming, shouting and stamping on their desks and the floor while Dennis and I kept tussling, and I kept jabbing away. It took the school's security guards to come in and break us up. When they finally pulled us apart, I immediately found out who the voice belonged to cheering me on. It was my friend and next-door neighbor. I couldn't figure out where he came from, and by that time Dennis and I were huffing and puffing.

"Yeah, Den! Who da coward now?" I said over my deep breathing. Dennis' nose and mouth were bleeding and that's when it all hit me. I thought, "Them Two-Two Ave Players gone kick my butt!"

"Mr. Campbell, shut up!" Ms. Kyles barked. "What's the problem with you two?"

I tried to explain to Ms. Kyles what happened yesterday, but even though she asked she wasn't trying to hear anything. All she did was tell the security guards to take us to the principal's office. Time didn't have mercy on my fears, after we left the principal's office it was time for lunch break. I had no idea that the word had spread throughout the school already about our fight, and that the Two-Two Ave Players were waiting to put a beat down on me.

So, what did my stupid butt do? I walked right to the Four-Way and when I got there the first thing, I noticed was that the Two-Two Ave Players weren't in their normal spot. Perhaps the corner they usually held up was too small being as though they had strengthened their numbers. It usually looked like fifty of them, but today it looked like there were a hundred easy. My mind started downloading stuff. The first thing I heard myself say was, take off running Sonny, but before I could heed my own voice those boys came by the dozens.

"Dere go dat sucka right dere ... "someone from the crowd yelled.

I struck out in the opposite direction, head centered, arms swinging, and feet running for dear life. I was almost home but as soon as I was about to turn the last corner, a rust-colored Chevy pulled up out of nowhere. When I looked I saw it was Dennis and three other dudes. All I know was I just took off again. As I made my way to freedom two things happened that would cause me to turn around and face my enemies. One, I was thinking that I had to face them tomorrow at school, and two I heard one of them yell for me not to run because they were going to let me, and Dennis go at it one on one. I weighed my options.

Dennis didn't have any fighting game, not when it came to me, so a one on one was right down my alley. I never thought they were trying to bamboozle me. I just stopped in my tracks and turned around. By the time I made it back to where they were, Dennis had his shirt off and his set up. He looked impressive, but in a matter of minutes, I crushed him again.

BLACK CATS, BAD LUCK

Three hundred sixty-five days and eighteen hours later, I found myself very upset as I walked home from school. There was a slight drizzle of rain coming down and it was giving my face a wet look, but that wasn't what had my nerves in an uproar. I mean, it's true I was praying it didn't start pouring down rain being as though I still had a little way to go before, I got home. Who had ever heard of water killing you if you're standing on top of it?

My head wasn't submerged under any of the puddles left by the city's poor drainage system. I walked through and sometimes jumped over them, so I was safe from drowning. In a sense, this is how I lived my life, walking around and jumping over trouble but coming just close enough to it that I could see, hear, and smell it however never actually being pulled into it. In a worst-case scenario if it rained I stood to get wet. That's it. There wasn't any sense in tripping when I had other things disturbing me.

All in all, it had been another one of those days at school when everything seemed to get on my nerves. Unlike the other day, today for some reason the bell rang too loud, the food tasted like crap and the teachers talked entirely too much about arithmetic, social studies, and science, etc. I was just sick of hearing all that mess and I couldn't wait to get out of class. When the bell rang, I was the first one out my seat heading for the door with good intentions of never returning.

On my way home I took the opportunity to think about that precise issue of dropping out of school. I knew that my father wouldn't agree, but I was seriously thinking I could convince him to let me do my own thing. To me, the streets were more lucrative in terms of making a decent living for myself, whereas that portion of my life where school was concerned, was just a waste of time. I mean, when you considered the products, the ghetto had to offer and the fact that you were intertwined to its diabolical apparatus, school seemed like a mockery.

This was my stable. The ghetto from birth to blossom had strong resemblances to the jungle where fierce lions, tigers, and bears were waiting to eat you alive. The ghetto, in contrast, had everything associated with blackness behind it. There was some type of negative connection designed to keep you from standing upright and to keep you stumbling.

It was like a black cat, a symbol of bad luck, blackmail, an expression of fraud or destruction, black ball, an intimidation strategy of which you're unwanted, and black nigger, a profound derogatory expression expressed to keep one struggling to survive daily. So, what did I need with higher learning? I was forced to digest knowledge on a day-to-day basis, but the knowledge they attempted to teach me had no direct correlation to my life. Nowhere in my school did the teachers explain to the students how to deal with life in the ghetto. I thought they were out of touch with my reality.

Besides, in my school, full of poverty-stricken students, most kids couldn't even spell emancipation proclamation more or less understand what it meant. Stabbings, cursing, cutting class, and other abnormal behaviors were the norm for us. How can a lesson about Christopher Columbus discovering America or George Washington never telling a lie effect a sixteen-year- old kid who listens to gun fights every night? For the most part, I could honestly say I never bought into any of that education crap. I had other learning mountains to climb, and they didn't include George Washington or Christopher Columbus.

On my way home my eyes impulsively scanned through the city looking at a facade barren of virtues. There in front of the Arab store, BoBo's, stood a few drunkards. One of which was in the process of chasing a black cat away and forbidding him to ever come back.

"I have enough problems ya scoundrel!" he barked defiantly, throwing a bottle at the cat. Broken glass splattered everywhere and once the drunkard knew the black cat was gone, he sat back on his crate and commenced to drinking his beer. I had a taste for some potato chips, so I walked inside the store to get a bag. I checked to make sure my money was in my pocket. When I felt the little bulge, I knew I could buy the whole rack if I wanted to.

By the time I made it out of the store I noticed the same drunkard. Now he was giving a youngster some historical notes about having seven years' bad luck and blah blah blah this and blah blah blah that. The youngster had inquired into the way the drunkard treated the cat and he insisted on giving him the entire run down on the way he saw life.

"For some reason, the ghetto seems corrupt," I heard the drunkard tell the youngster as I walked away, "but you'll find corruption in the four corners of your life as you commence to grow up and be a man... if you live to see it." The drunkard stammered and then took a long swig from his beer can. He held his head all the way back and sucked all the juices until the can was empty. "Ahhhh ... "he gasped before throwing the empty can on the ground. Then he let out a loud burp.

I cut through the back streets on my way home. The neighborhood dogs howled as I passed their gates, and some were even bold enough to chase me down the road to be sure I wasn't trying to trespass in their domain. I don't know how long I was walking but as soon as I got on my block it started pouring down rain.

My father's house was right up the street, but I took off running like it was nowhere in sight. As I took long strides, I couldn't help but wonder if anybody was home to let me in. I didn't have a door key unless you counted me crawling through the window to get in. It didn't seem like I had to go far but by the time I made it to the front door I was drenched. The worst part about it was that I found out quickly that no one was home.

"Daddy! Deloris!" I yelled at the top of my lungs, pulling, banging on the door. No one answered.

"At least they could've left me a key to get in," I mumbled under my breath. I kicked the door a couple of times before I headed to the back of the house to do a B &E. That's breaking and entering. My daddy hated when I got in the house like that, but I hated it when he left the house and didn't leave me a key. I was just about to remove the piece of wood that held the air conditioner up to the window when it stopped raining completely. Instantly, my mind started downloading other options. Since Daddy wasn't home and it was still early, I decided to hop on my bike and ride to my old neighborhood. That sounded better than me getting into an argument with him and Deloris anyway about how I got in through the window.

I hopped on my truck bike and started on my way. My truck bike was a three-speed with big handlebars to guide its big body. I bought the bike from a junkie one day for ten dollars, and ever since then it had come in handy.

When I got off my daddy's street, I took Seventeenth Ave. south towards Seventy-Ninth Street.

I decided that once I got back there I was going to cut through the back neighborhood and cross the railroad tracks that separated Miami Northwestern Sr. High School from the Zone. The puddles of water didn't stand a chance my big whitewall tires ripped through them unmercifully. I was pedaling long and hard and before I knew it, I could see my old neighborhood in the short distance.

I was thinking about going by Passion's crib, but I had to go holla at my grandmother and little bro first. That was a must. Once I checked in with the home team, I could do whatever I wanted to do after that. Marvin was languishing on the floor when I walked in, and my grandma was sitting at the table reading her Bible.

"Heeeey, babee! "my grandma said, obviously happy to see me.

"Whatchu doin' ova here? Yo daddy know ya here?" My grandma said, pulling me close to her and starting to hug, squeeze, and kiss me at the same time. As soon as I got a moment to talk, I answered her question.

"Yeah, my daddy knows where I'm at," I said, lying through my teeth.

"Well, get in there and fix ya some of that chicken and rice grandma cooked." As soon as I walked away, I felt a slap on my butt from my grandma. I was hungry and a plate of chicken and rice would do me a world of good. In fact, I couldn't wait to get in the kitchen. "Make sure ya wash your hands now, chil'," she shouted at me.

As soon as I finished washing my hands, I raided the pot like a roach raided a food cabinet. The chicken was still sitting in some gravy, and it was still hot. I fixed a big plate of rice and grabbed two pieces of chicken with my bare hands. Then I poured a big glass of Kool-Aid. In seconds I started grubbing down with both hands was feeding my face while the other washed my food down.

"I'm going to stay with mommy," I heard a voice say out of nowhere.

I looked around while still chewing with a mouthful of food. When I saw it was Marvin talking it registered to me what he had said, but I had to ask him just to make sure. I stopped chewing just long enough to get my words out.

"What did you say?" I was looking as serious as a heart attack.

"I said I'm going to stay with mommy," Marvin said nonchalantly, walking to the refrigerator. I hoped he wasn't looking for any Kool-Aid because I drank all that was there.

"You talked to mommy?" I asked.

"Yup..."

"Shoot, me too then!" I exclaimed.

I couldn't wait to get home to tell my dad, but first, I needed to find my mom and see what was up. I had to find out if it was true what Marvin was saying because he was known to tell lies. Summertime was in full effect when Marvin and I hooked back up with our mom. Out the gate, I could tell life was going to be lived under a different umbrella.

Case in point, my mom had finally initiated the first step in the life that would be a key factor to her and our survival, she began cleaning her life up and reaching for a different set of morals and principles. My mom told me in no uncertain terms that she was not going to let drugs kill her when she had so much to live for. She stated that to some people it might not look like she had that much, but to her, life was worth as much as Sonny, Marvin, Tiffany, and Cecelia in a nutshell.

What was more gratifying than hearing my mother talk with a new breath of life was her connection with reality. She understood that her giving up drugs wasn't going to be easy. In fact, most people who tried to get off drugs ended up using again in no time, but she was certain that wasn't going to happen to her. I believed her, save for the tears in her eyes when she spoke. Her voice had a deep sense of sincerity to it. It held a sincerity for love of herself and family.

What made me feel exceptionally well too, wasn't the glow she had and her physical cleanliness, but when she told me that ever since that night, when she and I talked, she made up her mind to give up drugs. That had been over a year ago and she was already looking replenished. She had picked up a couple of pounds and her skin looked fresh.

Until we had moved into The Village, I never really saw the place up close or inside. I never really imagined being inside where I could roam freely. In my mind, judging from all the things I'd heard about the place and seen like all the shooting and killing, The Village was the home of some of the most ruthless individuals the city had. I always tried to keep my distance, and I did a good job of doing that until destiny showed me it was in control of what happened to me and what side of life I'd end up on.

The Village, whose actual name was The Night Manner Apartments, wasn't dirty at all. In fact, they were nice one and two-bedroom apartment.

The only dirty parts of The Village were the drugs and gunplay that claimed so many lives almost daily. My mother had a new boyfriend too.

His name was Bobby, and he was an older man, perhaps with a little more focused than Cecil or Phillip. He fixed cars during the day and at night he was home taking up his manly responsibilities. Whatever that was. Fortunately, the apartment had two bedrooms or else Marvin and I could have found ourselves sleeping on the toolboxes that Bobby had spread out all over the house.

"Sonny, you and Marvin put your things in the room ... it's two beds and a dresser to put y'all clothes," my mother said. My mother also had a new job. Every day she would leave for work and return home around the same time, tired and beat. There was only one day out of the week that she didn't come home at her usual time, and that was Friday.

On Fridays, she'd get her check cashed at the liquor store on Thirty-Sixth Street and stop by the rental office to pay the rent. At that time rent was due every week, something like seventy-five to a hundred dollars depending on the size of the apartment. After she paid the rent, she'd buy groceries with whatever was left. She wouldn't spend all her money though as she would make sure to save enough money to catch the bus to work throughout the week. I figured that since my mom was making such a strong effort to change her life, I could at least do the same thing. So, the first thing I did was stop selling weed. I remember when I first told Mugbone I was through, he went off.

"Man, ya trippin' dogg," Mugbone said. "A brotha can make all kinds of bread, with dis scam, we got goin'. I'm tellin' you dogg. What ya get tin 'soft?"

"Naw Mug, it ain't dat "I said before Mugbone cut me off.

"Bruh, damn school, this da hood! Don't ya think anything ya do to put bread on da table is da right thang!" Mugbone lamented. I looked at Mugbone crazy after he said that. In all honesty, he was right. The only problem I had was I was truly trying to do the right thing for a change and make my mom proud. Mugbone and I posed arguments back and forth like two kids passing licks. It was like we were battling in a court of law. He thought his argument had more merit than mine and I believed otherwise.

Truth be told there was no winner or loser. I believe in the end he won, but save for my mind being made up I wasn't trying to hear anything else. At the time I thought I was doing the right thing, but as the old saying goes, "You plan and destiny plans, but destiny is the best of planners. "

I transferred to Miami Northwestern Sr. High School. Northwestern sat right behind The Village facing Twelfth Avenue and Seventy-First Street.

The school was so close I could yell loud enough, and everybody would hear me. The first thing I did when I enrolled was got in the Work Experience Program. In the Work Experience Program, I would go to school for half the day and then go to work for the other half.

According to my mother, I had to learn responsibility and the only way to do that was to get a job. My first job was working at the Burger King on Seventh Ave. and Eighty-Ninth Street. At first, they had me working on the fries until the manager found out I could count, then he put me on the cash register. For the most part, I liked my job. I gained a lot of business sense from it, and I got a chance to meet a lot of people, especially girls. What was interesting was I didn't know girls could eat that much. Those girls used to come in there and buy two Whoppers, fries, a large drink, and sit right down and eat it all. I used to say to myself, "Damn girl you gone eat all that?"

I had the motivation or should I say the energy to someday work my way up to the manager's position. Like I said, time and destiny would see to it that it wouldn't happen. I don't remember how it happened but one morning I woke for school with this terrible headache. When I showed my mother how hot my head was, she didn't waste any time getting me to the hospital.

"Boy, yo head is hot," she said, panicking.

My mother screamed for Bobby, and we all jumped in one of the cars he was working on and went to the hospital. Later I found out that I had pneumonia. I don't remember how I caught it, or for that matter what pneumonia was. I didn't even think anything of it even after the doctor told my mother that I had to stay in the house for the next few days. All I knew was my staying in the house meant no school or work, and I was down with that.

There was nothing like staying home from school chilln' like a villain. With all the attention the doctor told my mother to give me I was going to make the best of it! Since she was at my beck and call, I could live like a king for a few days. The only thing left to do was to let my boss know what time it was. I was thinking my mom should've let the school handle it, but she thought by her taking me it would look better. So, the very next day my mother ignored all the sneezing and coughing I was doing and dragged me out of bed. I was still weak, but she didn't care.

We just walked to the corner and caught the seventy-seven bus to Burger King. It might've taken us about twenty minutes, and they were agonizing ones, between waiting on the bus and the stop and go of the ride, but we finally made it there. As soon as we walked in the Burger King, I got this awkward feeling that something was about to happen. My co-workers had this look on their faces like they were shocked to see me. I figured it was the way I was looking. I hadn't even had it a complete twenty-four hours and already I looked like I had lost thirty pounds. I took a seat in one of the booths as my mom asked to speak to my manager, Mr. Charlie.

Mr. Charlie was a short, fat, white man that looked like Mr. Magoo. He also had a receding hairline that he always tried to hide by wearing a Burger King cap. All in all, for a white man, he was cool. What white man you know would work there if they knew they were working in the heart of the city? He had to treat everybody with mad respect or risk getting beat down. I was certain it wasn't going to be a problem once my mom told him why I had missed work yesterday.

The next thing I knew a short black man emerged from Mr. Charlie's office. "May I help you, mama?" the short black man asked with authority. He had a look on his face like, "What the hell do you want," but that didn't bother my mom. She pointed at me as she explained to the gentleman what was going on, when he looked at me, I could see his mouth moving but I couldn't understand what it was he was saying. All I know is that whatever it was caused my mom to curse. Then I felt my body being airlifted from my seat and ushered out the door.

I listened to my mom call the gentleman every name she could in the book. "Black punk, ugly M.F., S.O.B. dats why black people is messed up now. ..." she grumbled, "cause ya own people keep they foot on ya neck!"

A few weeks later I was back on my feet. Since the school never checked to see if I was still working, I used the other time I had to get my hustle on. My thing was I had to help my mom out, and since I could no longer do so honestly, I resorted back to the streets. I never called Burger King to try and get my job back either. I just moved on and didn't need alot of motivation to do so.

Just seeing my mother struggle from paycheck to paycheck was hard. I remember she came home one day and looked in the refrigerator only to find Marvin and I had eaten all the lunchmeat. She started boo-hoo crying, "Damn y'all ate all da food and didn't think about me!" That was the straw that broke the camel's back. It was no secret that in my heart I wanted to sell drugs anyway. I just didn't know how my mom would react.

As long as I stayed with my daddy it was cool since I didn't see much of him anyway, but my mom was a different story because I didn't have all the freedom. She was more in tune with Marvin and me. It was almost like she was our big sister and mother wrapped up into one person. People even asked us all the time if we were sister and brother. Now I had a legitimate excuse if she ever caught me. I wasn't in school and pushing pot was more lucrative in terms of making ends meet. All I had to do now was holla back at Mugbone.

"Man, I ain't foolin' with ya ... "Mugbone said with mad attitude, positioning himself to take his next shot. He didn't have the skill like Minnesota Fats, but he had a nice pool game. He never told me where he developed the gift from, but he made all his opponents dread the day they would bet against him in a game of nine-ball.

"Brotha, I'm the only one in the world who can shoot nine times without stopping. A Smith & Wesson can't even do that! It shoots six times and that's it. Eight ball in the corner pocket three times," Mugbone said, lifting himself up for a fraction of a second to point to where the black ball would hit. Then he keyed back on his target.

"Mugbone, I need to holla at chu man," I said.

"Brotha, can't ya see Mugbone trying to rake in these fools' cash," he exclaimed jokingly. I didn't respond. The bet was a c-note, a hundred dollars, and I just knew if Mugbone came up he'd break me off. For a moment the pool room was in utter silence. The only noise that was noticeable was the chanting all the bettors made hoping and wishing Mugbone missed.

Bets were made all over the pool hall, some in Mugbone's favor and some against him. Mugbone's tongue fell out of his mouth and rolled into a curl. Then with a slight motioning of his stick about three good times he sent the white ball crashing into the black ball. The black ball hit one cushion, then another, and then the third as Mugbone had predicted. Then it sailed towards its final destination.

I watched him smile and I listened to his opponents wait for the ball not to make it, but what happened next would break the hearts of many, including Mugbone. The eight ball went straight in the corner pocket and jumped back out onto the table. Mugbone had put a little too much tension on it.

"Mug, jack up!" the crowd yelled.

Leaving the pool hall, Mugbone finally responded to my question.

"C'mon Sonny... ya breaking my heart with yo crap. You done already switched out on me one time," Mugbone said still frustrated how he blew his shot. "Man, ya saw how that ball jumped out the pocket?" he asked as we walked home. Mugbone said his car was in the shop getting a new carburetor put on it.

"Man, stop trippin", I said impulsively. "I just didn't want my mom to start trippin on me. Now that I got fired from my job, she can't say nothing!"

"The hell she can't. She ya mom ain't she?" Mugbone was silent as he thought on it for a minute. "Alright! Why not. I'mma cop some weed with my car money. It's all I got to get my ride out the shop, so don't play no games!"

IT'S TIME FOR ME TO GRIND
- 1982 -

I had only one class per day at school to attend and I couldn't get through it fast enough. I was in and out so fast people never knew I had even been there. For the rest of the day, I was on the clock scraping the bottom of the barrel selling nickel bags of weed to my people. It didn't matter to me if you wanted to get high. If that's what you were looking to do, I was the man to see.

I ran up and down the block for hours at a time chasing cars and chasing sales. Sometimes things got crazy like when the police rolled through trying to arrest people, but I managed to duck them every time. All I had to do was just run into somebody's apartment until they left. Then I would come out after they left and get my hustle on once again.

I used to be so tired when I got home it was crazy. After a while I started getting lax and slipped up by leaving weed in my pants. I was so tired one night I forgot that I had brought the bomb home with me. While I was asleep my mom went through my pockets. I felt something shaking me.

"Sonny," a voice said a little above a whisper. "Sonny, get your butt up. I wanna tell ya something." When I opened my eyes, my mother was sitting on the side of the bed holding my weed in her hand. At first, I was scared. I immediately went to explaining but before I could get a word out edgewise my mother cut me off.

"Sonny, ya know I love you babe and I ain't gone tell you what to do cause if I try to stop you, you'll just find a way to do it anyway. So, babe, just be careful for ya momma, okay?" my mother asked softly. I looked into her loving eyes, perhaps a little fearful that she knew something I didn't. Her words engraved a sense of calmness in me. I know by her unspoken words and from what she actually said that it was time for me to grind.

The ghetto was seemingly in perfect harmony. Every teardrop, every bloodshed, and every time a brother or sister lost their life appeared in some form of balance; this harmonious appearance was a fabrication because it really didn't exist. In reality, just below the surface of the fabrication, people in the ghetto were dying every day.

Looking in retrospect my brother and I weren't given a fair chance to be productive in life. In terms of chance, such logic has no significant meaning by right and wrong standards. A chance is a chance, something you have towards something you're trying to gain, so you treat it like gold. In fact, back in the day having a chance was more precious than silver and gold. Simply because inside a chance there were hopes, dreams, and possibilities that if you took a chance and succeeded you could put aside all your troubles. However, today I'm forced to shun that frame of thinking. If you were in my position sitting behind mirrors, Plexiglas, steel, dead bolt locks, fences, and bars that prevented you from obtaining freedom you would too. That's the life of a "CONVICT", stagnated by the powers that be. It was nothing to hear gunshots blasting in the ghetto day and night, and it was nothing to later find out someone had been killed or seriously injured over a crap game, drug deal gone bad, or a love affair gone a little bit too far. Those things were the norm. We heard them so often that we didn't even flinch or try to find out what was up when they occurred. We just made sure our gates were straight and that was that.

After I finished high school, I got a job as a lookout man for Tiny. Contrary to what you think, Tiny was big. He was about a four-hundred-pound dude and looked more like a bear than a human. He had one missing tooth in the front of his mouth and a small head. His head was the only thing tiny on him, so I assumed that's where he got his name from.

Tiny was supposed to pay me one hundred and fifty dollars a week, but I never made it that long. I didn't like Tiny's regime for one thing. There was just something about it. I think it was the way he talked too greasy to his workers. He used to go off on them like crazy, especially when the books came up short. I wasn't going to let him try me like that. If he did, I was out of there, but it never came to that.

After about three days I was standing around guarding my post. I had this distinctive call I did whenever I saw the police to let everyone know they were in the area. Watching out for the police wasn't my only duty, though. I also had to watch out for the jack boys (robbers). That was the hardest thing to do because unlike the police who drove police cars that told you who they were, jack boys looked like everybody else. They could walk right up on you, and you wouldn't know what time it was until they pulled out their guns and said, "This is a stick-up ... don't make it a homicide!"

As I stood on the corner, I noticed a Jamaican walking towards me.

Jamaicans were known for robbing, so I made it my business to keep an eye on him. He was tall, light-skinned, with a big gold chain around his neck, and a face I would remember anywhere. That's all I needed to know. If a jack went down at least I knew how he looked in case we had to go looking for him, but none of that was about to happen. In fact, the Jamaican would turn out to be exactly what I was looking for.

"Hey mon, don ya come work for me? I'll look out for ya star," he said in his thick accent. "I'll pay dee five hundred dollars a week mon ... I tell ya be straight. I gotta weed spot and all ya have to do is guard my gates. If anybody disrespect me gates lick shot pun dem and I'll send ya across da water if me have ta."

The Jamaican studied my expression waiting to see what I was going to say. I had only one thought in mind, that I didn't even know this dude. The way he was talking and what he was offering made other things more important than to be tripping on not knowing him on a first name basis. Perhaps he didn't know it but as soon as he mentioned five hundred dollars, he had me' in his back pocket.

I mean, Burger King couldn't beat out that number not paying me sixty-five dollars a week, and Tiny couldn't beat it either. He wasn't giving me but one hundred and fifty and the crap you had to take that wasn't worth it. I already knew I wasn't going to take his crap even if I hadn't ever met this good Samaritan dude. Good thing I did though!

"Alright, dog," I said anxiously. "Where yo spot at?" Looking down the street for Tiny's workers I was wondering should I let them know I was outta there, but when I didn't see any of them, I didn't bother.

"Me gates on the other side of da village me son. Um tellin ya star in bout a week's time we'll have sooo much traffic mon ya won't even be able ta sit," the Jamaican said as we walked across the street.

There was a gray BMW waiting for us with this pretty sister sitting behind the wheel. She must've known her role already because as soon as we got in the car, she pulled off heading to another part of The Village. The minute we pulled away I felt a sense of relief overcome me. Although the Jamaican music was playing in my ears and I couldn't understand it at all, I understood it clearly that I was on like Mighty Joe Young.

"Oh, me bad star me forgot to tell ya me name QB, star," the Jamaican said, smiling from ear to ear.

"My name Sonny."

The first week QB paid me five hundred dollars in five- and ten-dollar bills like it was nothing. I swear that was the most money I had in my life, and it felt good. I tried to act like I wasn't excited while I was in QB's presence, but when the five hundred dollars and I were alone it was like intercourse. I counted the wad slowly and then I put it in my pocket as I walked around the apartment grabbing my crotch saying to myself, "I'm on now!" I took the money out, recounted it, and then put two hundred and fifty dollars in my front pocket and two hundred fifty dollars in the other. I then walked outside flaunting the notes in my pockets and hollering out loud to Tiny's workers saying, "Brothers I'm paid in full!"

I'll never forget when I got home, I looked in the mirror and kept repeating to myself how I was on. I felt so good I even told myself I loved QB, and I meant just that. The next day QB picked me up from my house. As soon as I got in the car, he handed me a nine-millimeter.

"If anybody disrespect my gates lick shot pun dem", QB said in a dry voice that told me he meant what he was saying. He had already mentioned the same thing to me once but with five hundred dollars in my pocket, I knew he was serious.

As soon as he handed me the gun, I felt a sense of power. For some reason I'd never felt that kind of metal before. It was amazing how I held in one hand a small piece of metal that had the power to take life and gain respect. I bit my lips, clenched my teeth together, and studied how my chest swelled up and down like someone had life projectors attached to it. I wondered how it will feel to shoot somebody with it. Since QB had my back, I was going to find out.

He didn't have to worry though because I was willing to do whatever it took to keep that money coming in. If that meant killing me a jack boy or two, then so be it. The sun hadn't even risen yet and I was knee deep in the trenches making sure everything was straight. As I moved in and out of the traps all kinds of things went through my mind. QB was a real cool dude, and I must've thought at one time or another he was rich. That's judging from how things were jumping off the hook. QB had said in a week we won't be able to sit, and he was right. Business was booming so hard we had to split shifts up and hire more guys to run the trap.

When QB discovered I was the smartest one of them all he took me out of the house and told me to keep count of his money. By me being good with numbers I was able to impress him even more. It was crazy how we just bonded. His problems became my problems and in turn, my problems became his. I remember I told him someone snatched my mother's chain while she was on her way home from work. He saw how upset I was and told me to tell my mom to find somewhere else to stay. He even told me to be sure to let her know not worry about the cost. He just told me to take it out the next money the spot made.

My mom found a nice three bedrooms one bath house on One Hundred-Twentieth Street and Fifteenth Avenue right behind Moped World. QB really won my loyalty after he did that. I mean. he was already good to me but that tilted the scales.

In my view, people came and went in and out of your life during your journey. Most of them sometimes appeared to shape who you were or what you became. Some you admired so much you patterned your whole world around them. That's what happened to me and QB. I loved QB so much, and all he was or would do for me that inadvertently I took on his culture. I started to speak like him, dress like him, and in all honesty, I prayed many nights that I could actually be him.

It was time to bring my brother Marvin into the drug game. Up until now, Marvin had pretty much been a silent instrument in my life. His boyhood ways, on a kid level, made us rivals, but little did I know that bringing him into the drug game would bring me much heartache, pain, and almost cost me my life. I brought Marvin, Snake, my future brother-in-law, and a few more knuckleheads from around the way into the game. I was still seeing Passion at the time, but my male desire lusted for other women too.

CHAPTER SIX

I CAN SNORT UP PERU

A lot of my homies started going to jail, and it was almost like an everyday occurrence. The main reason for that was they were always doing stupid things like falling asleep in the weed house or getting so high that by the time nine (the police) rushed in they'd be too loaded to run.

Our spot was called The Doorbell because we had this loud bell installed for all of our customers to ring when they came to buy. The trick was almost everybody rang the doorbell, even the police, and it would give us a heads up on who came and went before they knew if anyone was in the house. It didn't work out all the time. Sometimes the police would just haul people to jail for trespassing, and sometimes SWAT would come and just kick the door down.

The police had all kinds of tactics they liked to use. They would raid the spot in mail trucks, ambulances, and even funeral carriages. Since I wasn't working in the house and because I wasn't a lookout man I never got caught. I used to tell all my homies that only suckers went to jail. I didn't have any ill will behind my comment, at least not that I knew of. I was just trying to get everyone to stay on their P's and Q's. Liberty City had its forks in the road, but if you stayed straight and kept your mind on your grind the hood would reward you. That's what I was doing, keeping my mind on the grind.
and waiting to get rewarded at the end of the week.

At twelve o'clock I dozed off into a deep sleep after running back and forth all day making sure the spot kept dope. I was so tired I could hardly move. I didn't know how long I had been asleep before I had this weird dream. I say it was weird because of what occurred in it. It was very real as if someone was actually talking to me and saying, "You think you are smart, huh? Everybody goes to jail but you? You are going to get caught too, and you are going to jail!" I even saw the inside of a prison cell and the guards.

QB used to take me to the stash house. Every time we got there; I would make it my business to watch everything. I watched how he packaged the weed and even how much he would put in the bags. I kept my eyes open to the whole process because I wasn't crazy or stupid like those other fools. I knew one day I was going to have my own package. It was as simple as that. To keep QB from thinking crazy I played like I wasn't paying attention, but

I was learning the game from someone I thought of as a mentor. It didn't take long for greed to sit on my system and before long I had my own weed and packaged it up like his. I made sure my package looked just like his.

I knew he couldn't tell the difference because he handed me my own package one time and told me to take it to the spot. I was like bet that up and was laughing like crazy on the inside. Things were really moving for me. QB, like all Jamaicans, loved to sell weed. For some reason, they'd never touch coke, but that didn't have anything to do with me. I was on the come up. Ike was the biggest cocaine dealer in Miami. His fortune didn't come by chance though and let him tell it he worked hard to get where he was. Ike had all kinds of houses everywhere, for instance, a mansion that he and his wife lived in.

He also had a fully legitimate operating construction company. The cat was cold paid. What interested me so much about Ike was that he didn't have any attachments to his worldly possessions. He ran it down to me how he was able to accumulate the money to buy all those things. He told me and a couple of my homies one day when we were standing on the corner of Sixty-Eighth Street that the cocaine games was where the real money was.

"I'm tellin ya, jit, come holla at me. I'm going to put some real money in ya pocket," Ike said giving all the shorties there listening to him a derisive laugh. Ike was a heavy-set guy, not fat, but big. He was black and wore plenty of gold chains around his neck that only amplified the fact that he was paid.

For a young Jit breaking his way into the drug game, I had it all.

I had a boss, QB, who showed me much love and I had power over most young guys in my respected class. However, the problem with that picture was that I wanted more. I knew my position was temporary, a way in which brothers paid their dues. So, to think that I would live a life working for someone else forever was absurd. The truth of the matter was that I had to get in where I could fit in comfortably, and I knew the only way I was going to truly be comfortable was when the day came that I could have my own crew of workers busting kilos down and raking in money for me. The only thing was I had to pay my dues first.

There was a group of us who jumped on Ike's offer: Musclehead, Cosby (Silk), Convertible Burt, and me just to name a few. Actually, Musclehead, Silk, and Convertible Burt already worked for Ike. Ike had a spot in The Village where he sold quarters, half of grams, and grams of cocaine. He had two shifts, twelve to twelve. Musclehead, Silk, and Burt worked on the night shift. Every night they used to come down to the doorbell to cop weed, and that's how I met them. Our daily interactions are what gave birth to our friendship. In fact, after some time had elapsed, they were the ones who first stepped to me about getting a job with Ike.

As far as I knew Ike was the man. I kid you not, that brother used to have traffic in and out of The Village like Winn-Dixie. They sold nickel caps of cocaine and heroin, but when they saw the traffic and money Ike was raking in, they changed directions like a tropical storm. Like a lot of single African-American females busting their butt working two jobs to feed their families, I did the same thing but on a different level.

As soon as I finished my shift for QB I would go to work for Ike. The shift worked out good too. Since I was QB's lieutenant I could come and go as I pleased, and one duty never conflicted with the other. For the most part, the only problem I had, if you even consider it a problem, was dealing with peer pressure. Smoking weed came by chance, but in order to be accepted by a crowd like the Ike Boys I had to engage in a manlier drug' such as cocaine. Musclehead was the first one who introduced the drug to me.

Musclehead was about five foot ten inches tall and a hundred and seventy pounds. He got his name Musclehead because he had a huge head. He told me his mother was the first one who started calling him Musclehead and then everyone else followed suit, but he said the girls called him Musclehead for another reason.

So, I started snorting coke on the night shift. My first experience with the drug came at the expense of my own ignorance. I was trying to impress Musclehead and messed around and snorted a little too much for my young heart. Musclehead had warned me several times to take it slow but doing things slow wasn't the way I did things. I liked to move fast, fast enough to violate all speed limits and that's what I was doing, snorting coke like I was crazy.

"Damn, bruh. You hittin' that coke like you own it," Musclehead said teasing me.

"Head, dis ain't nothing," I barked. "I could snort up Peru if I wanted to." Perhaps that statement was true. The only problem was my body had a different point of view, and it said if you take another hit tonight after this warning, you're dead. My body shut down and I lost consciousness. I don't know what happened from there. All I know is when my eyes opened again Musclehead, Silk and Convertible Burt were standing over me with all kinds of utensils. All of them looked spooked out and for a moment, even after I had come to, no one said anything.

"Damn, man, you alright?" Silk finally asked, panicking.

"Man don't give that fool no mo coke! Dat brotha gon kill himself!" Burt barked.

It was an ungodly hour of the night. Thanks to the Florida heat the air was relatively still and there I was lying flat on my back thinking if I had known better, I would have done better, but somehow or another my ignorance almost cost me my life. I can't say it didn't hurt either. The coughing and gaggin trying to catch up with the oxygen flowing inside of me felt awful.

"Sonny, I told you to take it slow," Musclehead yelled, reaching out his hand to pull me up. Then as soon as everybody realized that the danger had been averted, what was almost a tragedy, the freak accident turned into a comedy show. Convertible Burt burst into laughter, then Silk, and last but not least Musclehead.

"Man, that's dat scutter... Ya talkin bout you like it fast,"

Musclehead teased. After all, I guess the incident was funny, but unfortunately, I would never live that experience down. Every time I looked around one of my homies found it amusing to remind me of that experience. From that night on I started taking it slow. I can't say that I exactly liked snorting cocaine, but it became more systematic than anything else. Cocaine sort of fit the mold when you worked in a drug hole during late hours of the night. It kept you alert, and as long as you were on coke you could deal with junkies from more of an animalistic standpoint than human.

It's sad to say but if you wanted to stay alive, because junkies or dope fiends got deadly when they didn't or couldn't get more drugs, you got with the program. That wasn't about to happen with my crew and there wasn't going to be any casualties among us. I would make sure of that. For the most part, we stayed strapped with nine millimeters and forty-fives while working on the night shift.

We handled business relentlessly and each customer got thrown against the wall and vigorously shook down. We didn't care who you were or what you looked like, deaf, dumb, pregnant, or adolescent, we dealt with you the same. Searching any and every part of a customer's body was enforced by us. It didn't matter if you were male or female - we took our customers through the whole nine yards and then some. Cocaine had us sprung out and heading for destruction at a breakneck speed of fast and furious. All of us were in the pursuit of happiness and willing to do whatever it took to obtain it. It didn't matter to us at all if we had ever noticed the difference, that we were defying our own love for our sisters and brothers. Or the fact that we were playing a major role in the scheme the "Powers that Be" had implemented to destroy us all.

All I know is, and I can only speak for myself, that I had these dreams that somehow made my destiny to become hood rich impartial and/or made me impartial to the struggle and pain my family and I had endured all of our lives living in the threshold of drug addiction and poverty, yet it made it so fair seeming that I, Sonny, can be the one to lift our cry above the hue even if it meant I had to sin to do so. I know, I know. Sometimes I cried to myself because somehow, I knew that the actions, I was taking on the streets were wrong. But what was I to do when I constantly had these dreams of being free of life's cruelty?

Sonny's Got Fans

If cocaine had become an addition to me, I never noticed it. If it did become a habit, as if there was a thin line between habit and addiction, I can't say with all honesty whether or not it was by my own will or if it just happened on its own. In terms of convenience, I'd have to say for the most part, where I was from, drugs and using drugs was a part of everyday life. It wasn't so much as the drugs, but the life drugs offered you that made you numb to the everyday struggles, and it gave you the courage to face your battles with a stick. The only problem with using drugs was that the illusions it painted in your mind only lasted for a short while. This form of escape let you dip in and out, repetitiously, until one day you woke up and found out something that you never knew about yourself, that you were a junky or an addict. In either case, you were a confused individual who couldn't discriminate between the two; so, you played with words and logic and said you had a habit when the truth of the matter was there was no difference. A junkie is a junkie because he loves to get high, and in contrast, an addict is an addict because he or she is addicted to drugs. It's just that the core of either sickness is summarized around one word. That is that they have a desire to get and stay high and just don't want to admit it.

I had to come face to face with myself and find out which label I wanted to use. I could not think of one that I would like to be called, being that both of them had negative connotations, and I had seen with my own eyes the damage drugs could do to *you*. Like I said, drugs were a part of everyday life in the ghetto.

I kept telling myself that was not what I needed in my life as I walked home after my shift. We had, had another night of craziness. My homies and I were on heavy dust (cocaine) and not only had the drugs altered our appearance making us look crazy as hell, but they had altered who we were. We used to act so crazy in the drug hole until everybody in the neighborhood became afraid of us, and that's something I didn't like. Deep down inside I knew I wasn't like that. My mom had raised me to respect people all the days of my life, so to see myself deviate from that pattern and actually have people become afraid of me was discomforting.

The first thing I noticed when I walked in the house was that everyone was asleep. It was like three in the morning and all I had on 'my mind was hopping in the sack and getting some z's, too, but I wanted to holler at my brother first and tell him about the latest events in my life to see what he would say. Sweet wasn't a dummy. He had plenty of sense and I was certain with our combined brain power we were going to beat the odds.

"Hey, Sweet ... Sweet," I whispered, shaking Sweet's shoulder for him to get up.

"Wake up man I need to holla at chu."

After a while, Sweet's eyes popped open. When I saw him break away from his stupor I felt a sense of elation, for whatever it was worth. My baby brother, my love, my other half was there for me even when I had stepped out of life's arena. One thing I knew was that with him I could be me. I could tell him what was troubling me, and I didn't have to worry about him using what I told him against me. That was done only in the judicial system, using whatever somebody said against them in a court of law. To us that was absurd. How could you give justice by doing that? Good thing that wasn't the case here. This was my baby brother Sweet. I could tell him anything and that would be that. I had no idea though that Sweet wouldn't even allow me to get a word out edgewise. As soon as Sweet got a good look at me he hopped out of bed looking petrified.

"Man, get away from me," Sweet shouted as he backed away from me with a look on his face like he saw a ghost. Maybe he had seen a human ghost, me.

"Man, what's wrong witchu," I said, trying to calm him down. He was acting paranoid like he was afraid of me. I even tried to touch him.

"I swear man if you don't get away from me I' mma call mommy, "Sweet threatened.

That's the last thing I wanted him to do was call my mom. I couldn't even think what I would say if my mother confronted me about using drugs.

The next day I made it up in my mind that I was going to stop snorting cocaine. My homies still offered it to me and I took it, but I used to fake like I was snorting. It wasn't like they were watching me do it. I'd just wait until they turned their back and make a sniffing noise like I was really getting down, and most of the time I even acted like I was high. To me this was the best part of my recovery. When I used to see how everybody acted on drugs, I couldn't believe that I had been acting the same way. All I knew was that wasn't me, and I kept putting on the hits until the desire was gone.

Most of the so-called big boys that you hear about today all came from that same coked out job. Convertible Burt, Convertible Fonz, Silk, Musclehead, Coop (Trick), Postal, and Boss (Liver Man) just to name a few. You all know their names. They're hood legends of yesterday living in the bottle (prison) being kept fresh like old wine.

A few months had passed, and I was steadily grinding, one slow motion at a time. I was no longer doing cocaine and both traps on which I worked for were clocking dollars like the US Treasury Department. It was 2PM and QB and I was just about to go grab something to munch on. I had a combo in mind, but QB wanted to stop by his favorite restaurant and get some curried goat. Sometimes it seemed like that's all he ate. I was wondering what was taking him so long. I left him in the house counting up the work, but I was thinking he should've been done. When I saw him emerge from the apartment, I knew something was wrong. He had this look on his face like he had just lost his best friend. I was like, "what done happened now?"

"I'mma bust shots in da blood clot boii," he mumbled.

"Look here, Star. Let me reason witchu."

I hopped in the car with QB, and we set out to grab a bite to eat. I knew we'd get there sooner or later but I had to listen to QB ramble on in his Jamaican vernacular the whole way there. This time, it wasn't so much his broken dialect that intrigued me, but what his broken English sought to express.

"Mon, I' mma do yo brotha something. I believe da Yankee boi stole me stash!" QB said angrily.

I didn't know what was going on. "What did he mean by saying my brother stole his stash?" I thought. My brother wouldn't take anything from him, especially when he knew that would make me look bad.

"Man, I don thank my brotha would do notin like dat without tellin me."

QB kept driving without responding to my words. I couldn't tell what he was thinking, and I didn't know what he had on his mind. Jamaicans were some crazy people who loved to do a lot of killing, and as mad as he was, I was hoping and praying it wasn't going to have to come to that. If it did, as much as I loved QB, blood was thicker than water.

Good thing QB and I had a bond. Our relationship went a little deeper than boss and worker. In fact, I knew QB had brotherly love for me by the way he treated me and the way he allowed my voice to stand firm outside of nonsensical things. QB even told all his friends when they would ask him about me that I was his strength. So, with his strong regard for me and trust in me, he squashed whatever it was about my brother that had him so upset. We hit Burger King first and headed to QB's favorite Jamaican spot to get his grub.

A few days later I was home looking for an outfit to wear. I never meant to bother Sweet's clothes, but I wanted to check out some shorts he had to see if I could fit them. When I pulled out the shorts wads of cash fell out onto the floor.

"Man, what dis is?" I questioned Sweet. He started looking dumbfounded.

"Playa, where ya get dis money from?"

"Man, why ya trippin?" He barked.

"Cause, I wanna know!"

Sweet never fessed up but I later found out he and his friend broke into QB's house just as QB had suspected. I was mad as hell at Sweet for doing that crap. Not only did he risk his life messing round, but he had put mine in jeopardy, too. I mean, it was just as easy for QB to think that I was down on the break in, but as he thought Sweet was the one who broke in. If he thought, I was involved then he would have come gunning to kill both of us. After we moved out of the apartment our family used to live in, it became our stash house. We paid the rent and utility bills like a normal family resided there. There wasn't a worry in sight and all of a sudden, the ghetto didn't seem so tough.

I copped me a fresh nineteen seventy-five Buick LaSable. It was a convertible, and that thing was hard. I used to have the top dropped so often you would have thought the car didn't have a roof. It had a roof, though, a white canvas top to be exact. I just loved driving with the top down all the time. It just seemed more appealing that way. In fact, the hood was the one who officially gave me the name Convertible Sonny. I don't have to tell you how much I love the name. Players and honeys gave me much respect, and if I can remember correctly, I believe I overheard a couple of shorties talking about how they wanted to be just like "Convertible Sonny" when they grew up. Now imagine that Sonny's got fans!

On a hot sunny day around twelve noon, it was business as usual. The big wheels kept turning and the crew kept on clocking dollars. We were raking in anywhere from ten to twenty grand a day in five- and ten-dollar bags of weed. We had a system in place. System was a word that made our organization sound sophisticated, but there was really nothing to it. Our apartment had a back entrance. Every time the bomb would get low, I'd beep QB to meet me in the back with the package. No one knew what I was doing when I used to branch off from the spot to get a new bomb and keep things moving. Anyway, QB used to meet me in the back. I would give him whatever money was made in exchange for a new package. Then I would clandestinely take the new package up to the stash house and bust the packs down into five-hundred-dollar bombs. I made sure my ledgers were intact. No fumbling around was my motto, at least not at this point in my life. QB loved every minute of it, too. My books stayed on the dime and my no-nonsense tolerance kept our workers on good behaviour. Well, all of them with the exception of Sweet. At every chance he had he rebelled against me. I kept telling Sweet the only reason he was back working for QB was because I vouched for him.

When I entered the stash house, I had every intention of cleaning things up. The place was a mess, and being a compulsively spotless individual, I let my guys get a little too comfortable. I even started laying stuff around and holding up on money to turn in after shifts. I never figured my actions had consequences and being as though I was young and handling large sums of money, I felt larger than life and untouchable. My mindset never came from the movie Scarface nor was it premised around any movies filmed in Hollywood. In the ghetto, you could easily be killed contemplating your actions around fairy tales. Bullets were real, death was real, and the production of building slaves, not actors, was in full swing.

I often think today there's a plan to subvert the black man. Maybe it's another conspiracy theory. I grant you that much, but in most beliefs, you can easily find substance. When I was young, I found my idols out of wretched men, who unbeknownst to me had no self-understanding, pimps with a string of hoes walking through the raindrops to get his money, or big drug dealers like Bo Dilly or Ike and countless others who shaped my destiny. That was such a simple thing to do. Living in poverty you'd always find someone out of thousands who just seemed to have the world at his feet. People loved him because he was smooth and drove around in the hottest cars.

Young cats like me lived for the day to duplicate his foolishness. In the end, we realized after we found ourselves in prison or dead that image that we held in high regards was a plant to lead the youth into the evil ways of man. You don't believe me? Take a survey. Ask any black man in the hood who was their idol growing up. You're going to hear names like J-Baby, Quartz, Rick Brownlee, Bo Dilly, Ike, Bonky-Brown and so on and so forth. They were nothing but plants, but not so much in the sense of them doing something wrong intentionally. They were manipulated and left alone for the purpose of destroying their own lives along with the myriad of lives that followed them hostilely saying, "when I grow up, I'm going to be like Ike!"

As soon as I entered the stash house, I heard someone pounding on the door. The knocks were so hard that they almost scared me to death. The first thing I thought of was that it was those gangster robbers trying to put the tax game down. The notorious robbers were known for that in The Village. They turned their greed on the dope man. This worked out good for them in the sense that dope dealers couldn't call the police. What were they going to say, "someone just ran up in my spot and took my dope?" For the most part, a drug dealer had to suffer the consequences of a robber and just bounce back, either that or have court in the streets. If a robber messed around and robbed the wrong hustler, he paid a dear price. Back in the day, most big boys, had hit men that didn't play. They made their living off of killing people, they went after robbers or cats who messed up the bomb money. That was one of the reasons I kept my books straight. I loved living too much.

I dropped everything I had in my hands, the gym bag, and the handful of money I was counting. At first, I looked around as if whoever it was outside banging on the door was going to bust through the walls and come charging at me, with such short notice, I couldn't even think straight, but something told me to look out of the window. The pounding continued relentlessly. "Open up!" I heard someone shout through the door. "Open this door or we'll knock it down!" I looked out of the window and saw policemen everywhere. "DAM!" I stammered as I hopped off the chair I was standing on.

I was in shock, but when I saw the door come flying off the hinges I pissed right in my pants. I just knew I was finished. The police ranted and raved about their successful drug raid. They confiscated at least fifteen thousand dollars in cash, ten thousand dollars in weed, ten guns, and another stupid youngster to add to the FBI files.

The Unseen Hand

Nobody ever told me that my criminal actions could have such serious consequences or repercussions. My peers schooled me on how to run game on a young lady and how to peddle dollar joints of weed and so on, but the most important part they lifted out. There is no eloquent way to say it. In terms of life lessons, I was pretty much left alone in this big world to fend for myself to the best of my abilities. I grew up with a skewed perspective of right and wrong. My limited ghetto-based education denied me the ability to distinguish the difference between right and wrong. Make no mistake about it, I was simply a tragic accident just waiting to happen. I went out into the world unprepared, and I was just going on about my merry way, trying to stay alive and trying to survive off of what I knew when life blindsided me. Before I knew anything I was in handcuffs and cramped up in the back seat of a police car. I was trying to sit calmly but all the commotion on the outside had me nervous. Beads of sweat dripped down my forehead and chill bumps frequented down my back. I wasn't scared, but extremely uneasy. For the most part, it seemed a little strange that even after seeing police cars many times in my life and watching them haul people off to jail that this time, I was the one going for the ride. My mind reflected on the time when I was young and watched Cecil being taken to jail. I kept trying to figure out if he felt the same way I was feeling, or did he have an I don't give a damn attitude. That wasn't the case with me because I started thinking about the dream I had, I was wondering was this it.

It wasn't long before my mother came and found me in the police car. As she struggled to get passed the police officers, I could see a look of desperation on her face. It was her look that hit me so hard because it caused me more pain than being in the back seat of the police car.

"Where is QB?" I heard her cry frantically as two officers restrained her. I tried to tell my mother that I was alright, but she kept screaming and hollering for QB. "Somebody go get QB! QB betta bond my baby out of jail!" My mom stood there defending me to the police, screaming that I hadn't done anything wrong, and threatening QB at the same time, but I couldn't do anything about it.

All in all, in my mother's eyes I was innocent because she knew her child was just a pawn in a bigger game who had somehow been set up since birth for failure. The real guilty party wasn't there, i.e., the system, and the unseen hand that had put guns and drugs in the black community for young boys like me to gravitate towards.

The whole time I sat there in the police car, which must have been for hours, no one moved. My mother had calmed down and she was standing a few yards away from the police car talking to a couple of girls who claimed they saw the whole thing. They tried to intimidate the officers by cursing at them, but none of it did me any good. I went to jail as sure as the sun rose and set.

By 4AM that morning I was walking out of jail a free man. I never even made it off the first floor. I was still in the booking process when I heard an officer walking the corridor yelling my name. There were numerous cells, and he was going to each one of them trying to find me.

"Albert Campbell!" The officer bellowed in a deep baritone voice.

"Yea dats me," I said, jumping to my feet.

"Date of birth?"

"January 9, 1964."

"That's you, you just made bail."

No, I'm not saying the experience of going to jail didn't spook me, but it was painless. I was surrounded by black brothers who were trying as best as they could to make bond but couldn't, and I made bond like it wasn't nothing. There were two bodies lying in the middle of the floor deadasleep and others clogged up the cell in different unsettled emotions trying to figure out their destiny, but mine was promising. I was being released so I could pick up the dice and roll them against the wall again.

The next day I was back in The Village. QB thought it was best for me if I would be the watch out man for a while. He didn't want me to handle any drugs, at least until things cooled down some. The only problem with that was every time I saw the police officer that arrested me, I would get nervous and go home. I still had the case pending and I just knew going back to jail wouldn't look too good.

When Passion found out about my uneasiness, she took me to a Root Lady. She said the Root Lady was her godmother. According to her, the Root Lady would make the police who arrested me disappear or stop bothering me altogether. I had no idea what a Root Lady was. Inside I felt like I didn't want to have anything to do with one, but Passion insisted on the matter. She kept telling me that there was nothing to it and that the Root Lady was only there to help me prevail over my enemies. Back in the old days, people used Root People in the place of lawyers or advisers. I don't know how true it was but when I finally went to see the Root Lady, she told me the case would be thrown out of court. She gave me some beads to wear and packages of dust to keep in my pocket. She told me to wear a pair of black underwear and to turn them inside out on the day I went to court.

Sure enough, when I went to court the case was dismissed. I felt like I had a new lease on life since I didn't have a case pending, and I thought it was time for me to start my game off from a different angle. I had already learned enough about the game from QB and now all I needed to do was put what I knew to work for myself. Shortly after my case was over, I started hustling for myself. The money was plentiful, the timing was right, and I felt as though nothing was going to stop me from selling my own drugs. In this way, I could call my own shots and make my own money.

I knew dudes like QB and Ike and a handful of others were making a killing in The Village alone, and there was no reason that I couldn't get mine as well. What I didn't know, and what no one bothered to tell me, was that with money came envy, jealousy, hatred, and animosity. Furthermore, by me simply cutting into what another man had built up on his labor, sweat, time, losses, and dope might cost me my life or someone else's theirs. But as the old adage goes, ignorance is bliss.

Nevertheless, I needed to make a name for myself just as QB had his trademark. His was the Doorbell and he had an emblem of a bell stamped on his bags. I went to the same stationary store that he went to buy his supplies and came across a stamp that said RUSH. RUSH was the kind of traffic I wanted coming to cop my drugs, so RUSH became my trademark.

I wanted to talk to QB and tell him it was about time that I started hustling for myself, but I knew he'd just try to talk me out if it. He would start by giving me this long speech about how he built the spot up and how he would give anything for me to just chill and I didn't want to go through that. For the most part, I simply didn't even want to face QB because all and all I knew he had been good to me, treated me like family, and I felt a little low even thinking about leaving him. I had to do what was best for me and my family. It wasn't time for fumbling around, at least not that day anyway. The spot was jumping so hard I used to sellout of what little weed I had like it was nothing. Every time I sold out, I would just go re-up and come back again shouting, "RUSH! We open!" I did this for about two weeks before QB realized what I was doing. I guess it wasn't that hard to tell since I stopped going around him and his workers were telling him I was selling weed close to his gates. The craziest thing about it was I thought I had just as much right to the spot as he did since it was in front of my old apartment. Not only that, but because I was the one who helped put it together, I felt I had the right to hustle there, too. Little did I know that's not quite how it went in the hood.

QB didn't like what I was doing at all. Every now and then he would even come through and threaten to do something to me. He said I was short stopping his gates, meaning I was taking his customers, and they usually gunned people down for doing less than that. He warned, "I'mma bust shots pun ya ras clot. Me don play bout me money!" There wasn't a doubt in my mind that QB didn't mean what he was saying. However, the point was that QB didn't love me because I was wise. QB knew I had a lot of heart, and if he messed with me, I was going to take him to war.

Cecil was hustling near our old apartment, he had been through a series of QB's threats, his antics didn't faze Cecil. Like father like son, we set out on a mission to conquer the city in a different kind of way. I think that both of us were thinking since we were family, we could make it to the top much easier together, and not with a lot of all that other stuff that went on between hustlers who were trying form a partnership. We moved up to buying a few pounds a week. We weren't making as much as QB, but we were doing well. As the plot thickened so did the hostility between QB and I. I knew it was just going to be a matter of time before things blew up. I figured the only reason why they hadn't already been because of the relationship we once shared.

I stayed on my p's and q's but I could feel the tension mounting every time I got to the spot. I knew death was like a common cold in the hood, and I didn't want to be added to the statistic. More so, I didn't want to be the cause of somebody else being added to them either. It wasn't like I was scared though. I don't know. I just needed a solution to the problem without looking like I chickened out, but I had no idea at the time what that was. Maybe, just maybe, we could all use a little compromise in life to get what we wanted. A piece here and there and a little give and take from both sides and you'd be surprised how things would turn out in the end.

One morning I was woken by a TV commercial. Sweet was watching some program and it never crossed his mind once that perhaps he had the volume up too loud. I would've told him to turn the TV down a little, but I wanted to hear the broadcast myself. It was a Job Corps commercial. I had seen that commercial I don't know how many times and never so much as blinked at it, but today, or that morning, everything that commercial said was like it was talking directly to me. I had to compromise in my situation with QB. I could either stand my ground and let it be known that my mom hadn't raise no punks, or I could dip for a minute and let things die down. I had pumped the spot up, too, but I just had this gut feeling that something tragic was about to happen.

I got out of bed and walked to the bathroom. I was just about to go inside when I heard my mom's voice coming from the kitchen. I couldn't exactly hear what she was saying but none of it mattered. She wasn't talking to Sweet or me.

"Ma, I wanna go to Job Corps," I said cordially. My mom was doing the dishes and cooking something for us to eat at the time. When I saw the steam rise from the pot, I know right then she was boiling water to make some grits. Grits and eggs were our favorite meal, and as much as she could my mom liked to fix that for us. When she heard my voice, she turned to face me. "Whatchu said Sonny?" She asked, wiping her hands dry on her shirt. She gave me this empty look. I couldn't tell you what she was thinking,
but I knew judging from the way she stared at me she was kind of shocked to hear what I had said. That's what gave me the idea that she heard me the first time, and when she asked me again that didn't mean she didn't hear me but that she wanted to be sure she heard me correctly. It took me to repeat what I said to better understand how thrilled she was to get me on my way. She didn't even discuss the matter any further with me. All she did was give me this big smile and she ran to grab the Yellow Pages. It all happened so fast.

The next day my mom was dragging me down to the unemployment office. That was where she said you signed up for the Job Corps. We had to catch two buses to get there. As soon as we entered the building my mom and I descended the stairs. It looked like she already knew where to go by the way she was moving. All I had to do was hurry along behind her.

I kept thinking it would be cool if she slowed down a little, but she kept her pace. As soon as we got to the top step, she slowed her pace and then stopped. Her eyes glanced over at the different people sitting at their desks manning phones and taking care of other responsibilities. I could hear a slight pant seep through her nostrils, but she never faltered. When she spotted a man, she felt could help us she approached him with the quickness. "Hi," she said politely. "I want to sign my son up for Job Corps. Where do I take him?"

"The gentleman smiled back at my mom and said, "Um ma'am step right over here and have a seat."

The gentleman gave me a cursory look and started rummaging through his desk. Within seconds he pulled out some forms and a pen and handed them to us to fill out. After we signed the papers, I could remember thinking, "am I really doing this?" I had only been to Tifton Georgia a few times with my grandparents when I was young. Now I was going to deal with the fact that I was going to be away from my family and the hood. I hadn't even gone anywhere yet and I already started feeling homesick. A big lump overwhelmed my stomach, and I felt a sense of nausea all of a sudden. All I wanted to do was get out of that place and never go back.

Little did I know soon I was on a Greyhound bus carrying two old suitcases full of cloths, a bag of food in case I got hungry, and heading to Morganfield, Kentucky. My mom didn't even give me time to cry or tell my friends good-bye. She just packed my stuff and sent me on my way. As far as the weed business, I left everything with Cecil, including a late model Volvo. My mom was a little upset about that, and I thought since Cecil knew the business things would be straight, but I was dead wrong about that. In fact, when the bus stopped, I called him only to find out that as soon as I left Cecil went on a rampage selling everything for immediate gain and not worrying about anything else. I was sick about that. I even tried to figure out a way I could head back home. As I travelled the winding roads that never seemed to end, I tried to make amends with my decision to leave. In all honesty I felt something really bad was going to happen to me with the QB ordeal, and getting away for a minute was the best thing I could have done.

My first week I had to attend orientation, and during the week I pretty much learned the center's rules, regulations, and how it was ran. The center looked like a school that had live in quarters to house other people who had come from all over the country. A few of the students even lived in Kentucky, but those individuals didn't stay on the campus for obvious reasons. What surprised me the most was that I quickly found out there were other people from my neighbourhood there, too. Cat-head, Nee-Nee, Trigger and a couple of others had been sent to Job Corps on court orders. They hated the place, and since getting an education to some young black men from my hood was like having AIDS, this was the last place any of us wanted to be. After only being there for a few weeks we were trying to figure out a way to make the center send us back home.

A few weeks later I was sitting in the TV room watching a movie when this guy approached me talking about, I was sitting his seat. "Hay man, ya sittin in my seat," the tall dark-skinned guy said with an attitude.

"Yo Playa nobody was sittin here, ya don't own dis chair," I said.

"Aye, I ain't no Playa and don't call me dat!" He responded.

"Well, Playa whateva but dis ain't yo seat," I said harshly, and before I knew it all hell broke loose.

I never saw it coming. Before I knew anything whoever they guy was, punched me in the jaw so hard my whole body went flying across the floor. Playa hit me so hard! I shouldn't say Playa because that day he gained my respect, but he hit me so hard I was out cold. The next thing I knew I was sitting up in the dorm with my jaw fractured. The next day when all my homeboys heard about what had happened, they came through to check me out. Nee-Nee was the first person I saw emerging from the hallway towards my room.

"Sonny, we heard what happened ta ya dogg. You wanna go straighten dem fools? He said with mad attitude."

"Yeah, let's go show dem cowards dat the homies from Da Bottom don play dat Let get busy!" Cat-Head stammered.

There was commotion in the dorm. People's screams echoed off the concrete walls and the place was in chaos, but that didn't stop us. We had to make a point so that everybody understood where we were from, Da Bottom. So, we took it to the TV area and put down. We started swinging on any and everybody and we didn't care who it was. In a matter of minutes' security and army base police officers had rounded all of us up and locked us down in Crab City. That's what they called the jail house that was on campus. As we sat waiting on people from the administration to come and talk to us, we made up our mind to tell them if they let us back on campus that we were going to kill those guys. We knew that would definitely get us sent home. Everything was tight that day. When the staff came by to ask us questions, we stood by the agreement we hatched.

"Um tellin ya, if ya let me outta here I'mma kill one of dem fools!" I heard Cat-Head and a couple other homies scream.

Within a few hours we were heading back to the crib. I already knew what I was going to do once I got there, and that was pick back up where I left off. Only two months had passed, and I knew things were pretty much the same. My only problem was Cecil messed everything up. I thought about QB for a minute, wondering if he was still beefing with me. I knew he had to know that I had gone into the Job Corps in an effort to avoid bloodshed, but now I was on my way back. When we finally made it home it was six in the morning. The Greyhound bus pulled into the downtown terminal to release its tired passengers. All of us were overjoyed to be back to the crib, feeling like we'd been gone forever. Everybody's parents were there awaiting them, including my mom. When she first saw me, she pounced all over me. The first thing she did was started telling me everything that went on since I left. I was glad to see her, too, but what surprised me the most was all the stuff that had happened in just a few months.

Sweet was working with Bob on Sixty-first Street. Bob was one of the older coons who had Sixty-first and the neighbouring streets from Sixty-second Street on back to Overtown and up to Fifteenth Avenue on lock. He was the heroin man who made plenty loot. Sweet gave me the run down on everything that was going on. In my opinion I wouldn't think a lot had happened in such a short period of time, but the city changed faces as fast as a chameleon changed colors. One day it was this way and the next thing you knew the streets were on a totally different course. In any event, Bob was the man of different faces I needed to holler at if I wanted to get back into the swing of things. Sweet told me Bob was cool and that I should holler at him about putting me down. At first, I didn't. I flinched at the idea because I knew Bob and his boys were straight up fools, but after my stomach was touching my back, I went ahead and hollered at him. Just like Sweet told me, Bob put me to work.

On the opposite side of Sixty-Second Street rested the city's main strip, Fifteenth Ave. We called it the Soul Train Line because of how people walked and drove up and down the middle of it. Fifteenth was famous for its weed, cocaine, crack cocaine, and heroin, distribution, but it was also infamous because of the many lives that were lost because of gun violence, and a complete miscarriage of human life. On the outskirts sat the ghetto inhabitants trying to escape stereotypes that constantly told them time and time again that black was ugly and white was beautiful. This was the very mindset ht kept an influx of traffic galloping through the dope stroll only to end up in graveyards or prison at an alarming rate.

The degeneration of the black man, by gavel or bullet or chemical or better yet ignorance, made a lot of people happy. The big-time drug dealer's pockets got fatter and fatter, the funeral parlor flourished, and so did the prison industry. Most people didn't land on the ghetto, the ghetto landed on them, so they simply lived by the sword to make ends meet to survive. The ghetto is a black man's rest haven. It's his heaven, too, if that's what he chooses to make it. It's also his own hell if he digs himself in deep enough that he can never get out.

Pump up the Volume

The reason why my days were cold and my nights were hot back in the day didn't have much to do with the seasons, but it was an indication of how my life was empty of God and his infinite grace. Granted, people told me stories about God and how I should be walking in the spirit. They even showed me pictures of Saviors and told me to try as best as I could to emulate them. Being a child, for the most part, I was obedient to my peers not knowing that I was being led astray. That's why I say I didn't have God's light to guide me through the valley of the shadow of death. THE GHETTO. Lacking His guidance caused me to run away from love and towards a life of crime.

My first day on the job was a challenging one. In fact, I think I would've quit right then had it not been for Sweet begging me to chill. Sweet kept urging me to stick with it until we found another way to get on our feet. It wasn't easy. I couldn't stand how Big Hound used to barricade us in the house like animals, and we couldn't get out unless someone on the outside let us out, and they couldn't get inside unless someone on the inside let them in. I thought that it was especially cruel and unusual punishment, because if the place caught on fire, we would burn to death, but that's how Bob ran his camp. The barricading was very simplistic, but the system around the barricade was very complex. The apartment had two doors, one for the customers to enter and the other for the workers. When the customers walked in the front door there was a reinforced wall with a hole carved into it the size of a golf ball. Every part of the apartment was super reinforced, and it took SWAT at least thirty minutes to get inside of the place. It also had a direct drain dumping system so we could dump the drugs in case the SWAT team turned the water off. That way when SWAT finally got inside the apartment, all the drugs would be gone, and we would lay on the floor like we didn't know what was going on. The most popular request we got was for a one-an-one. In ghetto terminology that was one capsule of boy (heroin) and one capsule of girl (cocaine).

The back door was used to change shifts, restock the house with drugs, pick up money, and to bring food. Every twelve hours when the lieutenants came to count up, they would bring us food and drinks. There were about six goons that used to come and drop off drugs and change shifts. They came deep like SWAT with heavy artillery just in case a situation arose such as workers stealing or the Jack Boys running up on the lieutenants while they were changing shifts.

One-day Sweet had just finished running a double. I was riding with the crew, as they went to put somebody else in the house to relieve Sweet. I was so tired that all I wanted to do was get home and crash. The lieutenants were jacking me off. They were taking a long time to change shifts. I had to see what was going on. I walked to the back door and knocked on the window.

"Who dat is?" I heard someone say.

"Sonny man what's takin ya'll so long?"

No sooner than the words came out of my mouth did the back door open. One of the lieutenants came out of the house looking crazy. When I saw how he was looking I knew some foolishness was going on. Face was one of the lieutenant's name. I wished I never knew him, especially after when I heard him say, "Man, yo brotha count came up short four hundred dollas." The minute he said that my mouth dropped. I was thinking, "I just know this fool didn't mess up these people money when he knows how crazy those cats are!" That meant that Sweet had to be dealt with. My heart pounded like crazy. If that was the case, I wasn't going to sit back and let those fools hurt my brother. If I did that my mother would hurt me. So, the only thing I could do was get into it with him.

I was thinking maybe things wouldn't be that bad. The last guy that got caught stealing or came up short, they striped him naked in front of the apartment building and beat him near to death. Then they put him back into the house to work the money off he was short. The problem with this picture was that we weren't going to let no body beat up on my brother and do nothing about it.

Sweet and I didn't have a cold chance in hell to win a war against Big Hound and his crew, so I did the next best thing. I begged them not to beat my brother. I just told them that I'd pay the four hundred dollars that he came up short. The lieutenant who walked out and told me about the money walked back in the house to discuss my offer with the others. As he walked away, I had all kinds of thoughts running through my head. Something was telling me to dip, and just suit up on the tail end and be ready for whatever they wanted to do. Something else was telling me that I was crazy as hell for even thinking like that.

I heard the door slam, waking me from my daydream. When I looked towards the door the lieutenant had disappeared into the apartment. All that was left for me to ponder on was the babbling of voices inside, of which I could barely hear, but couldn't understand. About thirty minutes rolled around with no sign or no one coming out. I was just about to get worried when the back door swung open. At first, I heard a bunch of laughter and then all the lieutenants came out of the house. They didn't look mad or anything, but I knew you didn't have to be mad to hurt somebody in the hood. It wasn't that personal if a fool violated, he got dealt with. It was up to him to respect the game or not.

All the lieutenants passed by me like it wasn't anything. I was about to ask them what was up when Face hollered and told me it was their mistake. He said they made a bad count. I felt good as hell. Not so much knowing that I was right all along, but also knowing that Sweet was learning how to keep it clean.

Big Hound knew Sweet, and I were from The Village, and since The Village was jumping major drugs, they wanted to put a spot down in The Village. The catch was that they would let us be lieutenants, and that was like signing our own death warrant. Hit Man was a big-time cocaine dealer, who already had The Village on lock and anybody who dared to try to put down in his spot got dealt with. Big Hound had to know this so his idea of trying to set up shop there seemed suicidal. The problem was I wasn't ready to die. I let Big Hound know off the bat I wasn't trying to get down like that. I could stand being a lieutenant somewhere else, but not in The Village. Those fools would kill me if they caught me bringing some other hustlers in who didn't live around there talking about selling dope.

After SWAT got me a couple times out of Big Hound's heroin house and they didn't get any drugs off of me, I decided to go back to sell drugs in front of my old apartment in The Village. I knew I had gotten busted there too, but it didn't matter because I was getting nervier as time went on.

I thought The Village would be sweeter for me, but that wasn't the case. The police had gotten so bold that they would sit in the spot all day for weeks, and no one would be able to make any money. They wanted Hit Man bad. We used to call Hit Man a one-man SWAT team. That fool was as crazy as a bessy bug. When Hit Man got upset, he would start biting on his lip and wouldn't stop until it bled. Most cats used to try to figure out what they could do for him before it got to that point because they knew if his lip bled then somebody else was going to bleed too. They were going to get shot or beat down, but in either case, they were going to bleed. When Hit Man saw nine, (the police), still sweating the area he parked his car and sat on the side of The Village. I watched him sit in his car pondering his problems. He looked over at me every once and a while but quickly got back to his situation.

Usually, I would be in violation of strict ghetto laws being that I was trying to do my own thing, but a big player like Hit Man didn't pay me the least amount of attention. He knew I wasn't a threat to him, or his empire and he didn't care about how much weed I sold. though I did well I was in no position to alter his traffic. If anything, he had bigger problems than me, like the police, and he knew it. Besides, there were other hustlers around like Ike and QB getting major case flow, so if he was going to take the heat to anybody, it would be one of them. Each of them had their own individual sections. The way the apartments were built different pusher could utilize different angles to serve their own individual needs. As long as no one got too close to the next man's trap peace was maintained.

After a while Hit Man got out of his car. I heard him complaining and talking foolishly about the police stopping him from making his money. When I saw what was going on I hatched a plan. I figured I could straighten his problems out for him if he'd just give me a job. I had to let him know so I bopped over to where he was standing. My stride was smooth yet strong, and I had the kind of evil on my face no evil could match. From that moment on I was so wrapped up in this living I was willing to kill or be killed. All I needed was for a boss player like Hit Man, the ghetto Savior, to push my button.

"Wassup shortie?" Hit Man croaked as he gazed into my immature body, not even a string of hair on my face.

"Ya'll youngsters' betta be careful round here, ya see nine sweatin," he said, trying to obscure his anger.

His frustration was almost hidden, but I wasn't a fool. I just knew he was hotter than the sun and I was trying to get down on his line. So, I said…

"Man, I'm straight dogg, dem crackas always sweatin ya dogg, give me a job off da streets and an AK-47 and' I'll blast dem crackas fo ya," I said as serious as a heart attack. There was a cold silence for a split second. Hit Man and I exchanged glances. I couldn't read his mind, but I knew he could read mine. He knew I was foolish enough to do it.

"Naw Sonny, we jus gotta wait dem crackas out." Hit Man said as he dug in the pocket of his neatly pressed khaki outfit.

"Here, Sonny. Just chill out," Hit Man said as he passed me five crisp hundred-dollar bills. His anger never faltered by nine sweating his spot, but he had enough humor to smile as if it wasn't a problem.

I think Hit Man had come to appreciate what he had just by seeing me showing how foolish and ignorant I was. I was willing to act a fool that day at the expense of my pride. The only problem was Hit Man realized what he had and what he stood to lose by some youngster who didn't have a clue of what was going on. Hit Man knew the rules down to a science. That's why he glanced around, made sure nine wasn't looking his way and dipped.

Hit Man never said it, but I could tell from that point on he liked me. He knew I had heart and he wanted me to learn how to govern it. The first thing I needed to learn, if I wanted to work for Hit Man, was that you never shoot at the police. At times Hit Man would ride through the area and come talk to me. He called it getting me right, well schooling me in ghetto etiquette, and trying to make sure the entire kill a cop crap was out of my system. I could tell he had plans on hiring me, but he had to make sure he wasn't hiring an out of control zealot.

One day I went ahead of myself and asked Hit Man for a job. I thought I had the rules down packed, and I made sure he knew I wasn't about to do anything crazy like shoot at a police officer. If a fool got out of line that was a different thing altogether. Hit Man gave me and Sweet a job that same day. There was no need to keep grooming me. That stage was over. It was time to pump up the volume and get paid.

Nothing Unusual

Most of the guys that worked for Him Man grew up in the Village. The Village was their livelihood, and the drug game was their validity towards living. I remember when you were asked to state who you were and what set you claimed? You weren't talking that "I'm black and I'm proud" thing! Not in the hood anyway. You were talking about "Playa I'm real and I'm from da Ville, now play wit it!" That was the attitude in the game where I'm from. You lived, ate, pissed, and crapped the drug game.

From a young G's perspective, I always loved the drug game. It was sort of like my refuge. Since the ghetto was holy it made sense for me to view the hood as the Bible.

Sometimes I even followed the scriptures according to my limited understanding. If I'd read that God said something about warring or how Jesus feed the multitude, I followed the Word. I even planted seeds in the earth. At the time when I was looking for a job from Hit, Man Corenthia was pregnant with our baby. That was one thing that I liked about Hit Man was he respected family ties. One day he pulled me to the side and said ...

"Sonny I be seeing you walking around here holding your girl's hand with her big belly, stop being so quick to result to violence, remember you have a family to support, and you can't do it from behind bars or in the graveyard."

It was September 17, 1985, and Hit Man words didn't really sink in until I held Katrevia in my hands. I looked into her bright eyes then back to Corenthia and at that very moment, my life meant something to me. I had a purpose and a reason to do as best as I could to stay alive and support my family. It was the happiest day of my life.

In between me fulfilling my parental role with Corenthia, I still had to deal with other virtues of the street life, of which my own personality had become a product of. The Bible also helped me while I was on that destructive path. So, I constantly prayed ...

"Yea though I walk through the valley of the shadow of death, I fear no evil; thy rod and thy staff comfort me, every step of the way ... "

Most of the hustlers who went to jail got right back out in a few years. It didn't matter what the crime was, from murder to getting busted for drugs. In a few years they were back out on the streets and bigger than there were before the left. Seven years would be the most you'd spend for killing somebody. If the crime was robbery those seven years varied from three to five, and sometimes even a year and a day.

I remember, Happy Tat walked right up to Bert and shot him in the head in broad daylight. He might have spent eight months in jail if that. Happy Tat was a fool. He didn't care who he robbed or killed. It didn't matter that all of us grew up together, struggling together. If you messed around and got caught slipping, you became fair game. That's what happened to Happy Tat. He got so wrapped up in robbing and killing cats until his discretion got blurred. He forgot the hood was filled with killers and notorious bandits like him. Nobody messed with them unless there were willing and ready to go to war. He was on a roll for a while and built up a name for himself. I can't forget the day Happy Tat robbed Ray Ray. Ray Ray was the bomb man for Hit Man on the day shift, who feared Happy Tat. Well, the whole hood feared Happy Tat. When he threw down on Ray Ray he was crying like a baby.

"Com on Tat-man, don't kill me," Ray Ray pleaded. Happy Tat even sat down and talked to Ray Ray while he robbed him and made Ray Ray's watch-out man go get all the drugs to bring back to him. Tat had his hand in a brown paper bag like he had a gun. Nobody knew if he had one or not and nobody wanted to flinch and find out.

Tat was the kind of fool that if you just heard he was in the area it was enough reason to be scared to death, especially if you were hustling. Even fools like Happy Tat had an end. My mom used to tell me all the time when I was young ...

"Boy, one day you gon meet your match." She also said, one-day Happy Tat gon run up on somebody just as crazy as he is."

How does the night look before and after a murder? Before everything can seem normal. It didn't necessarily have to be a full moon or any signs that warned you that a disaster was imminent. Just out of nowhere all hell could break loose and the next thing you've got a dead body lying on the ground and everybody trying to figure out what the hell was going on.

One day I was unaware of the time. It was one of those good nights, like a Good Friday, when the wind swooped through the hood leaving a tolerable sensation on anyone who was lucky enough to be standing in its path. It had rained earlier and most of us were standing on the corner kicking it. A cat named Barerug was standing on the end of the Circle K Store popping game to one of the ghetto queens. My homey Ty and I were standing at the other end making a bet that Barerug couldn't get the girl's seven digits. Barerug was a dangerous cat who lived by the gun. So, I'm thinking a dude who was more so a fool in the hood didn't have a lot of sense not to pull any girls, especially like the one he was popping flavor too. Boo was so pretty and fine that cats thought she was out of their league. Before Ty and I knew anything, Happy Tat hit the corner with his gun in his hand.

"Alright ya suckas, it's tax time!" Happy Tat said.

Ty and I gave up Hit Man's package like it was nothing. We didn't have time to be wasting with this fool. Barerug bucked the jack, and why he did that was beyond anybody's guess when he knew Happy Tat was a known killer.

"Playa, I ain't giving you notin, ya gotta kill me," Barerug stammered as he stood in front of the frightened girl protecting her from Happy Tat.

Oh, Playa ya wanna buck huh," Happy Tat said right before busting off two shots. One hit Barerug in the leg. The other one ricocheted off the ground and hit the wall. Ty and I ducked behind a car. We heard a couple of people screaming but we couldn't identify who they were. We saw Happy Tat run passed us as we listened to Barerug grunt in agony for somebody to call an ambulance. Nothing was unusual about that night. People came and went as they normally did, and motorists traveled back and forth down Seventh Avenue as if it was any other day.

A month later a number of us were chilling in front of the same store. This time, Happy Tat was up there, too. He was hanging around like it was all good just chilling with some of the guys he'd robbed before. It was crazy but hustlers were so spooked of Happy Tat that even when they caught him slipping, they didn't do anything to him. The craziest things about it was that Happy Tat wasn't even a threat because the police had just run us out of the Village, so no one was strapped. Well, no one but Barerug. He came from around the corner with guns blazing. He fired several shots at Happy Tat. One of them hit him in the leg and Happy Tat took off running. Barerug ran behind him, and a crowd ran behind Barerug. Everybody wanted to see what was going on. Happy Tat was running fast, but Barerug was right behind him. Happy Tat ran across 7th Avenue and into somebody's house. Barerug was still in hot pursuit after him. For a moment we heard a lot of commotion going on inside the house. Then all of a sudden, we saw Barerug dragging Happy Tat out by his leg. Happy was begged ...

"I'm sorry Barerug, man you know I got dat monkey on my back. "

There were about fifty of us standing around looking at this drama unfold right before our eyes.

"Naw ya no good robbin sucka, ya shoulda thought about dat befo ya shot me, don cry now!" Barerug shouted at the top of his lungs. Then in an instance, between a burst of tears and wailing from Happy Tat, Barerug squeezed his killer steal. Shots rung out like crazy and Happy Tat's body danced around on the ground like a snake being splashed with a pot of boiling water. His body only stopped jumping after Barerug's gun was empty.

CHAPTER SEVEN

ARE YOU SMART OR INTELLEGENT?

I ran the bomb (the man who does the drug transactions) on the night shift and Ty and Twin were my lookout men. Ray Ray ran the bomb on the day shift and Sweet and Pep Brown were his lookout men. To me, I had the sweetest shift because in the wee hours of the night I could make things happen. It didn't take me long either. As soon as I learned HitMan's system, I started tapping his package like I tapped QB's. When I saw a roll of heavy-duty aluminum foil in the trunk of Hit Man's stash car my mind went to thinking of a scam. I was thinking those were some fat twenty-five-dollar sacks of cocaine that Hit Man was selling. I could take a little bit of cocaine out of each quarter then repackage it in the same aluminum foil and even Hit Man wouldn't be able to tell the difference.

After studying Hit Man's folding technique, I would break down a hundred quarters pieces and make one hundred twenty-five quarters. Fifteen quarters I would sell off the bat making three hundred seventy-five dollars every day for myself, and the other ten quarters I would break down into dime sacks and send them on Fifteenth Avenue where I began building my own trap. My homeboy Maurice had a game room up there, and that's where I put it down. I knew if Hit Man ever was to find out I'd be dead, but for some reason, I wasn't deterred.

We started off small so the hustlers who already had Fifteenth sewed up never noticed what we had going on. That was a good thing. As long as everybody was happy there wasn't a need for any gun play. I didn't need that type of activity going on, not so soon anyway. If something did jump off though there were just a couple of goons, I knew that had my back. One, in particular, was Ray Ray. Ray Ray was tapping Hit Man's sake too.

Our scam used to run so smoothly that Ray Ray and I got caught up in who did more and was getting more money that we fell out again. It took a material device to show us that our beef from school days when I whipped his butt still existed.

One day Ray Ray took me to see a 1975 Chevy with lime green interior. The car was clean and in the back of my mind I was mad that I hadn't seen it first.

"Man, dis Chevy raw huh Playa?" Ray Ray said excitedly as he walked back and forth.

"Yeah, dis thang like dat," I said nonchalantly.

I didn't show much excitement but deep down inside I was trying to hatch a plan to get it instead of him. When the salesman came, he and Ray Ray started talking. I saw Ray Ray trying to explain to the salesperson about how he was going to try and get up the money. I would I've thought Ray Ray could buy the car easily with what he was trimming Hit Man for on the side plus the four hundred and fifty dollars a week salary he was making, but that wasn't the case. Ray Ray had habits, obviously one bigger than what he could afford, like getting high, and having a few cats sweating him like they were groupies. That kept him broke as a joke. Three weeks had passed and when I saw Ray Ray still hadn't bought the car I went behind his back and bought it. The car was on Seventy-ninth Street at this little buy-here-pay-here car lot. When I got there and showed the man, I had the money to purchase the car on the spot, he didn't hesitate or mention the fact that Ray Ray had left a two-hundred-dollar deposit to hold it. I came through the Village cruising in that thang it felt like I was floating on air. When Ray Ray saw me and the paper tag in the back window, he caught instant beef. He flagged me down and walked towards the car with the quickness.

"Damn, dats how ya playin?" Ray Ray said with mad attitude.

"Dogg, ya acted like you ain't want it so I just copped da dam thang," I said grinning like a Cheesy Cat.

"Man, dats messed up! "

"Homie, stop trippin I! if ya get da bread I'll jus letchu get it fo forty-five hundred."

"Forty-five hundred? Da car don cost notin but two grand."

Boy Ray Ray was hot, and he didn't speak to me for days. Every time he saw me, he had this sour look on his face like he wanted to jump on me. Ray Ray knew I could fight. He had another option of dealing with my so-called good fighting butt, though. He ran and told Hit Man that I was tampering with his dope.

I remember the day Hit Man came and scooped me up to discuss the matter. I was scared out of my wits. The first thing Hit Man did was check his packages to see if it had been tampered with. I couldn't tell what he would've done if he had found out that what Ray Ray said was true, and God knows I didn't want to find out. When Hit Man looked at his dope, putting it to his nose, weighing and tossing it around in his hands, my nerves were going haywire, and if I wasn't mistaken, I saw him biting on his lip. I soon found out, though, that I had done such a good job repackaging his dope that even he couldn't tell the difference. He just game me back the dope like it was nothing and told me to put it up and ride with him. I was like, "oh no this cat bout to take me somewhere and beat me up. "I hesitated to get in the car, but I knew if I didn't it would point out my guilt. One way or the other I thought I was doomed, but I climbed inside anyway. Hit Man had a big four-door Benz. All I knew was that it was so pretty that I couldn't believe he was going to let me ride in it with him. As soon as I got in, I felt like I was sitting on top of the world. It would take me to see Hit Man's chrome pistol laying in between his thighs for me to realize how close I was to having six inches of dirt sitting on top of me.

When we rode across the railroad tracks on Seventh Avenue and Seventy-fourth Street Hit Man made a left turn. There were no streetlights, and he could have just as well as shot me and dumped my body on the side of the road. As soon as Hit Man pulled in a dark alley and put his car in park, I noticed for the first time that he had an awry look on his face, and a brushed lip.

"Sonny, what would make a dude smart as opposed to intelligent in da dope game?" Hit Man said with a menacing look on his face. I shrugged my shoulders in response.

"Okay Playa, let me help ya out. Da choices we make in life define who we are. If you made some messed up choices nine times outta ten you a messed-up dude. Now how you make those choices one way or the other depends on whether you think you're smart or intelligent." Hit Man said as he drew closer to my face. He was so close I could feel the air seeping out of his nose and mouth. My body shriveled up.

"So which one is you, Sonny, smart or intelligent?" Hit Man asked with the same menacing look on his face.

"I'm smart," I stammered, as my back flattened against the back of the seat and the door's panel as Hit Man drew even closer to my face.

"Datz da wrong answer Playa, ya see a smart cat can read and write so he think he can cheat a hustler like me cause I can't, but ya know what, wit all a smart cat's knowledge he still can't out think an intelligent hustler like me, if ya wanna last in dis game Sonny, you betta be intelligent like me and play by da rules, cause if I ever come by my spot and see yo lil smart behind done found a way to tap into my package thinking I won't know or can't tell, I'mma letchu know right then and there that you made a bad choice and I'mma kill ya!"

The Night Shift

Hit Man liked to party. One year he made so much money hustling that he invited all of his workers to the Jazz Festival in Atlanta. It was his way of showing his appreciation for all the work we had done making him hood rich. It was the Budweiser Super Feast, one of the hottest festivals on the planet. Pattie Labelle and Luther Vandross were the headliners, and everybody that was somebody was supposed to be there. Hit Man was definitely somebody, and by right since we were on his line, we were too. My homey Ty chose to stay behind and keep the spot going. We kept telling him to roll with us, but he wasn't with it.

At the break of day, we set out to join Pattie and Luther in Hotlanta. By the time we made it to the Georgia Dome it was packed with people. I'd never saw so many black people packed into one place in my life. I kid you not, the short time I was there I felt like I was in another dimension. The moment we entered the dome, I realized Hit Man had power. Not simply because we had front row seats, but because I witnessed him intermingle with Pattie and Luther's entourage. Now that's real power, at least from a young G's perspective. I was fantasizing as I watched him. I imagined that he was me and I was him, and I was the one standing up there like I was the King of Miami.

The stage was set, and the show was about to begin. In an instance, the stage man working the electronics dimmed the lights down low and all types of multi-colored green, red, blue, and white lights popped out of nowhere. They were flashing across the stage and the people as well. Ray Ray and I sat motionless in anticipation for whatever was going to happen next. I had a stomach full of butterflies. All I could think about was if I was actually about to see Pattie Labelle and Butler Vandross in real life. Those same voices that I'd heard over the radio and snapped my fingers to or sung the chorus line with were going to have a face. The crowd stood frozen for a moment. Then no sooner than the host did his customary greeting did Pattie strut out onto the stage wearing this red sequenced dress. The crowd went berserk, and Ray Ray and I stood there with our mouths agape. Her hair was sharp but her long sensuous fingernails were even sharper. In sum, the homegirl was beautiful, and her voice was intoxicating. I felt all of Pattie's songs deep down in my soul. The music just made me lose control. Everybody in the Georgia Dome was on fire. My homeboy Twin was messed up so bad he started crying like a baby. I think for the most part Pattie and Luther spoke directly to our broken spirits in a soulful way. Everyone there was up on their feet hooping and hollering like crazy. We stayed throughout the whole show. Finally, around three O'clock in the morning we arrived back to the suite, still in a state of bliss. All I could say was, money made conditions better in this wretched life of mine.

We stayed in Atlanta for two days. The night we were about to leave, Ray Ray and I had a good talk about the streets and how we were going to get some money one day, and travel all over the country like Hit Man did. We were so fired up about the show that we even squashed our beef.

"Yeah, Playa ain't no sense in us beefin, when we got money ta get." Ray Ray said earnestly.

I think Ray Ray meant what he said, and there's no question in my mind he was being honest. The question was, was I going to be foolish enough to believe that one Jazz Festival was going to be enough to squash a conflict he and I had since we were kids? One way or the other, since the mood was set, I went along with the truce.

Hit Man emerged from the back room wearing a light blue Puma sweatsuit shouting ...

"Alright ya'll let get ready to get on da road, I got money ta make, we can't make it up here in the ATL lolly gaggin round."

I stayed up the whole drive back home thinking of a master plan. I was getting a little money, but I wanted to be on the level with cats like Hit Man. I knew I had to step my game up, but the problem was figuring out how I was going to do it. I certainly, couldn't keep tapping Hit Man's package. That crap was going to play out sooner or later, and I just knew it was going to be bad for me if he ever found out what I was doing. He had already started looking at Sweet and me funny after we bought new cars. I copped a 1978 Cadillac Sedan and Sweet copped a Chevy Caprice Classic. We hadn't put but a little money down on the cars, but I'm sure Hit Man didn't see it that way.

I pushed my face against the window and started counting the streetlights as we rolled past them. Somewhere in between the trees and the roaring of the van I lost track of time. The next thing I knew we were back in Miami. When we got back to work the first thing Ray Ray and I saw was that Ty had mixed his package in with Hit Man's dope. We didn't know how much money he had made but we knew he made the packages way too small. Not only that but he used the wrong bags to repackage the drugs in. Ray Ray refused to sell the drugs on his shift, and I was afraid if I tried to sell the drugs, one of the customers might turn around and show it to Hit Man. I was just thinking how in the hell I would explain that when he already suspected that's what I was doing. I told Ty I wasn't going to sell the drugs.

"Man, you can sell da stuff," Ty said loud as he tried to put me on blast.

"Man, I ain't messin wit dat," I complained.

After Ray Ray and I kept refusing to help Ty sell the drugs, he accused us of telling Hit Man on him. I didn't know where he got that from, but I knew I didn't tell Hit Man a damn thing. Ty wasn't trying to hear nothing. After going back and forth with him for a few days, Ty decided to take it to the next level. One late night while we were working, he upped a Mac-11 with a thirty-round clip on me.

"Sucka I should blow yo freakin head off!" Ty screamed as he pushed the gun's barrel in my face. My heart almost jumped out of my chest. I started thinking this cat is trippin hard. I didn't move, and the minute he pointed his gun at me I lost my voice. Ty was talking crazy too.

"I thank you and Ray Ray told on me anyway," he yelled violently. I still didn't say anything. I could see Ty's temper rising and I was just hoping and praying that he would put the gun down. I kept whispering to myself and hoping he didn't lose it and squeeze the trigger. I guess Ty felt like he had made his point without firing a shot because he finally lowered the gun's barrel from my face and walked away mumbling to himself.

I didn't leave right away. I waited for a while just to make sure everything was cool. I was mad as hell, but I couldn't do anything about it at the time. After about an hour of pretending like nothing had happened, I told Ty that I was going to count up the drugs, but instead of doing that I went home and got Sweet. I told Sweet what had happened and how Ty tried me. I knew I didn't mind being a chump for a moment or so, or even an hour, but I wasn't going to be one for life. I made up my mind that somebody was going to die that night. I asked Sweet to lay in the back seat of my car, with an AK-47 and if Ty acted like he wanted to do something to blast him.

When I pulled in front of the spot, Ty was still sitting in the front chilling like nothing had happened. I jumped out of the car. The car had dark tented windows. When Ty saw me pull up, he didn't budge. I was out of the car so fast, that he understood right then what time it was. His eyes kept trying to penetrate the tints, until Sweet cracked the back door open.

"Playa why you were trippin," I said with an attitude. I was waiting on Ty to get slick out the mouth.

"Sonny boy ya couda sold da drugs fa me," he stammered.

"Nah, how I'mma sell dis?" I barked as I showed him the drugs. The package looked crazy. What really upset me was he was beating me getting mad like he and I were in cahoots together. After I showed Ty how crazy his package looked, he took it and sold it himself. Then he walked away mumbled something back at me and we left it at that.

Drama

One day a bomb of eighty-quarters of cocaine was sent to Ray Ray. For some reason, he thought he could get over on Hit Man. He came looking for me to tell me about this plan he'd hatched. I was chilling in Fifteenth Ave. with my own hands in the cookie jar. When I spotted Ray Ray, I knew he was up to no good.

"Sonny ... Sonny ... "Ray Ray said excitedly.

"Wassup?" I blurted out, interrupting him. I was anxious to see what it was he had to say.

"Sonny, I got eighty-quarters, dem lame jokers dun slipped," Ray Ray said looking around like he was expecting somebody. It took a minute for me to digest what he was saying. I knew, I heard him say something about, eighty-quarters, and dem slipping. The part that confused me was how could they lose two thousand dollars' worth of dope. That made me wonder.

"Man, how dya jus gon slip like dat?"

"I don know dogg, but dya did."

"Ray dem cats might be try in ta set chu up, jus put da bomb up in da apartment fo a few days, if dya don say notin, den we'll see wassup, "I said.

A few days went by and sure enough, Hit Man began to ask about the missing quarters. The first thing that came to my mind was somebody was dead. Hit Man had on his Rambo outfit, and he was looking foolish in the face. I didn't say anything because I didn't have anything to do with it. Hit Man wanted me and Ray Ray to ride with him. I started thinking, oh no not another ride. I just knew, this time, Hit Man was going to move something. That day he was riding in his Bronco. I let Ray Ray climb inside first since he was the one responsible for the drugs. I figured if Hit Man started shooting Ray Ray would get hit first.

It was mid-afternoon, and our daydream was suddenly invaded by Hit Man telling us he wanted his dope. When Ray Ray said that he didn't know anything about the bomb, Hit Man started biting on his lips.

"I'm about to hurt ya'll bout my dope!" Hit Man barked. I was scared to death, but I still didn't say anything. I was wondering why in the hell Ray Ray ain't just give the man his stuff. All he had to say was it was misplaced, but he didn't want to do that.

I knew Hit Man wasn't faking about his money. What I didn't know was, that Ray Ray had spent all but three hundred dollars of the stash. What messed me up the most was that I had somehow gotten dragged into the middle of his mess.

When Hit Man notice Ray Ray and I weren't saying anything and playing crazy, he drove us back to the spot and dropped us off. Before he pulled off, he made sure we understood that if his dope didn't come up he was going to punish me and Ray Ray and get a fresh crew. After Hitman dropped us off Ray Ray and I didn't exchange any words. We didn't have too. Not when he already knew that I was hot for being involved with his foolishness. I just went to Corenthia's house holding a boat load of bad thoughts in my mind. All I could see was death at the end. That night I held my daughter, and Corenthia like I was already missing them.

A few hours later Ray Ray came around to Corenthia's house where I was and called me outside. He was waiting on me to come out so he could shoot me. Good thing Corenthia felt something was up and told me not to go out the door. I wasn't afraid of Ray Ray at all. Sure, I had some reservations about killing him, but that was only to the extent that I didn't want to go to prison and leave my family. Nevertheless, I had to confront him.

Later that day, I walked out of the house, strapped with my pistol, with intentions to confront Ray Ray about Hit Man's dope. When I saw him walking through the cut, I yelled ...

"Aye Ray Ray, let me holla at chu." He spun around and walked towards me with much pep in his steps.

"Man, why ya trippin? You and I know you got da man stuff," I said. Before I knew anything Ray Ray poked me in the face and said ...

"So, what Playa! Ya gotta gun?"

"Yea punk," I said and backed a few steps away from him. I pulled out my chrome .38 Snug nose pointed it at his stomach and squeezed the trigger. I was expecting a loud boom and Ray Ray to fall to the ground but neither happened. The gun just clicked. I was so surprised that I froze, thinking at the same time what the hell just happened. Ray Ray must've been shocked too, by the way, he looked at me and then at his body. When he realized he wasn't shot he took off running. I ran behind him still pulling the trigger. All I could think about was the Barerug and Happy Tat incident. In the back of my mind, I felt a rush, thinking people were going to talk about me like they talked about Bareurg, but God was looking out for Ray Ray that night. The .38 I had wouldn't shoot for anything in the world. Every time I squeezed the trigger it just clicked.

When I got home Sweet and Maurice were there. As soon as I walked inside the house I was besieged by Sweet's words when he said ...

"Man, dat sucka Ray Ray shot at me when I rode through da Village," Sweet said panicky. I could hear Maurice talking over my thoughts, saying something about killing Ray Ray, but I was so busy trying to figure out what the hell was going on, that I couldn't really register anything. Then seemly out of nowhere I said ...

"Yeah man, I just tried to kill em," I said confused, "but dis gun wouldn't shoot, see." I pointed the gun's barrel towards the floor and squeezed the trigger to show them the gun wouldn't shoot but this time, it went off. The loud noise scared the daylights out of everybody. I dropped the gun, and all of us stared at it.

Around 11:30 that night we got word that Hit Man wanted to see all of us up at the Circle K Store. When we drove up, we saw, Hit Man, Ray Ray and his brothers, Ray Ray's do boys Pep Brown and Big Mel, were up there chilling too. There were a lot of different people up there also. They all heard through the grapevine what was going on and were waiting to see what was going to happen. For the most part, since everyone knew about Ray Ray and his big family and how they went for bad, they were whispering that we were going to be their next victims. The odds may have been against us, but

I had to go for broke. This fool was about to get me trapped off in something I didn't have anything to do with, and I wasn't about to go for that.

When I saw Pep Brown and Big Mel, I knew right then those fools helped Ray Ray spend the money or had something to do with it. Ray Ray was still tripping and trying to act like he didn't know what was going on. I was about sick of his crap. Since Hit Man was up there, I told him everything. I let him know I didn't have anything to do with it. As soon as I said that, Hit Man started looking at Ray Ray funny and biting his lip at the same time. Ray Ray had an ashen look on his face. He started talking crazy to me and we started arguing back and forth. I could not believe; he was really acting like he didn't know what was going on. He did everything he could to try and shift the blame on me. He even called me out.

"Sucka let go in da back of da store." Ray Ray said. Impulsively, I responded.

"Let's go punk!" I barked. "Nah chump let's do it right here!"

I was so hot, before I knew anything I punched Ray Ray in the jaw. It had some force behind it too, by the way, his knees buckled. Then we tied up, but I wasn't getting off like I wanted too though. I wanted to stomp him but every time I got the fool down, people were pulling me off of him. There were only two people up there with me, Sweet and Maurice. There was a lot of commotion going on, but it became obvious to us that we couldn't win against everybody that was up there.

"Man, dam dat!" Sweet said with mad attitude. "Let's go get dem guns," he shouted.

The night lights flickered across my face, but I didn't have time to think about it. Before I knew anything we were back on the corner with not the least bit of understanding except somebody was about to die. We rolled up on Nick and one of the twins. Before I could get out of the car Nick was walking towards me running off at the mouth.

"Sucka ya tried to shoot my brotha!" Nick shouted. It was on and popping from there. O'Neal aligned the car with the quickness and pointed the chrome .38 Snug nose at Twin's head.

"Playa whatchu wanna do? Die!" He squeezed the trigger, but the gun just clicked. I couldn't tell you what was up with that gun, but every time you squeezed the trigger it wouldn't shoot. Sweet and I were in the back seat holding Tec-9s. As soon as we heard O'Neal's gun click, we jumped out of the car. Sweet, started shooting at Twin, and I was shooting at Nick. I was so anxious to kill him I hadn't realized that I forgot to put the clip in good enough. Nick was trying to run but I had him in scope. I stood in a police stance with both hands on my weapon and squeezed. In my heart, I wanted to kill Nick, but God had other plans because as soon as I squeezed the trigger the clip fell out. Man, that was crazy. Sweet was doing so much shooting till I thought some of the shots were coming from someone else on the Twin's side. To keep from getting hit, I ducked behind a car. I reloaded my weapon but by the time I got back up Nick was long gone and so was everybody else we were shooting at.

As the plot thickened in my life the rapture seemingly cooled down for a hot moment. The old western day shoot-out was the beginning and the ending of the kill or be killed drama which left everybody engulfed in the episode who was still left standing. Enough had been said and done, and I guessed Ray Ray and I both felt that we'd made our point. I realized that all of us were a bunch of deranged shorties searching for our own individuality in a disrespectful way. It was the only way we knew how.

Hit Man's empire suddenly collapsed. I guess, despite his love and desire to remain the King of Liberty City, fate had its way with him. One day we woke to learn he had taken on a deadly illness. Rumors had it that he had contracted AIDS. Some people even said his wife or immediate girlfriend was feeding him ground up glass in his food and had some type of spell on him. That was the talk about town. All types of rumors surfaced around the ghetto grounds from different people, never mind if they were true or not. No one cared so much to even seek the truth one way or the other.

The thing about it was that Hit Man was a ghetto celebrity, and his business was everybody's business no matter how true or false it was. The last thing I heard about Hit Man was that he had cancer. At the time I didn't know what cancer was. To me, it could have been another fancy way to say he had AIDS or whatever. I didn't really know. Hit Man never said anything to me about what was going on with him, and before I could build up the courage to ask him, he had passed away.

CHAPTER EIGHT

PROJECT CHICK

A few months before all of the drama went down QB moved his spot into the victory Holmes Projects. He was smart, and when he learned or saw different people moving in The Village he got missing. After hearing about the war, we were forced to go into with the Jenkins Boys QB didn't have any problem putting Sweet, Maurice and I down on his line.

The Victory Holmes Projects were very quiet. That's despite the fact that it was a lot of petty drug peddlers running up to cars making sales day in and day out. The spot was a money maker too but unlike the village people weren't killing themselves and dying because of turf wars. One thing victory Holmes didn't have was law and order. Everybody pretty much just did whatever they wanted to do, but all that changed when the Door Bell Boys hit the spot. We put a sense of order in the area. We had to bust up a few knuckleheads to let them know we weren't playing any games, and from there on everything worked out like a smooth operator. We even made some of the small-time peddlers Doorbell Boys since they were more likely familiar with the customers.

We made the customers park in the parking lot down the street and walk to where we were selling the drugs. This kept traffic from getting congested and gave us a handle on those desperados who would come in acting like they wanted to buy drugs only to attempt to snatch the drugs out of the workers hands and take off. This also helped if the police came up posing as customers trying to invoke a Sting Operation. We weren't having any of that crap. In order to purchase any drugs, you had to be on foot.

There was one more thing the Door Bell Boys did to ensure that the operation ran smoothly. Most of the guys that came from The Village had to find a girlfriend in the projects. A sense of residency was a key factor because we would have a place to run if the police rushed the spot or wanted to arrest us for loitering and prowling. Even though I had a newborn baby and a woman of whom I loved dearly, I was no exception to the rule. So, I got me a girl to kick it with.

No matter how bulletproof and smooth we thought we were, the spot still occasionally ran into opposition. Most of that opposition came from the police. Some of them not only knew us from The Village, but a few of them had grown up with us in the neighborhood. They were the one that kept the heat on us. This was where your girlfriend came in handy. She could walk right up to the police, let them know you were her man, and you were in the projects visiting her.

There was this girl named Brenda who used to sweat me. I wasn't really the aggressive type, so I never approached her. One day I was standing on the corner rapping with my homeboys, and she thought she'd put me on blast. I saw her coming before anybody else did. I was hoping she'd just keep walking by us, but little did I know she was on a mission. Brenda got right in front of where we were standing and started fronting on me.

"AyeSonny," Brenda said with a smirk on her face. "Boi, you scared of dis huh?" She said, pointing down at the crotch of her black biker shorts. I wanted to tell her I was, but I just let her slide. Brenda was a nice girl I just wasn't into her like that, but when I started thinking about the benefits of having a girlfriend in that location, I took her up on her offer, and she became my Project chick.

Brenda and her mother used to hold the big bomb. They would distribute the weed to the guys that worked for QB. I would've loved to be the bomb man, but I had to build myself up first because the drug game had protocols too. You started off doing field work and you worked your way up the ladder. One day I had just taken over my shift. I packed my .357 magnum in my waistline and went to riding up and down the street on my ten-speed bike. I hadn't even been on my route a good thirty minutes when things started to get crazy. One of the Dixon Boys came through to cop some weed and as he was riding through his car broke down right in front of the spot. The Dixon's had a reputation for getting money and killing people. They were cool with me, though, but regardless of whom they were or my personal feelings towards them or their killer reputation, I knew that if I didn't get Jonny to get his car from in front of the spot, gun shots were going to start popping off at any minute. I didn't want that to happen, so I thought I had better help him. I had it in the back of my mind that if the gunman saw me out there helping Jonny, they would give him a chance to move his car.

"Yo Playa keep it movin," Jarvis yelled aggressively.

"Aye ma car broke down, ya can't see dat," Jonny said, acting as if he wanted to approach Jarvis.

"Dam dat Playa push dat junk in da parking lot," Jarvis said angrily. Then Jonny shouted back.

"Make me move it tough guy!"

"Bam ... bam ... bam ... bam ... "The first shot hit me in the ankle. I screamed, cried and yelled in agony. As soon as I fell to the ground more shots rung out. "Bam ... bam ... bam ... "Bullet were ricocheting off the asphalt and walls like crazy. All I did was kept yelling.

When Jarvis finally noticed I was hit he ran behind Jonny popped round after round at him.

Seemingly out of nowhere I heard somebody scream "Jump Out". Apparently, they were on their way to raid our spot. Then I heard sirens blasting through my ears. The next thing I knew I was at Jackson Memorial Hospital with my ankle wrapped in bandages and an IV stuck in my arm. I closed my eyes for a few minutes then I heard the door swoop open, and Sweet approaching me with the quickness.

"Man do ya want me ta get at Jarvis?" Sweet asked.

"Nah ... da man wasn't tryin to shoot me."

When I got out of the hospital, I went back to the projects to resume my job as a watch out man. Things were pretty much back to normal except for the guy, that was running the bomb kept coming up short with the money. QB must have remembered how tight I kept my books, so he gave me the position of running the bomb. That mean a two-hundred-dollar raise. I started making five hundred dollars a week. Since I couldn't run if the police came, QB hired another guy to stand right beside me to run with the drugs if the police showed up. Now that used to be crazy. As soon as Nine came through the guy used to grab the drugs and take off running into the rear of the projects. I would be sitting there looking like I didn't know what was going on. Most of the time Brenda would be close by so when the police did come, she would walk up and sit on my lap.

Brenda has access to QB's drugs. At first, that seemed innocent that's until Brenda's greed took her personality down a different road. I knew for a fact QB was breaking Brenda and her mother off proper. So why she got the notion that she had to start stealing from QB's stash was beyond my comprehension. I guess she did it for the same reason I did my dirt.

Every time Brenda stole from QB she would bring the drugs to me. That girl was crazy. Sometimes she would give me a few thousand dollars' worth of weed. I used to be paranoid at first, mainly because I knew QB would do something to Brenda if he ever found out what she was doing. How would he not find out when she was hitting him for such large amounts? The whole thing reminded me of the Ray Ray incident, except in this case I was the benefactor and the one manipulating the strings behind the puppet. Brenda was the puppet and my interest in her was the strings. In the dope game, it didn't matter who you were, somebody could easily get killed, and Brenda was playing with fire, never mind that she didn't believe so. I wasn't trying to go that route again. My concern was the bigger picture. I figured I had to let her know what she was up against, yet I couldn't bring myself to do so. Strangely enough, I left it for her to figure out that what she was doing was against the odds on her own. Since I was benefiting, I just couldn't bring myself to tell her to stop. All I did was give her those puzzled looks every time she brought me something like, "Girl you messin round da man gon kill ya." Then I would take whatever it was she had to give me.

"Boi don worry bout notin, I got dis." Brenda would say after she'd dump weed in my lap. Then she'd walk away, as proudly as she came, feeling satisfied that she'd pleased her man.

An Eye for An Eye

We didn't see Jarvis for a few days after he shot me. I guess the word had gotten out that even though the shooting on his part was accidental that there might be some repercussions. On a breezy evening, I was chilling up on my stomp and grind, when all of a sudden, a car pulled up seemingly like out of nowhere, I thought to myself whoever was driving should've known the rules, park in the parking lot and walk back. That was my first thought until the back door swings open. No one stepped out and in a matter of seconds I grasped the image of Javis parlaying in the back seat, scrounged down with an AK-47 in his hand pointed at me. My heart jumped and all kinds of things ran through my mind.

"Sonny wassup Playa, we good or what?" Jarvis asked. He had a mischievous look on his face.

"Ain .. ain ... notin ... erarie ... thang ... cool ... we ... good, "I stammered nervously. I was spooked to death. My pulse raced and I knew if I'm said anything that sounded remotely close to having a problem with him shooting me, he would've gunned me down. Fortunately, for me and Javis no one made any move that could have been detrimental to either of us. Jarvis' reasoning turned out to be innocent. In fact, the situation was so harmless that he even came back to work.

A few days later a black Buick Regal made a right turn off of 7th Ave. and headed in our direction. As usual, all of us were standing around chilling. The car drove slowly then all of a sudden, a guy sitting in the back seat caught my attention. He rose up, leaned out of the car's window with his arms stretched across the roof. He shocked us when he began firing an assault rifle unmercifully. We weren't at war with anyone at the time, but it was obvious someone was at war with us. Everybody was scrambling around running for cover. Those of us that were close to children grabbed them, trying to keep them from getting shot. **"Bam ... bam ... bam ... "The** shots went off. Bullets hit the ground, cars, walls, and some even penetrated people's homes. It was a hectic situation that no one could make any sense of. I don't know exactly what jumped into me, but as the shots and the car moved hurriedly down the street, I jumped in my car and started to follow them. I was hoping they didn't open fire on me being that I didn't have a gun. I just got caught up in the moment, I guess.

"Y'all got dem suckas." I yelled out of the car's window. Our cars hit Fifth Avenue one right after the other. I think with all the drama going on, at some point, they didn't even know I was following them. I trailed them all the way back to the Large Mount Projects. I made sure not to forget the apartment they went into because Large Mount was big, and you could easily get one apartment confused with another. One thing was for certain, though, I had the car they were driving locked in my memory. I even locked in a few of their faces as they got out of their car. I drove back to the spot to see if anyone got hit. When I found out everybody was good, I hunted QB down. By the time I caught up with him the news had already found its way to his doorstep.

"Yo, mon what up wit dem bloodclot boi dem shotin up me gates star?" QB said as soon as he saw me. He was hot, too. I saw death in his eyes. His attitude was intense, and he was eager to maintain the hood's status quo, "an eye for an eye, and a tooth for a tooth." Even though QB had already been briefed I told him what had happened again. This time, I had a little more information than he already had. I knew where the guys were from and more importantly what some of them looked like.

QB gave me a few guns to arm our crew with. We already had several handguns, but I took the ones he gave me anyway. I rode back to the spot to get Maurice, Sweet, Brown, Tyjoe, Block and I went back to the Large Mount Projects. It was twelve midnight when we pulled up on their spot. There were about ten or so goons standing near the Black Regal. There wasn't any time to think because before I knew it, I was out of the car screaming ...

"Yea suckas, wassup now." There was six of us in all but when we started busting shots you couldn't tell if it was twenty or thirty of us, with all the different shot going off. We were getting the best of them. We watched their crowd part like the Red Sea. I don't think we hit anybody, nor do I believe that was really our intentions, nor the cats that shot up our spot, despite believing that we or they were trying to kill somebody.

It took a split second to reload my gun when seemingly out of nowhere, I heard rapid gunfire being returned. Bullets zoomed across my head. "Darn nit." I gasped. "Ya'll lets bail," I screamed to the others, but they were still shooting back. I ran and jumped inside my car trying to get somewhere. As soon as I got in the car, I heard my front windshield break. Glass shattered everywhere. It seemed like two or three bullets went through my windshield at the same time, in the same spot. All I could do from there was duck and pray, and If I hadn't, I wouldn't be here to talk about it.

I tell you that's something, that even in our madness we looked for God to protect us. That night I wasn't only looking for God, I was praying He'd bless us to return home safely.

Sweet was behind one of those big green garbage bins. The gunfire was coming back so rapid, and I kept praying, saying ...

"Please God, don't let my brotha get killed." That was the scariest night of my life. I went over there with all intentions to get some things straightened out, but it turned out that straightening found me. I don't know how many times I prayed to God to let me live. It must've been at least a hundred times. I know one thing, though, I was pissed with QB. I couldn't believe he had sent us around there with handguns when those cats were shooting AK's. I was still paranoid, but I had to go back and give QB a piece of my mind.

"Dread ya gave me handguns, and dem cats were shooting back at us wit cannons," I screamed.

I was still shaking like an old 57 Chevy. The whole window thing told me that I was supposed to be dead, and I immediately understood that I had a lot to be thankful for. I had the will to live, all of us did, and God hadn't amputated that will from our lives. In a sense we were death struck, unwilling to turn around when we knew the road, we were traveling lead to a dead end.

The next day I went to the gym to workout. I had to calm my nerves so I could think straight. The crew went back to Large Mount and put in work without me. I wasn't about to go anywhere near that spot until I found out what was going on. We did some investigating of the matter. In a matter of days, we finally found out exactly where the guy lived that did the shooting. The information came from one of the guy's baby mommas. She told us everything we needed to know, she also said ...

"I don't care if ya'll kill em, cause he ain't doin notin fo my baby anyway." That same evening, we called QB and gave him the rundown. After hearing what we'd said it was understood that it was on and popping again. The thing about it was there had been two drive-by shootings and no one had been killed nor shot. To me, not only did I think that was rather odd, but I had to question what was the purpose of the guy shooting up our spot in the first place. Nobody asked that question, perhaps for the obvious reasons. Nobody gave a damn, I'd imagine. I did have some reservations though. I thought we should quit while we were ahead, but QB's nephew Ray wasn't trying to hear that. Sweet and Maurice stayed behind this time to run the spot, while Ray and I went to settle the score. This time, we had a little heavier firepower to work with. Ray had a fully automatic Oozie, and I had a brand new Iraqi Styled AK-47 with two banana clips. When we got to the guy's house, we noticed the street was clear. Even the area where we had shot up days earlier was nothing like I'd seen it the first time I went around there. When I saw that I thought this was the best time to call the shooting off, so I said ...

"Ray something don't feel right man, let's come back later," I said looking into his eyes.

"Naw mon, me can't go back empty-handed, me have ta show me uncle dat INI is a Rude Boi and a guardian of his gates," Ray said with a screwed face.

We swung a left turn up the one-way on Eighty-first Street and entered through the back way of Large Mount Projects.

"Stop da car here," Ray said. I pulled the car over to the curve and he hopped out. We were just a couple feet away from the guy's house. After seconds elapsed, I heard rapid gunfire going off. I don't know how many shots I heard, but I knew a fully automatic gun could easily spit thirty or forty round in a fraction of a second, with the squeeze of the trigger. Every time I heard the gunshots blast, I winced thinking death would certainly be my ruin. Ray was nuts, I watched him stand from the sidewalk and shoot up the guy's house and a Cadillac Servile that was parked in the yard. He unloaded his Oozie like it was nothing. The whole thing was repugnant, but it was how we lived, an eye for an eye and a tooth for a tooth.

"Come on man ... let's bail," I yelled out of the car at the top of my lungs, and we dipped.

The Bandit

Some say the presumption of innocence and guilt can be measured by the way one cares for his family. Being young, believing in the Bible's teachings that God looks after children and fools, we always believe that our deeds were justified and innocent within themselves. If someone struck you on the cheek, it was simply childish to think that anyone out of the hood would turn the other cheek. He hits back and perhaps hit harder. That's what we were stuck between in the ghetto, a bunch of cheek hitting and hitting back. However, if that's the case, if the presumption of innocence or guilt could be measured by how one cares for his family, am I guilty or innocent? Life says I'm both, innocent and guilty, at the same time. Innocent of being black, yet guilty of thinking that I can use my color as an excuse to violate my neighbor, when he too is innocent and guilty at the same time. If we beat our neighbor over the head with" sticks and stones or degrade our women with words, life measures our worthiness and life hands out its own punishment in the way it sees fit. Some people call that karma.

***

We've all heard old adages thousands of times growing up. We have used old adages ourselves, to get a certain point across. My mom used to tell me, "Boy-what goes around comes around," she'd say that pointing her finger at me and giving me that face like she was serious. I used to hear adages like this all the time from her. What her words meant to me was more than the nothing I understood about life, and my mom didn't always have to scold me, nor my homey's mom scold them. Being "deficient in caution and in showing prudence in love", sometimes "life" would just get sick and tired of all our foolishness and say, "hol up ma' I got dis". Life would teach us that we were not in control.

***

As we made our escape to freedom the next thing that happened brought my mom's words into the perfect view of my mind. I could see and hear her say, "Boy what goes around comes around."

"Bam ... bam ... bam" I heard a series of gunshots rang outta nowhere. They were swift, loud, and over with, seemingly as soon as they started. My mind couldn't move fast enough to figure out what was going on before I felt my heart skip a beat as Q.B.'s nephew Ray, screamed in agony. Frightened to death and remembering the window incident I ducked for cover. I was steady trying to steer the car and hide at the same time. In the back of my mind, I thought Ray wasn't as lucky as I was. Someone had fired back at us, at least. that's what I thought. The only thing I didn't hear was the window shatter, nor did I see glass anywhere. Ray was definitely shot, blood was everywhere. I couldn't believe it, that silly joker had shot himself in the knee with a fully automatic Mac-10.

When QB met us at the hospital I told him what happened. I even let him know that before we shot up the house that it didn't look good, but Ray insisted on doing the job. We dropped Ray off at the hospital, and as we were driving off, I looked in the rearview mirror and saw a police officer writing something on a piece of paper, I'd imagine he was writing down our tag number. We didn't know what was happening, so we parked the car. Everything kept going from bad to worst. What really made the whole job bad is that we shot up the wrong house. The Seville that was parked in the yard belonged to a guy named Fat-Pimp. Fat-pimp was a known killer. When he found out the Door-Bell-Boys shot up his house and his car he came around to the spot riding with a six-car entourage. We spotted them as soon as they hit the corner. If we wanted to, we could have opened fire on them, but we had already been told that Fat-pimp wanted to talk. They pulled in the parking lot. All of them exited their vehicles and walked to where we were. Maurice, Sweet, Ray, Jarvis, and some more trigger-happy niggas, and I waited. I was representing QB, and everybody else was there to represent his muscle.

"Wassup Fat-Pimp," I said. I looked around at all the goons he had with him. None of them brandished their weapons, but I knew they were armed to the teeth.

"Man, dat was a mistake ... somebody tol us da wrong house. "

"Playa dat waz my baby momma's house... "Fat-pimp said, interrupting me.

His voice started to rise. I knew they had us outnumbered but by the time it would have taken them to get to their cars we would have gunned them down. I didn't want to see any more bloodshed, so I offered a compromise to the situation.

"Man, da beef ain't with you ... some cats come 'round an' sprayed our spot up-we."

"Playa jus get my car fixed," Fat-pimp said interrupting me again. I was thinking in the back of my mind, this fool bout to piss me off, but I just humbled myself. I learned that from my mom. She taught me to always think. That day if I hadn't been thinking, somebody could have easily been killed, preferably Fat-Pimp, the way he was trying to shrink my manhood to the least common denominator.

"How much ya car cost?" I asked.

"$3,500. "Fat-pimp said. I watched him utter the price like it was nothing. I couldn't help but notice a glow appear, on his face, all of a sudden.

I let Fat-pimp know straight up that I thought the price was steep, nevertheless, I told him to come back in 'bout an hour.

"Dem dem fools dogg," Ray said, as soon as Fat-pimp and his entourage slowly drove away.

"It's whatever dya wanna do." Ray was still talking crazy even though he'd almost lost his leg. The insane part about it was that now he was in a wheelchair.

I met QB and told him what was going on. He didn't want to pay the money. I had to agree with him that the price was high, but we were dead wrong.

"You wanna go to war with those fools for our own mistake," I asked QB.

"Because if we do-every-body-lose." I had to put it to QB that way because money was the only thing that made him listen. What I wanted him to understand was that he would risk losing a twenty to thirty thousand dollars a day spot over a thirty-five- hundred-dollar bill. He pondered for a moment then finally agreed to jack up the bread.

***

After the drugs kept coming up short, QB decided to park a car behind the back of the building. The sole purpose of the car was to keep the drugs in the trunk, so the guy who did the transactions could go back and forth to it. He would be the only one with the key to the truck. He did this, also, so that Brenda would no longer have access to the drugs. This worked out well for a minute until it got out, we had drugs stashed in the car. We even found out, outta all people, Jarvis was plotting to rob the spot.

We heard Jarvis was hanging around in the back of the building. People who actually saw him told us he was wearing army fatigues, looking like he was Rambo, or a one-man army. Jarvis was a nut case. He was the type of person that had no sense of reasoning. That's why that day Jonny Dixon's car broke down in the street in front of the spot he started shooting.

We hadn't seen Jarvis in a while, but knowing he was in the area trying to pull off a gank move (robbery), kept everybody on their pees and cues.

***

It was in the spring of the year 1987, my homies, Maurice, Tyjoe, Block, and a couple other dudes my brother Sweet and I were sitting around smoking weed. Sweet, Maurice and I were just about to go to the crib when this guy came where all of us were sitting, asking to hit the joint. He then said ...

"Hey ya'll, ya'll know Jarvis is sitting on da back street?" All of our eyes widen. Hearing Jarvis was somewhere lurking made us all freeze.

"Man, we ain't worrying bout dat fool," I said. I was trying to keep everybody cool, but before I could even finish my sentence three of the workers jumped in a car and left Maurice, Sweet, and I sitting there. We weren't stupid. We knew they were going to check Jarvis, we just didn't know how stern that straightening would be. In about five minutes, we heard a series of gunshots go off. They sounded like fireworks, but all of us knew better than to believe our first impression.

It didn't matter what happened, small problems or big problems, if QB felt he had a problem, he had to send somebody to straighten it out.

One day, QB was going home to check on his stash. He had a couple of houses in Carol City that he kept all his dope. The main house was on 177th Street and 18th Avenue. When he pulled up to the house, he noticed that his gate was open. Sensing something was wrong, he parked his car alongside the road and walked inside, brandishing his pistol. As soon as he entered the place, he noticed someone had broken in. Things was scattered everywhere. Clothes were all across the floor and furniture was turned upside down. The first thing that came to QB's mind was that he was glad this time, he didn't have a lot of stuff there. He had only brought a few pounds there because he was planning on taking them to the city later on. Those two pounds were nowhere to be found, QB looked for them, but he couldn't locate them anywhere.

That same evening QB called me at the spot complaining that somebody broke into his house. All I heard him kept saying was that he wanted his stuff back, and then the phone went dead. He never mentioned to me that he wanted me to come out to the house, but since I knew where it was, Sweet, Maurice, Ray, and I jumped into my Caddy and drove out there.

"I want me stash back ... "QB ranted. His face was askew, and his attitude was boiling hot. He didn't even give us a chance to get all the way out of the car.

"Um tellin ya ... if I don get mi stash back, uma kill some blood clot body. "

I already knew what his killing meant. It meant he was going to stay his butt home and send us to do his dirty work. In my mind, I was trying to figure out why he was even trippin about two pounds when he had hundreds of pounds stashed elsewhere. It wasn't like we couldn't have easily made up for the lost. That was too simple for him. QB had to flex his muscles, trying to appear as though he had the power to say "Be" and it is. So, he put us on yet another mission in Carol City to find two measly pounds of weed, and in our naivety, we were stupid, blind, and dumb not to suggest otherwise.

We had the whole hood under surveillance. As soon as we got back to the city, we armed ourselves with pistols. We already had a defacto mindset so only God knows what was about to happen next.

Maurice, Sweet, Ray, and I cruised the city blocks in search of the drugs. We were in the Cadilac and Maurice was driving. Ray was riding shotgun and Sweet and I parlayed in the backseat, looking blankly out at the streets.

"Hey letz go check dem cats' ova dere ... "Sweet said, as he pointed in the direction of a group of guys. They were just standing around in front of a store minding their own business. They looked harmless, but so did we until we hopped out of the car waving pistols around. As soon as Sweet and I got out we made them fools get flat.

"Com on man don kill us. "One of the guys cried.

"Playa shut da hell up!" I yelled, as I examined the packages of weed, they had cuffed in their pockets.

"Man ... we don no whacha talkin 'bout ... we ain't take nothin ... "the other guy stammered.

The few crews we did jump out on acted like they didn't know what we was talking about, and that was cool. But just to let them know that we were serious about our business, we slapped a few of them upside the head with those pistols. That was the telling part. The irony of it all though, was that we never got QB's stuff back. All that came about, as a result of our pseudo-investigation, was that we'd secured a myriad of enemies trying to do the impossible.

It wasn't so much the fact that QB's house kept getting broken into, or the fact that we'd accumulated so many enemies along the way trying to flush out those jagged edges the game had sown for us. Nor was it so much even the power I assumed QB had, in as much falsely obtained, that made me decide to check myself; but the fact was, I realized QB was faking; building his legacy off of a bunch of brain-dead youngsters, like me. To be honest, I think QB was afraid of us knowing our mentality was to act outside of our nature. That's why he played psychological games, like talking about killing all the time and using his Jamaican accent; that had a kind of ring to it that made you wince, to keep us off his butt.

After running the streets all day, I finally made it home and was ready to crash. When the lights went out, I laid awake in my bed thinking, who exactly could it be that kept breaking into QB's house. From a hood's perspective I didn't think it really mattered or if I really cared. I mean it wasn't my dope, but I felt like I owed QB some form of loyalty, at the very least for all that he had done for me. I was thinking in the back of my mind whoever it was had to be somebody close to him to keep hitting the right spots at the right time, and that's another thing that bothered me. I was just hoping and praying it wasn't anybody I knew. I don't know why but the first person came to my mind was Sweet. I don't know why I thought of him. I swear on everything I love I don't, but I knew my brother. He was sneaky and plus I just knew that he was capable of doing something like that, and then have us on a mission looking for the bandit while the bandit be sitting right in the car with us. Yeah, I had to laugh inwardly about that too. My brother Sweet? He was something else I thought. His image overlapped in my mind. All I could see was that devilish smile he wore every time he done something he didn't have any business doing. I understood my thoughts were conflicting with our passion as brothers, but I was seriously thinking it was him. The only thing about it was, the fact that he was with me most of the time. Plus, the fact that he wasn't exhibiting any changes in his lifestyle, kept me thinking that something was amiss. That wasn't nothing though because he was as sly as a fox. Knowing him, he could have had somebody else breaking into the house, somebody else getting rid of his portion of the weed, while he was sitting back stacking his money. The thought even ran across my mind about the time when I found all QB's money in the closet.

I realized I couldn't sleep so I hopped out of bed, threw on a pair of jeans and laced up my shoes. Everybody else in the house was still asleep, so I just eased out the door undetected. I had it in my mind to ride by the spot and chill with my niggas. As soon as I walked through the path, I noticed QB was chilling like a villain. My first thought was trying to figure out what he was doing in the hole when he tried to make it has business to stay away? My attention was on Sweet's face trying as hard as fuck to read his mind. He was chilling too, pulling on a stank one, like there wasn't a damn thing going on. I wondered what he would do if I all of a sudden yelled; "It's Sweet!!" Umph, he probably would crap in his pants.

Take A Rest

It seemed like I wasn't there five minutes. When I started to regret that I got out of bed. Jump-out swooped in and raided the spot, and it just so happened that QB was present. They were wearing plain clothes and ran right up on us. At first, we thought Fat-pimp and his nephews had made a move on us since QB refused to pay the money. But it wasn't them. I'd never thought the day would come when I was happy to see the police.

"Why da fuck you grabbin on me," Sweet bellowed.

"What's your na ... "

"Man dis is crazy, we ain't sellin no drugs," I said cutting the officer off in mid-sentence.

Minutes later Sweet, QB, and I were handcuffed put in the back of the patty wagon on our way to the County Jail.

As soon as we got to the police station, I felt irritated, not that I was sweating the situation, because, we were only arrested for Loitering and Prowling, I just regretted not staying home.

Jail was a world inside of a world, and you had to be just as tough inside there as you were on the streets. It was crazy too, even though I knew we were being put in jail, I was looking for ways to get over on the system. So, my eyes were glued on our money that the Officer took and sat on the table in front of us. That's when I hatched a plan to at least get some of it back. When the police officer walked out of the room, a big smile formed across my face. QB was sitting within arm's reach of the money, Sweet was next to him, and I was on the end. "Starr grab da bread," I whispered to QB. I even signaled "with my head for him to get it, but he was scared. Sweet wouldn't even make a move, so I reached across them and grabbed three one-hundred-dollar bills and tucked them in the seam of my sweatpants. Moments later the officer came and escorted us to the holding cell.

I think we might have stayed in the holding cell for three hours before they transferred us from the sub-station to the County Jail. As soon as we got there, we were booked, informed of our charges, and allowed to use the phone.

The County Jail was a mad house, you could hear the horror, screams, and shouts echoing off the walls. People were coming and going and arguing their innocence, and some refusing with violence to be crammed in a cell. Knowing the procedures, I wasn't worried. Like I said, I was still looking for ways to cheat the system. Anything I could do, to make my short stay as comfortable as possible, I was willing to do.

When we walked into the cell my face zeroed in on a white boy whom I overheard telling another guy that he had stashed two hundred dollars. The thought of his two hundred dollars put a smile on my face; his two hundred, plus my three hundred equal five hundred, that had me excited. That's just how it was, a cracka ain't have nothing coming with me.

QB and Sweet were looking crazy and I was trying to figure out the best way to get this money. I figured if I simply asked him to let me see the money, I could snatch it out of his hand. But I knew he wasn't going to go for that, I was just going to have to get it like "Drack," in blood. Sometimes skin color didn't matter because a lot of white boys grew up with us and know how to fight, and dude was kinda thick.

I bent down untied my shoelaces and tied them again tighter never taking my eyes off of him, then I sprung to my feet, and I walked over to buddy and said ...

"Ai yo, ya said ya got two hundred dallas?" I asked all, cool, calm, and collected. He didn't answer through; I guess he figured something was up.

"How much chu got-man?" I asked with a mischievous look on my face. I wasn't expecting it, but even though he was the only white person in the cell, he tried to act tough. That's when I took it to him. I hit him with a crisp three-piece, bem ... bem ... bem. He never saw it coming, after the last punch to his jaw, he balled up in a fetus position and started yelling for the guards.

"Cracka shut up," I quipped with a muffled voice. When the officer did come, he came and called a guy's name and let him out of the cell. While the officer was at the bars, the young white man stood with his back up against the wall looking at me and breathing like a bull. That's when I knew I had to give him the business.

As soon as the officer left, we went back at it. I connected with a two piece, that knocked him to the floor.

"Cracka, where dat money at!" I said gritting me teeth together. I was breathing hard like crazy too. Just as I was about to kick him, I heard QB's voice in the background ...

"Left em lone starr, ya crazy ah wa." I turned my head in his direction and said...

"Man, I ain't tryna hear dat crap, dis cracka bout to give up dat bread."

When I turned around to face the white man again, I noticed him going into his crouch, when I began walking towards him, he extended his arm up in surrender, and with the other hand he come out of his crouch with the money and handed it to me. I snatched the money and walked away with a smile on my face.

Another guy had smuggled a few bags of weed in, when I looked in his direction, he tossed me a sack and a sheet of 1.5 rolling paper. I rolled one fat joint, then walked over to the guy and got a light. I took a long draw off the joint and immediately I began to gag, as I was trying to catch my breath, I passed the joint to Sweet. I don't know what kind of weed that was, but I was high as a kite. When I looked up through blurred vision, I couldn't believe what I was seeing. I blinked my eyes a few times because I thought I was tripping. I saw QB posted up in the back of the cell sweating like crazy. I walked over to him and asked.

"Man, what's wrong withcha?" He looked back at me with a blank look on his face, turned around sharply and started pacing the floor. I thought he was claustrophobic or something.

"Man, de-I cann stay in dis place, me hav to call me sista fe bond," QB stammered.

"Star, da letchu use da phone didn't da?"

"Yea me try ta call me sista, but nobody picks up da blood clot phone. Me hav ta make bond Rude Bwoy, me have ta make bond now, bum-ba-clot!" QB shouted.

"Man take it easy, we only in here for trespassing, we'll be out in a few hours, bredren you trippin."

I turned sharply when I felt somebody tap me on the shoulder.

"Sonny, you wanna hit dis?" Sweet said as he passed me the joint. I grabbed the joint took a long-calculated draw and blew the smoke in QB's face. It was right then and there that I peeped QB's ho card. He was soft as cotton.

In the back of my mind, I knew it was the money that made QB appear to the naked eye to be ruthless. For an instant, my life with him flashed before my me. Come to think about it, he never went on missions with us, he would just simply send us to do his dirty work, while he took the credit for it. All the crap he used to be talking like everybody feared him suddenly diminished from my mind, and his appearance from then on looked suspect. After seeing his weakness, I could never look at him the same again.

I figured it was about time that I made my move. I understood that my services to QB' s establishment were greatly needed, but I had an obligation to myself and my family. So, I started doing my own thing. I used to go up on Ali-baba to cop an 8-ball, (1/8 of an ounce of crack cocaine) from Rick Brownlee's spot or I would cop jugglers from Convertible Burt's spot in the Graveyard Projects. They were called jugglers because the rocks were so big that you could cut them in half and double your money.

Things worked out pretty good too. I made some good ends with my side hustle, and I didn't have to tamper with QB's drugs.

QB heard that I was making money on the side. One of the workers told me that QB wanted me to come to the stash house right away. I didn't know what to expect of him, but I knew it wasn't about to be no drama. I hopped in my Chevy, keyed the ignition and drove in silence to my destination.

As soon as I walked in the house, QB stood up and in two long strides he was standing in front of me with a wicked look on his face.

"Yo Star, me hear dat ya sellin crack pun me gates."

"Yea man, I go up to the Bab and get me an 8-Ball for a hundred dollars, cut it up into nickel pieces and make a profit."

"No mon, ya takin me moni an' buying da bum-ba-clot, crack, me feel fe bust shots upon ya ras." Then he spun around quickly heading in the opposite direction.

For a minute I didn't quite understand what this fool was talking about, me using his money. I used my own money, although using his money would have increased my supply. However, I was straight up with QB so that thought never crossed my mind.

QB was looking at me crazy too and sweating like he was doing that day in the County Jail. My mind suggested all type of things, but I didn't feed into them. I just played it cool, to see where he was going with this conversation. I knew QB was soft, but he still had a bunch of goons on his line ready and willing to carry out his orders.

Then he stopped dead in is tracks and turned back towards me.

"Man take a rest."

"What!" I responded with my ears at attention.

"Ya firing me?" I questioned. "Look, Man, you know I got a family to take care of, if ya don't won't want me to sell crack on yo gates, all ya have to do is say dat an' I'll stop, ya know dat." My argument was sincere, but from the look on QB's face he wasn't hearing it.

"Jus take a blood-clot rest, hear me now."

"I hear you bredren," I said then turned around leaving out of the house feeling some type of way.

One thing I knew about QB was that he was a shrewd businessman. Regardless, of what I thought of him as a person, I had to give him his props. He didn't bar none when it came to his empire. If someone posed a threat, he dealt with them before the threat became a reality, and that meant that I was on my own.

I can't say I wasn't fazed about being fired because I was. I was messed up, because even though I did my own thing on the side, I was still loyal to QB. So, I couldn't believe he was actually firing me, after all, we'd been through.

It had been months since I last saw or heard anything from QB. And since I was no longer working for him, it wasn't like I missed seeing him. I just went on about my life, staying focused on why I was out here in the streets in the first place and that was to get paid in full.

I moved directly across the street from QB's spot and sold my crack. Sweet and all the other guys I used to work with, were still working for QB. At first, I didn't see him that often, then all of a sudden, he started hanging in his spot daily. I figured he must've thought I was going to come back to him begging for my job back, but, from time to time, we would just make eye contact. When he saw that that wasn't happening, he did what any smart businessman would do in the drug game, he sought me out and told me that I had to move my spot somewhere else.

I couldn't believe that he told me to move. Here I was, trying to make ends meet, to support my family, and QB was trying to intimidate me. I felt the heat in my body rising. For a moment I even stood stiff on the sidewalk, looking foolish in the face. My first' thought was to tell him to make me move. But I didn't say anything. I just acted like I didn't hear him.

For some strange reason, I didn't feel threatened by QB because I knew the guys that was working for him wouldn't think of coming against me. When I was working for QB, I used to organize his entire crew. I would tell them, when we go on missions, things like don't forget the guys that are shooting from the front side of the car, stay ducked down at all times when the guys behind the car are shooting, be careful and don't leave anyone behind, and all kinds of tactics to ensure their safety. I never lost a man on our missions. QB on the other hand would just send them out there on their own, with no instruction and no support.

If he wanted to do something to me, he knew he would have to get some other guys to carry out his orders. I wondered if he understood that I still had a measure of influence over my brother and the rest of his crew.

I knew QB very well, and when he wanted some serious action taken care of, he would fly in some Rude Boys from Jamaica. One of his hit-men name was Jew-boy, and he had a few unidentified cats that we only saw around when QB had murder on his mind. When he began threatening me with them standing by his side, I knew he meant business.

"Ai pussi boi, me see ya hav nuff wax pun y're ear, me catchu roun here again, me gonna kill ya battie hole, me make ya madda cry."

After he flexed his muscles, I thought it would be a good time to take a rest, close shop and call it a day.

CHAPTER NINE

FAT PIMP

I didn't get much sleep last night because QB' s hitmen weighted heavily on my mind. Nonetheless, it was ten o'clock in the morning and in spite of all the drama that was going on in the spot I was going out there to get my hustle on. I got dressed and headed out the door.

It was a beautiful day for a change, the sky was clear and there was a nice breeze blowing through the hood and felt like it kissed my face. The crazy thing was, as rare as the day seemed to be, instead of enjoying the cool sun rays, I felt a sense of trepidation stirring inside of me like a tornado. I couldn't help it, I knew when people made threats in the hood, nine times out of ten they carried them out. The fact of the matter is, I could have backed down and let QB take the spot and moved somewhere else, and started all over again, but I didn't want him to capitalize on the hard work I put in building up my clientele. However, when QB flexed his power yesterday, I had second thoughts about his ability to take my life.

As I drove down Seventh Ave. on my way to the spot that's when I noticed that my gas needle was on E, I pulled into the Amoco Gas Station. As soon as I pulled up to the gas pump, I spotted Fat-Pimp coming out of the store. My first thought was to pull off, but I didn't want him to think crazy like I feared him. I turned the car off, hopped out and started looking up at the sign acting like I was reading the gas prices. What I was really doing was getting myself in position to grab my Colt 45 revolver off the seat and squeeze the trigger if he started tripping.

From my understanding, QB hadn't paid Pimp all of his money, and from his point of view, I was still working for QB. I started thinking of how messed up it would be if I killed Fat-Pimp, or he killed me over him and QB's beef when QB and I had severed all ties. Before I made any sudden moves, I watched him to see what he'd do. As soon as Fat-Pimp saw me, his eyes lit up, and he had a Kool-Aid smile on his face.

"Sonnnnni, wassup, nephew," he said, grinning between his teeth. "Oh, wassup, dogg," I said. Startled as if I hadn't noticed him. "Um jus chillin," I stammered.

"Boy I been tryna catch up witcha, to ask you, do you wonna get with a playa like me and start gettin some real money, cause I know dem Jamaicans feedin you crums," Fat-Pimp said. He was still grinning, and I was trying to figure out his angle. The last thing I was expecting was for him to come at me like he did. I didn't know how to respond. I was just looking crazy.

"Whatchu finna get some gas? Hurry up I'll watch yo car."

"Nah...um straight," I said as I thought that I didn't want to leave my gun on the seat.

"Man go ahead, I'mma watch yo car." Fat Pimp insisted.

Now what was I going to do? I had the fat joker pretending that he was my friend on one side, and I was standing on the other. Like a fool I walked inside of the gas station to pay for my gas. I was so paranoid when I got inside, I just laid a twenty-dollar Billy Bob on the counter and rushed back outside.

I hooked up with Fat Pimp that same day. Don't ask me how it happened because I don't remember. All I know is that Fat Pimp liked young cats that had heart and I fitted right in with his plans. Fat Pimp had a lot of young goods working for him that was my age that he called nephew. All they did was ride around all day robbing and kicking jokers butt for their dope and then distributed it.

One day I was riding in the car with Fat Pimp talking about getting some dope from him. We had four cars trailing us with four of Fat Pimp's nephews in each car. I think he wanted to impress me by showing me all tha he had going on for himself. We rode by five of his spots and watched his nephews pick up money. On the last stop we pulled up to this guy's house that lived in Aswan Apartments. Fat Pimp and I were parked directly in front waiting on the guy to come out. He never told me what was going on, but something told me something was up. One of his nephews knocked on the door and as soon as the guy opened the door all of his nephews rushed the door and pulled him out. They started beating on him like crazy. After they beat him enough, they put him in the trunk and drove him to the Sugar Hill Apartments off of Seventy-third Street and Fourteenth Terrace. I'll never forget it. As they commenced to whipping, they guy I watched him slip in and out of consciousness before I heard a series of gun shots go off.

The thing that stood out to me the most about Fat Pimp and all his nephews wasn't how brutal they were, but the way in which they would brutally beat, and torture people was just unbelievable. I said to myself; these fools are cray for real.

The first thing I said to myself or promised myself after several long uncomfortable moments of saying nothing, was that I was going to be straight up with Fat Pimp. I was going to pay him for whatever I got from him. I would make sure of that.

After Fat-Pimp finished his violent demonstration, he dug in his crouch area and pulled out what appeared to be cookies. They were wrapped in a zip lock bag with a couple of rubber bands around it.

"Here, take dese five ounces Sonni, an' give me $4,500 back," Fat-Pimp said, never taking his eyes off of the road, but for some reason, it sounded more like he was giving me an order.

We road by a few more spots and ended up circling around the block of QB's spot, while I called myself inspecting the cookies. I thought the price was kinda steep when ounces were only going for $500 at the time, but since I hadn't moved up to purchasing ounces yet, and he was giving them to me on consignment, I didn't hesitate I grabbed them out of his hand with the quickness.

Now, it was official I had back-up, and just like that, all my fumbling worries about QB's hit men was a fleeting memory.

When QB's workers saw me getting out of Fat-Pimp's car, I knew the word would get back to QB, and that's all I needed. Normally, nobody was allowed to park in front of QB's spot, customers had to park in the parking lot down the street and walk back to the spot to cop their package, but Fat-Pimp and his wrecking crew parked right in front of the spot, five cars deep, and none of QB's workers said anything. I understood Fat-Pimp's actions to a tee, it was a physical statement that said, Fat-Pimp got Sonny's back, now play with it!

I quickly went from making five hundred dollars a day to a thousand. I worked for myself, so the only person I had to pay was Fat-Pimp. Things were going well too. I had all Fat-Pimp's muscle, and I was getting at least five ounces a week on my face, or as much dope as I could sell, because Fat-Pimp kept plenty dope, at least that's what I thought at the time.

Fat-Pimp was basically a robber and a gangster. He didn't have spots of his own, he just had people he supplied drugs to after he took it from somebody else. However, Fat-Pimp would hit rough patches and when he couldn't find anybody to rob or tax, he would be out of dope maybe for weeks at a time, that's until he taxed somebody else. Being taxed meant that people like Fat-Pimp would constantly demand money or drugs from hustlers without paying for it. If whoever he taxed didn't cooperate, he would simply take them to war until they conceded or put-up resistance. That's why Fat-Pimp had so many enemies and was constantly at war.

All that macho crap was cool, but when he was out of dope my business suffered at lot. Although I saw Fat-Pimp and his crew commit some of the most violent acts on human beings that I had physically seen, I began to get irritated with the fact that he kept running out of drugs, so I decided to save my money, and when he ran out again, I'll be straight. So that's exactly what I did, I saved up forty-five hundred, that way I could buy nine ounces for what he charged me for five. Then I could afford to make my rocks bigger and outsell Reggie. Reggie had a spot across the street about a half a block away from where I was. I used to wonder where he was getting his drugs from because I knew I was going to need a new connect soon.

One day I hit the corner on my way to my spot and I spotted Fat-pimp and his entourage of multi-colored Caddies. Before I could make it to where they were, they pulled off seemingly like in unisons heading in the opposite direction. I drove up in Reggie's spot and hopped out of my car, and said ...

"Aye Reggie, wassup."

"Ain't not en Sonny, what da do?"

"What Fat-pimp wanted, was he lookin fo me?" I asked, knowing he saw me when I hit the corner.

"Nah, he was jus droppin ma sack off."

"What!" I shouted.

"Dat joker given ya dope too, how da f*** his fat stank a** playin, what dat fat a** n**** tryna do, lock both of da spots down?" I said yelling at the top of my lungs. I called Fat-Pimp everything but a child of God.

I couldn't fathom what his point was, giving Reggie dope when he knew Reggie was my competition. I couldn't wait to see him and ask him what was going on. More importantly, I couldn't wait until he ran out of dope again, so I could cut all ties with him, but what I didn't know was that the words I spoke against Fat-Pimp would come back to haunt me one day.

A few days later, when I went to pay Fat-Pimp, he was acting kinda strange. When I mentioned to him about him giving Reggie dope, he just brushed it off like he didn't hear me.

After that I didn't see Fat-Pimp for a while, and I made no attempt to contact him either. When he finally did show back up, on the scene, I was copping a few kilos of cocaine and business was booming, and that meant his services were no longer needed. He pulled up at the spot and beckoned for me to come to his car.

"Wassup, nephew, I see the streets been good ta ya since I been gone," he said with a mischievous smile that made me wince.

"Yea Pimp, dis thang dun pick up like crazy."

"I got some of dem thangs fo ya, wassup?"

"Nah, playa, I'm straight, I'm copping a few bricks now, no thanks homie, I'm good."

"You good, what da f*** dat mean, you good?"

"Dat means I'm doing my own thang now homie, and I don need nothin from you no mo," I said with a little uneasiness in my voice.

"Okay nephew, I'mma get atchu." Fat-Pimp said nodding his head with a devilish grin on his face.

As he drove away that smile left an impression on my mind. I noticed that same look on his face when I used to take those rides with him and his nephews a little over a year ago when they went on their missions.

Playas Wanna Play, Ballas Wanna Ball

On a crisp summer's afternoon in the bottom (Miami), I was standing in the Victory Holms Projects, on 73rd Street and 6th avenue, chillin like a villain, about to smoke me a joint, when fate came knocking on my door, talking crazy, whispering ...

"Hay Sonny, it's about time to pay the Piper." I was watching my investment and trying to make sure that my ends was panning out the way I had planned. I was trying to build an empire, and I didn't need any fumbling around. You hustlers know exactly what I'm talking about. For example, workers trying to run game, talking about Nine (the police) found the package or spreading some other lame crap on me that sounded utterly ridiculous saying ...

"I had to give my baby momma a couple of dollars so she could buy our baby some pampers."

Right now, I wasn't trying to hear any of that lame crap, not when every dollar counted. If the workers needed cash, they had to wait until they got paid on Friday. None of that mess was going to work, not today anyway. I had a birds-eye view on my business, and I wasn't taking a penny short.

I'm assuming, that there are a lot of things I could be doing besides sitting in a drug hole that could've saved me a lot of trouble, but I was one hustler that had his priorities in check. First the money, next the power, and then the keys to the city. Thus far, everything was copasetic. I had the whole set-in view. I could see the pistol man standing on his post, the bomb man (the guy that's selling the drugs) working in unison with the customers, and I could see the hoochie mommas too, prancing around in skimpy miniskirts, screaming ...

"Where da ballas at?"

No doubt today was a good day. There wasn't a jacker in sight, nor a green and white, and I had a smile on my face that was so bright I could've lit up the whole city. I knew if I could've kept this up, I would be hood rich in no time.

I licked my joint nice and slow along the top, then around the edges to make sure it burned evenly. Afterward, I popped it in my mouth as I grabbed my green Bic Lighter out of my pocket. When I lit it up, I watched the miniature fire burn the paper, and it receded. At first, there was a slight glimpse of white smoke that shot out of my nostrils like it was fleeing from a smoke detector. It felt so good I had to tilt my head back. Then I closed my eyes for a split second to let the smoke work its way in and around my brain. I held some of the smoke in for a few seconds before I opened my eyes to release it in the air. As the smoke oozed out of my nostrils, my peripheral took a snapshot of a five-car convoy heading in my direction.

The first thought that comes to mind was that Fat-Pimp was coming to put in work on somebody. Him and his crew was the only ones that rolled in fixed-up Cadillac's like they were apart of some type of junior mafia, riding around looking for trouble. I knew his M.O. all too well because I took a few rides with him when I first started out. I never got down and dirty with his foolishness, but I watched him, and his nephews beat the daylights out of dudes that either owed him money, messed up his drugs, or they were simply putting the extortion game down on somebody.

There was no doubt he thought he was tough. He often argued he was because, even though he left some cats for dead, and others paralyzed, he was met with very few repercussions. Make no mistake about it, Fat-Pimp was no joke, and everyone knew it. This cat had a lot of run-ins with some of the most ruthless hustlers in Miami, from Bonky-Blue, to Tick Lee or any other up and coming hustler in the hood. I was wondering, since my name is ringing bells now, was he thinking about adding me to the list of people who he taxed.

When you saw Big-Pimpin in the area, you never knew what he was coming to do. But for anybody that stayed in as many beefs as he did, it was no telling what could or would happen, you just never knew when somebody was going to come by spraying the area with bullets try to kill him.

In any act of fate, I was thinking, whatever he was doing in the area it didn't involve me. But I was wrong, dead wrong. Before I could take another puff of my joint, he and his wrecking crew were right in front of me.

"Wassup nephew," Big-Pimpin said as the dark tinted window of his Doo-Doo Brown Cadillac Fleetwood Brougham slowed down. A gush of smoke seeped out into the air, and somebody from on the inside turned the music down, but I could still feel the bass beating from the outside. The music sounded so sweet I wanted to ask him, what he was working within the trunk, seeing his facial expression made me renege on that thought.

On the real, Big-Pimpin and I were down, like four flat tires stranded on a dark country road. Yeah right! I was no fool. I felt that he had something on his mind. So, I spoke a little too soon when I said, there wasn't a jacker in sight. I finally replied.

"Oh, it ain't nothin, just playas tryna play, and ballas tryna ball. You know what it is yo, what dya do?" I said sarcastically.

"Dya do what Pimp tell 'em ta do," he says, giggling feverishly through his stomach.

"Why don chu come ben a few corners witchu main man, ya no fo ole time's sake.

We can catch a few skeezus down on the Boulevard and get sucked up." He giggles again.

"I don know Pimp because right now I'm tryna keep a birds' eye view on my trap."

"Awe Playa! Dem cats ain't going nowhere. I need to holla at chu, I got some of dat good oily dope, da hole thang comin back twenty-eight, and I'mma letchu get it at a good price." Big-Pimpin says with a smirk on his face.

As soon as he mentioned oily dope, the ounces of cocaine that came back twenty-eight grams after you've cooked it, and at a good price; I let my guards down, and I didn't give a second thought of whether I should ride with him or not.

I mean, truth be told Big-Pimpin wasn't my main man, but when drugs were involved and I was trying to cop, the source didn't matter. Besides, I didn't think Pimp had any beef with me, not when we had broken bread together when I was struggling, trying to come up. He was the one who put me on my feet by giving me ounces on consignment, not to mention him holding me down after QB had put a hit out on me. So, I figured the least I could do was bend a couple of corners with him. I'd imagine he wanted me to ride with him while he put his tax game down, and then give me a deal on some bricks that I couldn't refuse.

It was usual for me to carry my .45 on my waistline. What was unusual, was for some reason, tentative to my understanding, was how I decided to leave my pistol behind. In my mind, Big-Pimpin was going to ride around the city with his entourage trailing behind him and do what he does best. I didn't go for that we were going to get sucked up by some prostitute crap. But why I left my gun was a mystery to me. On the other hand, I was under the impression that everything was copasetic between Pimp and, so I didn't feel the need to bring my pistol.

As soon as I passed my gun to one of my workers, I spotted Reggie Biggins in the back seat of Pimp's car. He had a stupid look on his face, but nothing registered to me that something was wrong. I just figured he was trying to cop some work as well.

"Sonny let my nephew ride witchu." Big-Pimpin hollered. His glittered voice interrupted my train of thought. At the sound of his voice, I saw Man, Big-Pimpin s chosen nephew, hop out of the car and started walking towards my jeep.

Man, and I hopped into my jeep I keyed the ignition slammed the stick shift in first gear headed towards Seventh Avenue and made a right turn. I reached for a joint out of my ashtray and fired it up, hit it a few times then passed it to Man.

We started talking like we were the best of friends. I thought that, since Man and I were cool, I could ask him what was going on.

"Ai, where we goin?" I asked him just as he began to gag.

"Playa you can't hit dat Sensi like dat, dis dat fie." I said as I chuckled.

"We goin to the condo on 1-1-9." He stammered, trying to regain his composure.

PSK was one of my favorite rap songs and I had it booming out of my fresh Alpine sound system. I was bobbing my head and chatting ...

PSK makin dat cream ... people always say what da hell does that mean ... P-is for the people who can't understand ... how one homeboy became a man ... S-is for the way we scream and shout ... one by one I knock dem out ... K-is for the way my DJ kuttin ... sucka MC's boi ... ya ain't seen nothin ... "I turned the music down a notch when our convoy cruised up along beside a police car. I didn't want to draw any attention, a five-car convoy already looked menacing enough, I thought. It's a good thing the police officer didn't look our way. I suppose he must have gotten a call, by the way, he sped off while the light was still red. As soon as he was gone, I pumped the volume back up and took another hit of the weed, before passing it back to Man. The dew was blowing, the sound system was bumping, smoke was thick on the inside, and the convoy crept through the ghetto at a slow speed. "PSK makin dat cream ... people always say ... what da hell does da mean ... "The convoy arrived a few minutes before we got there because I had to stop to get some gas. It only took us a few minutes to gas up, but it gave me extra time to question Man about the dope that Big-Pimpin claimed to have. I had no reason not to believe Big-Pimpin, but I could estimate the amount that I would receive if I knew how much he had. I knew he would show me some love on the price since he was getting it for free anyway. All I could imagine was, who was he taxing this time. Man pretended like he didn't know anything.

We finally arrived at the condo. I saw five multi-colored Cadillacs, Midnight Blue, Candy Apple Red, Pearl White, Smoke Gray, and of course, Doo-Doo Brown all dressed in their own unique style.

Man, and I walked up to the second floor, and headed towards the door. I had been there before, so I knew exactly where we were going.

Man tapped on the door, using some kinda rhythm. I figured that must have been some kinda secret code they used. Blue opened the door, and we entered.

"Wassup Blue." I said as I walked by him.

"You tell me wassup Playa." He said aggressively.

As I walked inside, I noticed there wasn't any furniture in the place, and right then an eerie feeling surged through my body.

Loose Lips

I bounced into the living room, where I saw Big-Pimpin sitting in a chair.

"Pimp, what's up Poppa," I said smoothly.

"Reggie tol me whache said bout me, don't ya know dat loose lips sink ships," he said.

"Pimp, you know ain' t carrin it like dat, talkin about chu. Man, what I gotta say 'bout you? We ain't beefing, my face is clean witchu you, I paid ya what l owed ya, even doe ya charged me way too much." I said sincerely, while looking at Reggie, and the rest of pimp's crew.

Suddenly my nerves took on a different mood swing when out of my peripheral I spotted somebody peeking from around the wall in the kitchen. I turned towards the direction of the Peeping Tom, but whoevex it was, quickly drew his head back so that I couldn't see him. Big-Pimpin was silent, and everybody else including Reggie looked like they wanted to jump on me. I was about to say something, when the cat who kept peeping from around the corner of the wall, ran out of the kitchen with his hand inside a large brown paper bag and screamed ...

"Hog, you want to dump in him, right now!" He scared me so bad, I almost pissed on myself. I was relieved when Big-Pimpin said ...

"Not yet." Then he waved his hand at him to go back into the kitchen. "I'll call you when I'm ready."

I looked at Reggie and he looked scared. I wanted to tell him "Don't get scared now, you the one got me in this mess." He had a couple of knots on his face like they had been whipping his butt already, but I wasn't sure what was up. Maybe he was just scared because he was thinking that I was about to pay the piper behind his lies.

"Sonny, I know you da cross." Fat Pimp said, interrupting my train of thought. When he said that, I looked at him in bewilderment. I was about to say something when this fool runs out of the kitchen again.

"Pimp please let me gun em down!" He said grinding his teeth together like a maniac.

"Please Pimp, I been waitin ta kill him fo a long time."

"Not now Muddy-eye, chill out," Big-Pimpin told him. Then he disappeared into the recesses of the kitchen.

I started thinking, so this is the way I'm going to go out huh? Damn, and to think that I haven't had a chance to enjoy my life and these fools are about to take me out. I wondered where they would find my body. Would Fat Pimp take me to Alligator Alley so the alligators could have me for dinner? Or would he simply leave me here stinkin in the apartment? Where would he shoot me, in the stomach or the head: Would it hurt? Or would I die instantly? Just BANG, and it's over.

Then a passing thought jumped in my head saying 'No Sonny, you can't go out like this. You gotta do something man. What about Corenthia and our daughter Katrevia? What are they going to do without you? My daughter's image appeared to me. Her smile tradiant. I could see her when she she was trying to impress her daddy by taking her first steps. I could also remember hearing the first time she uttered the word daddy. What about you theme Sonny, I asked myself. "Playas Wanna Play and Ballas Wanna Ball.: You haven't even made your mark in the hustler's Hall of fame yet and your're about to get taken out.

"Playa what type of hustler are you? Hell No? I ain't going out like Willie Lump-Lump the Chump. I gave all that other stuff some serious thought in the short time I had, but what got to me the most was when I began to think about my mother. She always told me "There would be days like this, but you've got to keep a level head and there's a good chance that you will come out of it ok.

I started scanning the place looking for an escape route, I looked at the glass door thinking that I could run right through it, but it had bars behind it. Okay, think Sonny, think.

"Yeah, Sonny you da cross," Big-Pimpin said.

"Let Reggie out, so we can deal wit em." By this time Muddy-eyes came out of the Kitchen holding a .357 magnum down to his side. I figured since they're going to kill me, I might as well go out knowing that I tried to save my life. It wasn't time to freeze up, right now I couldn't afford it. Besides, I didn't need anything clouding my thinking. I thought as soon as they open the door to let Reggie out, I'm going to make my move.

When I heard them unlock the door, I rushed Reggie from behind and said ...

"Why you tol da man da damn lie?"

"Get off me, I retorted as I snatched my arm from his grip. I had gotten so mad I was ready to strap it out. It was looking cray anyway. I couldn't get out of the glass door, I couldn't get out of the front door, and I was on the second floor. I wasn't about to go out without a fight though, and if they were looking for me to beg for my life, I wasn't going to do that either.

There was only one bedroom, but I figured that it had to have a window. I didn't know how it was going to turn out and I didn't have time to think about it. It was a do or die situation. Either I do it die wishing that I would have done it. I took a couple of steps ahead of the guy escorting me to the room. He was talking crazy too.

"He, tryna get away, put his ass in da back room." One of his nephews grabbed me by the arm.

"Get ya hand off me," I said as I snatched my arm from his grip.

"Man, I ain't gon try nothin." I said repeatedly, so he would back off me and give me some space. For the most part, I wasn't paying him any attention. All I had on my mind was the window and getting a few seconds on him so that I could come up with a plan of escape. I knew one thing, that if the windows have bars on it, I was through dealing.

As soon as I crossed the door's hasp, I spotted the window, and I noticed the window it was barless and my eyes lit up. I heard Fat Pimp say something in the background, but I didn't have time to grasp or think about what he said. It happened so quick, I took a few long strides then I felt my body crashing into the window, headfirst. I heard glass shatter, then I was airborne, sailing through the sky. That's when I realized that I wasn't Superman and couldn't fly. I think I felt my feet kick, but I really couldn't tell. Time at that very moment was precious. It was either death or glory. As faith would have it, I somehow grabbed onto the window's pain and jerked, causing my body to flip upright, case in point, by the grace of God I landed on my feet on top of the roof of a car foot first.

Man, I tell you, God must have sent one of His Angels to catch me because I was definitely a goner.

I still had to make my move. I didn't know if the dude was going to start shooting out of the window. I wasn't about to hang around to find out either. My adrenaline was pumping, and I was still six seconds away from freedom or death. I still wasn't going out without a fight. Blood started dropping out of my nose. That meant somebody was going to die tonight. I hopped off the car's roof and ran as fast as I could to safety.

I ran down the street, and across the avenue to T&A Performance, then I went to the phone booth to call Sweet. As I was fumbling trying to get my nerves under control, I noticed blood was still dripping out of my nose. I dialed Sweet's number, and he picked up on the first ring.

"Hello."

"Sweet, Pimp tried to kill me," I said huffing and puffing like crazy.

"What!"

"Yea, strap down and come get me from T&A."

"How ya got dare, never mind, I'm on my way."

Sweet came with the rest of our crew, they were three cars deep and armed to the teeth. The first thing we did was drive back across the street to the condo. I had to get my jeep and I wanted to see how crazy Pimp was. If he was still there, then I knew that fat bastard wasn't working with a full deck. If he was gone, like I was hoping and praying, then he wouldn't be as stupid as everybody thought he was. When we got there, all of the Cadillacs were gone. I hopped into my jeep, keyed the ignition, and my crew and I headed to Reggie's dope spot.

When we arrived there everybody was looking crazy. We did what had been called "setting the record straight". A war was going on. We jumped out of our vehicles, waving guns, and talking crazy. Half of the crew were asking where Reggie was, and the rest of them was taking money and drugs from his workers. I even had to stop Maurice from shooting one of those cats in the mouth.

"No, Reese," I shouted just in the nick of time, as Reese was pointing his pistol in one of the guy's face.

"We ain't got no beef wit dem homie, it's Reggie we want!"

"Yeah, but I don like da way he lookin at chu."

We waited around in the spot to see if Big-Pimpin would show up. When he didn't show I felt good. I mean, I know what he did to me was messed up, but I didn't want to go through anything with him. I just couldn't back down. If I did that I wouldn't ben able to make any money on the set. Jackboys would have been trying me left and right.

One way or the other I had to come up with a plan on how to deal with Fat Pimp. I knew he was a killer, and he wasn't going to stop until somebody was dead. The problem was I hadn't killed anyone in my life and didn't know if I really could.

When I noticed my crew getting restless, I decided that we would leave and go camp out at my crib.

When we got to my house, Maurice, Sweet, Block, Tyjoe, Charlie Red, O'Neal, and I sat round in the front yard on high alert. All of us were talking crazy about what we were going to do when we saw Big-Pimpin and his flunkies.

"I'mma blow his brains out," Maurice promised.

"Naw, leave dat fat Kentucky Fried Chicken eatin joker for me," Black said sternly.

"I'mma put dis 41 magnum down his throat, and squeeze dat trigger jus like dis,"

Sweet demonstrated as he shot his weapon on the ground. BOOM! The sound echoed off the still streets. Everybody started laughing and commenting Sweet for having so much heart.

"Boi, you crazy," Brown said jokingly.

"Naw playa, I'm fo real."

All of us had something to say. Now whether we meant it or not was a different story all together. One thing was for sure, was Fat Pimp was known for killing people.

The phone rung and all of a sudden everyone got quiet. Then it rung again before I answered it.

"Hello," I said hesitantly.

"Surprise, surprise, you coward, I'll be round dare, in a black van, be looking for me.

"How fast could you get here," I shouted through the phone's receiver, then hung the phone up.

As soon as I hung up the phone, my crew started busting open package of dope that they took from Reggie's workers, and began snorting cocaine, and lighting up joint after joint. I hadn't snorted coke in years, but that night I took a few hits. I started positioning my crew like I was an army commander. "Brown you and Charlie Red, get on the roof with the AR-15. Maurice, you and O'Neal take the back yard, block you get in there," I said pointing in the direction of a tree. Sweet and I went in the vacant lot next to our house. We were in the perfect position to lay an ambush. I don't know how long we were waiting on Big-Pimpin, but he was a no-show. I called everybody in and gave them their instructions for the next day and we parted ways.

***

A week later Corenthia and I were chilling in the front room watching TV when we heard somebody knock on the door.

"Go see who dat is baby." She got up and walked to the door.

"It's somebody name twin," she said and came back and sat on the couch.

"Twin," I mumbled. Then I jumped up and headed to the door.

When I opened the door Big-Pimpin was standing there with this greasy smile on his face. I also caught a glimpse of cars parked in front of the house.

"Let me hang up da phone, I'll be right back." I spun around and walked back into the house.

"Hol up Playa I'm tryna holla at chu."

I went to the back room and got my Colt .45 and held it firmly in my left hand and walked back outside.

"Man, mi nephews tol me I was wrong, but we were really tryna tax Reggie, butcha ran jumped out da window," Big-Pimpin said, with a half-smile.

"Letz jus get back down like was used ta be."

"We can't do notin no moe Playa," I said keeping a weary eye on him.

"Man, urn da one dat help you get on yo feet."

"Yea ya did dat, but dat waz crazy wha chu did ta me, I was loyal ta ya, I knew ya was ova cha ... "

"Sonny." I turned my head in the direction of Corenthia's voice.

"Ya, betta hurry up boi yo food gettin cold."

"Urn comin!" I yelled, then snapped my head back towards Pimp.

"Yeah, I knew ya were chargin me too much, but I, I paid you, and when ya didn't give me no mo dope, I bought my own and ..."

"Man dats some sucka s***," Fat Pimp interrupted.

"Naw dogg…fo real…fo real. I'm posed to take ya a** to was… but since ya did help me get on my feet I'mma leave it at dat," I said looking crazy. "So, man jus leave from in front of my house…and don come round here no mo."

Fat Pimp grew silent. He walked away and I turned and walked back in the house. I ethink he knew I was willing to kill him that day.

THE RUSH MOB

I had finally reached the point in my life that I had been working for. Not only was I doing well, but I had my own thing. It was funny how life seemed to play out. When QB fired me, I was devastated. I didn't know how I was going to work things out, having a family and all, but things fell right in place Little did I know QB had taken me as far as I could go with him, and there was nothing else or no other reason for me to stick around him. I didn't know it at the time, and perhaps he didn't either, but life did. That's why life created a situation that would lead me towards the inevitable, which was being on my own. Just think, if QB hadn't fired me I'd be working for him getting paid a salary and taking orders. I was doing so well now that I hired my own workers. Now I could pay salaries and give orders. You see how it all worked out? I just had to pay my dues first. The workers took care of the streets, and I had another crew handling the packaging and delivery of the drugs to various spots. I was getting plenty of money too.

Corenthia and I even moved into our own place. We copped this cozy house that sat in the cut behind the Rolex Strip Club off of One Hundred and Twenty-second Street off of twenty-seventh Avenue. For a young hustler on the come up I'd say it was plush, especially if you looked at it from the outside where I had all my toys parked. There was a Jaguar XJ6, A Mercedies Benz 500SEL, a Mustang 5.0, a Bronco, a Maxima, and a 1975 Chevy convertible. Anyone would have sworn I'd instantly graduated on the level of Hitman overnight.

QB's spot was out of weed for about four days. I didn't know what had happened to him or what was going on with his suppliers. All I knew was that it wasn't like him. He never let his spot run out. I noticed the first few days he would come stand around and then all of a sudden, he just up and stopped coming around period. When I saw that I was like, 'I'm going to get me a few pounds of week to put out there.' I mean, there wasn't any sense in letting the spot go to waste, I thought. Knowing the way QB packaged his product I did mines the same way. I knew people would think it was coming from him, so I put it out there like that. I started making thousands of dollars a day just on weed. The word spread quickly too. When QB heard, I was selling weed he drove around the spot to put his threat game down. It just so happened that I was standing in the spot when him, his brother, and Jew Boy pulled up.

All three of them jumped out of the car like they were going to shoot me up right then and there. "See dis bum ba clot boi, me wan ta lick shots pun da blood clot, ya no, da boi dem pier disrespect da I an I," QB yelled as he stammered along his words.

I could tell he was mad. I kind of froze in my tracks being the the whole thing caught me by surprise. I was trying to watch QB'S brother and Jew Boy while I thought about what was about to happen to me at the same time.

I was glad when I heard Brenda's mom's voice penetrate the air.

"Sonny give me da weed, I'll freakin sell it, I live 'round here, they can't do a freakin' thang to me," Ms. Mattie yelled. Her words broke through QB and his boys' threats like it was nothing. When I looked over at her, I noticed that she was walking towards me like she meant every word that she said. I was still at a loss for words. I couldn't believe how things was just falling into place. QB was a smart businessman, so when he saw way was happening, he and his little wrecking crew hopped inside of his BMW and pulled off. Now I was making at least five grand a day in weed sales, and my crack cocaine sales skyrocketed. After the incident with Ms. Mattie, QB never came back around, and that's all I needed. I stamped Rush on the bags, and we started calling our crew "RUSH MOB".

It's A Brand New Day

    I heard that Fat Pimp had went to jail, and when I didn't see him come around, I know something was up with him. He usually had to make his presence known. He just up and disappeared all of a sudden. I didn't see him for about a year. I guess I can say it was a good year too, since I didn't have to be lurking over my shoulders wondering when he was going to show up with the foolishness. The only thing I wished was that the year would have gone on forever. By the time Fat Pimp had made it back to the set I was strong. My name was ringing all over the place, people would be saying, "dat cat Sonny bank is on swole, or Dat Boy doin it." That's how everyone that they respected QB. Man, it just felt so good being able to look the ghetto in the eye and say, "now what."

    A year later my business had expanded. I had a spot-on 15th Ave. it was doing as good as the one on 73rd Street. I opened two more spots, one in the Pork-an-Bean Projects and one on 18th Ave. Some of the guys that already had their hustle going on, that was getting money near the spots I had, started buying from me. Some of them I fronted dope to, and this kept a lot of beef down. It was nothing about the drugs because I had plenty. I had Cubans literally throwing me drugs every time I got hooked up with one of them, shortly afterwards they would give me whatever I wanted to consignment. I could go with no money and get ten and twenty bricks like it was nothing. My name and word was as good as gold.

    One day I was riding around checking on my traps. As soon as I pulled up on fifteenth Ave. I saw Sweet walking towards me with much pep in his steps.

"Aye, guess who came round here."

"Who."

"Big-Pimpin." I was outraged, but I managed to stifle a response.

"What did he want." I asked.

"I don't know, he ain't stop."

    I knew if Fat Pimp had been through once, it wouldn't be long before he came back. So, I decided to chill for a minute just to see what was up. By the time Fat Pimp wasn't a threat, at least not to me. I had a crew and I was down with whatever trouble he wanted to bring. A few hours later, I spotted Big-Pimpin bend the corner on fifteenth and Sixty-Second Street. At the time I was engulfed in a game of C-Low. There were maybe about ten or fifteen of us betting hundreds like they were one-dollar bills, and I had the bank. I also had a choice. I could have kept my head bent over in the crap game and let one of Miami's most dangerous robbers walk up on me, or I could let the bank ride, I just knew I had another head-crack in me that would have broke everybody. The only thing that was with the time it might have taken to throw the dice Fat Pimp could've head cracked me, I chose the latter.

"Wassup Sonny."

"Whatchu mean, wassup," I asked walking towards him, staring in his eyes.

"I'm fresh out da joint, let me hold a lil someten."

All I could do was crack a smile. It was funny how the tables had turned. I reached in my pocket, counted out five hundred dollars, and handed to him. A few days later Big-Pimpin called me on my cell phone.

"Dis Sonny?"

"Yea, what's up Playa."

"I need you to loan me some money to get my car fixed."

"Whatchu need?"

"Five grand."

I started thinking to myself, 'is this joker trying to tax me.'

"Pimp, you thank I'm sweet huh," I said screaming through the phone's receiver. Big-Pimpin was trying to say something, but I was steadily talking over his voice.

"As a matta fact, don eva ask me fo noten again!"

"Damn man, it's like dat!"

"It's a brand-new day Playa, I'mma kill ya da next time I see ya!"

"Oh, we'll see bout dat," he said. Then the phone went dead.

One day Brenda come to where I was on 15th Ave. and told me that Big-Pimpin came by the spot five cars deep, looking crazy. I made up mind right then and there that I was going to kill Big-Pimpin.

I summoned eight of my workers and armed them with AK-47s and AR-15s, with extra clips. We parked on 15th and stood by our cars. There were two of us to a car. We had the guns in the trunks, but the trunks weren't locked. I told the workers on 73rd Street to tell Big-Pimpin to come up on 15th Ave., if he came around there again. I commanded my guys ...

"If dey ride down dis street, we gon to kill all of dem."

While we were waiting, two police cars cruised slowly by our spot, evaluating our cars. When they turned off the avenue, I yelled to my crew ...

"Let's go to the Pork-n-Beans. My intentions were to unload the guns into a young lady's house that worked for us. While we were headed to unload the guns, the same police cars that we noticed on 15th, was behind us watching every move we made. When they left, we pulled up in the Pork-n-Beans Projects, then Sweet, Block, and I exited my bronco. The cars following us pulled in also, I had one guy driving Brenda's car, and another guy driving Corenthia' s car. We had almost finished unloading with only two assault rifles left in Corenthia's car. Then we spotted the police officers, one of the guys panicked and threw the gun back in the trunk of Corenthia's car, the gun went off, ("BOOM"). From there, things went berserk. All my homies started running in different directions.

Sweet, Block and I ran with our assault rifles. The guns that were in Corenthia's car were registered to me, and I left a 41 magnum in my bronco.

I ran through the projects, across the street, through an alley, and hid behind a house. Moments later I peered from behind the wall of the house and saw a door opened to a duplex. Instinctively, I ran into the people's home brandishing my AK-47.

When the four people of the residents saw me, they quickly dove to the floor, they must've thought I was robbing them. To calm them down, I place the gun on the floor beside on of the guys.

"Aye, ya'll get up, da police were chasin me. Yo Playa, you got some clothes I can wear?" I was talking fast, and stammering on my words, when one of the guys said ...

"Yea man hol up," as he turned around and headed in the other direction. Moments later he returned with a gray sweat suit and handed to me.

"Bet dat up dogg, I gotchu."

As soon as I put on the clothes, I cautiously walked outside. Sweet startled me when he came from around the corner of the duplex.

"Damn man, whatchu thank, whatchu thank I should do?" I asked nervously.

"I don know."

"Da guns registered to me, and da bronco is in my name, and one of da cars is in Corenthia' s name, um jus gon claim da guns."

Sweet and I walked back on the scene where the Miami-Dade Police Officers, and the ATF, had the area roped off, taking pictures of the cars and the guns. Minutes later I walked up to the officer with the ATF letters printed across his jacket and said ...

"The guns belong to me." When I said that he drew his revolver, pointed it at my face, and yelled ...

"Get on the ground now!" His comrades rushed to his aid brandishing their pistols. Within seconds I was lying flat on the ground, with an officer's knee on my neck. Then I was handcuffed and placed in the back seat of a police car.

I was taken to jail and charged with Reckless Display of a Firearm. After testing the guns to see if they were converted into fully automatic, which of course they were not. I was released.

"Beep ... beep ... beep ... "I heard my beeper go off as soon as I got my property. I stopped at the phone booth and punched in the unknown number on the keypad.

"Dis Sonny." I heard a woman's voice say.

"Yeah." Then she handed the' phone to Big-Pimpin, and he said ...

"I heard ya had guns waitin on me." I took the receiver from my heart and stared at it for a few seconds, and said ...

"Yea Playa, I jus thought I'd letchu know, it's a brand-new day, and your days are numbered," I said. Then he hung up the phone.

My Bahamian Connection

The few Cubans I was dealing with was out of dope. That happened at a bad time too, because it was the first of the month, and around that time business be booming.

My Cuban connections kept telling me to wait, but they had me on hold for nearly a week. I needed some work bad too, because I didn't want my customers to go elsewhere, and risk losing my clientele. I needed to get something to hold me down until they got straight. The rule to the game was, if your connection ran out of dope, it would be wise to wait until their supply came in, since the streets were filled with tricksters, desperados, and bandits, waiting to find somebody, running around looking for dope during a drought. It was best to deal with people that was established and that has gained your trust. But my back was against the wall, so I broke the rule.

I bought a few bricks from this Bahamian guy name Willie. He tried to sell me dope a few times, but I was always straight. On this rare occasion, I beeped Willie from the phone booth in front of Mr. Wonderful store. I hadn't been waiting five minutes when the phone rang.

"Hello, somebody beeped Willie."

"Yeah, Willie, dis Sonny."

"Oh, hey Sonni, wassup, ya ready to ... "

"Yeah, I need three of dem thangs," I said interrupting him.

"Okay, where ya at?"

"On da ave, in front of Mr. Wonderful's store."

Thirty minutes later Willie pulled up in front of the store driving in a blue Grand Am, with dark tinted windows. He beckoned for me to get in the car. When I got inside, he handed me large brown paper bag on my lap and said ...

"Check dem out mon."

"Nah, I don't need to check dem, da straight right?"

"Yeah, mon."

I rolled down the window and signaled for Sweet, who brought me a Gucci bag filled with money. I took the money out of the Gucci bag, put the bricks in it, and hopped out of the car, and into Sweet's convertible, and dipped.

I went straight to the crib and started breaking the work down, I dropped a half a brick in the glass cooking bowl, measured the baking soda, added water, and put it in the microwave. Moments later, when I saw the amount of oil that had settled at the bottom of the bowl, I knew it wasn't going to weigh out right, so I immediately beeped Willie. He called right back, and I said ...

"Ayeman, dis thang ain't comin back right," I said with agitation in my voice.

"I'll be oba dare in bout twenty minutes Poppa."

When Willie came, he cooked the reminding two and a half bricks. He used all kinds of gimmicks, but the drugs just wouldn't come out right. After he finished cooking the dope, he weighted it and, disappointment appeared on his face. After cooking the three kilos, it came back to a little over one brick. Then he turned to me and said ...

"Aye mon, jus work wit dis, I'mma get atchu early in da morning."

"Okay," I said with a serious look on my face. Then I escorted him out of the house.

That next morning turned into three, and then four days. On the fifth day, I was getting ready to wage war against Willie. I ran into him at the Bahamian Restaurant on 54th Street and 14th avenue.

When I entered the restaurant, I saw Willie sitting at a table with an exotic looking young lady. I couldn't hear what they were saying, but they were laughing, and having a good time. When Willie turned his head in my direction, and our eyes met, his mood swing changed in an instant.

Before I could make it over to where he was, he got up from the table and approached me.

"Hol up mon, I know ya hot wit me, but if ya jus give me a few mo dayz, I promise you'll never have ta buy no mo dope." He was saying as we walked outside.

I had to do some quick thinking, to figure out my next move. I could have reached in my waistline, pulled out my pistol, and gunned him down, or I could give him a few more days and see if he would make good on his promise. A few more days couldn't hurt I thought, so I agreed to his terms. A couple days later, Willie beeped me, when I called him back, he said ...

"Aye, ware ya at mon?"

"I'm at da crib, wassup?"

"Youa see when I got dare mon" When he came, he gave me the two bricks he owed me, fronted me five, and we became partners.

During the next eight months, Willie and I was ballin out of control, that's until word got back to me that he was telling people that I worked for him. I don't know why, but that rumor really upset me, I felt disrespected. Willie and I discussed the issue, and I chalked it up as just a rumor.

One day, my homie Convertible Burt asked me if he could touch Willie, and he wanted me to set it up. He said ...

"Man get Willie to bring me ten bricks, I'mma take em, and bust dem down with witchu."

"Playa, don ask me to do no slimy crap like dat, cause I don cross mi friends, and if anybody try to rob em, uma go at'em wit all I got," I said.

Willie didn't have spots in Miami, he sold bricks, he also had cats coming in from other states copping bricks from him, and he had dudes he used to send to Atlanta Georgia to run a spot for him.

Willie and I were getting major loot, but over time I felt that something wasn't right with our chemistry. I could feel tension, I could feel deceit, and I could feel the cross coming. I couldn't quite put my finger on it, but anytime this gut-feeling surged through my body, that meant something wasn't right.

The Game Is Slimey

I very seldom stayed out of my house overnight, when I did, I'd chill at Brenda's crib. Most of the time I'd just stay over late and then I would leave in time to make it home before the sun came up, especially when I wasn't conducting business, to avoid arguing with Corenthia. Willie used to call Brenda's house whenever I was over there in the wee-wee hours of the night, checking up on me. I'd usually tell him where I would be crashing for the night since we were partners. Whenever he called her house, she'd answer the phone and pass it to me, like she normally does.

One day while I was cruising down 15th Ave., Convertible Burt flagged me down, when I pulled over, he said ...

"Aye dogg, ya know ya partna bustin yo girl Brenda?" He said with a smirk in his face.

"Homie, ya tellin me dis foolishness, cause you want me ta letchu touch da man."

"I do wanna touch' ern, but he is knockin yo girl down dogg." When he said that I began to think about all those times that Willie used to call be checking up on me, when I stayed over Brenda's house late nights.

It was two o'clock in the morning, and Brenda and I had just got finished taken care of our business when the phone rung. I was laying across the bed about to doze off and didn't realize that she had passed me the phone when I heard Willie's voice say ...

"Wassup boi, ery thang alright?"

"Yeah urn straight, meet me at da Ham and Eggery in da morning, I needz ta holla atchu," I said before I handed the phone back to Brenda and dozed off.

The next day I never got a chance to talk to Willie about the issue with Brenda. I was planning to confront him about what I had heard, but since we had to go out of town to collect his money, I decided to wait until we got back.

We hit the highway headed to Atlanta that same day. While he drove, he struck up conversations about his spot, I'd answer him, but for the most part, I couldn't vibe with him the way I used to.

By the time we got to Atlanta, it was late. Willie and I checked into the Days Inn Hotel. The next morning, we went to one of the workers to handle his business. While Willie was in the house talking on the phone, two of his workers were outside talking to me. They were complaining about how he was charging them too much, and how greasy he talked to them. That's when I came up with a plan when I told the guy.

"Tell Willie, the police raided the house last night and took the money, and they were asking ya'll did ya'll know anybody named Willie Bain."

We're going to split the money three ways, and I'm going to start bringing ya'll dope at a better price. I followed the guy into the house, he gave me twenty grand all in one-hundred-dollar bills, and I stuffed some it down in my pouch and the rest in my pants along the waistline.

Willie and the guy were in the room talking, and moments later he burst out of the room and said ...

"Sonny lets dip," nearly running like out of the house. When we got in the car he headed straight for the expressway, and we rode back to Miami in silence.

A week after we came back from Atlanta, I was thinking about Willie screwing Brenda, and Convertible Burt's words came to my mind when he said ...

"Get Willie to bring ten bricks, so I can take 'em."

I called Willie and told him to bring me ten bricks to the house, and within an hour he came with the package. I grabbed the duffle bag of bricks, took them to the back room, gripped my 41 magnum and walked back into the living room, holding the gun to my side, and said ...

"Aye potna, I heard dat ya screwing Brenda." As soon as I said that Willie's face balled up in a knot. He started speaking in his Bahamian accent so loud and fast that I couldn't understand a word he was saying. Then I said ...

"Since ya wonna play like dat, uma take dese ten bricks, and yo spot in Atlanta, and you can have Brenda, or I can jus take yo life potna," I said grinding my teeth together.

"Man, whoeva tol ya dat liein, I ain't never screwed dat girl mon! I...

"Whateva, potna, I ain't sweatin it, jus don't let me catch chu in Atlanta," I said and nodded my head towards the door. He got up and walked away.

I never mentioned anything to Brenda about her and Willie, I just charged it to the game.

CHAPTER TEN

SONNY'S BRIDGE IS FALLING DOWN

In all the dope spots I had, things were going really well for me. It's safe to say, at the young age of twenty-four, that now I was really at the top of my game. It was nothing for me to open a new spot, brand it with my labels, and have it in a matter of weeks pumping major drug traffic and cash flow. I don't have to tell you that from a young G's perspective it felt good to be able to buy anything I wanted. Hell, it felt even more exhilarating to be able to buy people. Sometimes I bought love, other times I paid for friendship, and sometimes I even paid for people to leave me alone. You had to be a hustler to understand that.

My homeboys Gary and Ty was doing their own thing in the dope game, but it wasn't anything compared to what I had going on. One day I asked them did they want to invest some money with me, I offered them 50% return on their money within thirty days. They put up twenty grand apiece, I put up sixty grand, and we patched up and brought ten bricks. In less than three weeks, I paid them both, but Ty kept re-investing. From time to time, I'd look at Ty and smile. I think about how he wanted to take my life, back in the day, when we were working for Hitman. Now we are partners. I guess time has its way of changing things.

Corenthia told me that this Root Lady wanted to see me. I heard about and knew of Root Ladies, Voodoo, and Yoruba, so I felt that all she wanted was to try to make some money off of me. She would tell me a few lies, get me all worked up, give me a bag of dust for protection, and then charge me a few grand. So, I wasn't too enthusiastic about going to see her.

"Sonny please jus go see da lady, please" she pleaded

"What do she want".

"The lady just wonna talk to ya." Corenthia was so persistent, that I finally agreed to see her. This wasn't the same Root Lady I'd been to see years ago. She was some lady from the islands who was supposed to be able to tell the future. It was on that Saturday night when we drove to her place in North Miami Beach.

As Soon as Corenthia and I entered the lady's apartment I felt an eerie feeling subdue me. Corenthia was on my side holding my hand, but I swear it was like she wasn't standing there at all. Maybe because I noticed her staring at the different artifacts, picture and candles the lady had everywhere. I can't tell you what it was but the whole thing was strange. A heavy-set lady emerged from the back room wearing a multi-coloured dress. She had her head wrapped up and she was toting a Bible. I believe it was the King James Version. She also had this smile on her face, or this look that kind of made me feel invaded. At that moment something told me this wasn't a joke.

She invited us into her kitchen, where she prepared a table for us to sit. As soon as we sat down, she started humming and hissing like a cat. The whole thing caught me by surprise, I was spooked. Then she said ...

"Sonny, how are you doing?"

"I'm fine," I said.

"There's no need for you to be afraid, I won't hurt you, my only desire is to help you. Your girlfriend told me about you not wanting to come and see me, but I'm glad that you changed your mind." I looked at Corenthia, thinking to myself, 'why she had to tell da lady dat.'

"Well, I tell you what, I'm not going to charge you anything for this reading; if what I tell you don't come true, you don't have to worry, we're out of this as though we never met before. But if you find what I'm saying to be true, you can give me whatever you wish." She continued.

"There are some people watching you Sonny and not the regular police, it's the ones that wear plain clothes. I don't know who they are, but they told the regular police to leave you alone.

Three days later, I saw what appeared to be two undercover police cars sitting down the street from my house. I don't know if I was paranoid, after hearing what the Root Lady said, or what. But I stayed inside the house for a few days, until they left.

My next move was to find a spot to stash my drugs. I found a condo in the same building that Big-Pimpin tried to kill me in, I even rented the same apartment. The moment I got the keys I moved all my drugs and guns inside the condo.

A few weeks had passed, and I had the condo in full operation. Sweet and a guy name Block were my lieutenants. I had other lieutenants too, but they were the closest to me, with access to large amounts of drugs and money.

One day we were sitting in the apartment counting money, when I thought about the money Brenda, and I had got caught with at the Airport in East St. Louis. I was thinking that since I was already close by the lawyer's office, I'd roll by him to see what was going on with the money that the agents confiscated. Something told me to take the one hundred and fifty thousand dollars we had counted with me, but I decided to play it safe, and get it when I came back.

After leaving the lawyer's office, I passed right by the condo on my way to 15th Ave. As soon as I parked my car, one of my lieutenant's name Brown came up to me crying like a baby, then he said ...

"Man, I went to the apartment, and everythang is gone."

"What! Man, what da hell is you talkin bout, I just left da condo, and it was straight."

"Sonny, um tellin you, everythang gone."

Brown and I headed back to the condo. When we walked in, I noticed that the place was ram shacked, I almost fainted.

"Man, you can kill me if ya wonna, but I swear I don have nothing to do wit dis. I'll stay witchu until ya find out who did dis, but man I swear, it wasn't me."

What puzzled me the most was that I knew there was only three of us there who counted the money. And after we were done, we put the money in the drop ceiling in the bathroom. The rest of the drugs and guns were in the closet. I had to asked myself if I were a robber who entered a house and found thousands of dollars' worth of drugs, and firearms in a closet, what would make me go into the bathroom, remove one piece of the ceiling, and go right to the money? It would have to be an inside job I thought.

There were only two people that I suspected of robbing the house, and they were Sweet and Block. I got right on the phone and called Block and Sweet, and told them to meet me on 15th Ave. When I got there, I didn't even ask them if they did it or not. I just told them, if they didn't get my stuff back in that condo, that I was going to kill the both of them. Later that evening I got a phone call from my mother, she said ...

"Come over here right now, and I mean now!"

"Okay, I'm on my way." When I drove up, I saw my mother standing in the front yard. When she saw me, she turned around and headed in the house. When I walked in, she told me to sit down, and she said...

"Boy is you crazy, Sweet is your darn brother, have you forgotten? That boy Block loves you like he's your brother! Sweet almost drove off of the side of the expressway, and almost killed himself, after what you told 'em, you scared em' so bad. You better not bother neither one of them, is that money getting to your head, what the hell is wrong wit chu!" She said as I listened with a confused look on my face.

As I was driving home in silence, I recalled my mother's words, but they still didn't shake how I felt about the situation. When I got home, I discussed the situation with Corenthia before we fell asleep. The next morning, I started to ask her to book me a flight to St. Louis, but I changed my mind and took the long tedious ride up there. When I got there, I collected the thirty-five grand from the remaining portion of the drugs that I had left.

When I returned to Miami, I brought a brick, called Sweet and gave him half of it. I also gave him all the workers, and all the spots save the one in Victory Holmes Projects. I had every intention to never have anything else to do with him ever again, as far as business was concerned.

I took that half of brick, and started grinding, and within a few weeks, I was up to a brick. I decided to send the brick up to Atlanta, and make a quick flip, but the guy got busted on the road with it. After that, I fell into a critical depression, and Remy Martin became my best friend. Every morning I would get up and drink until I couldn't drink anymore. I called myself freeing my mind, so I could think of a master plan on how to get back on my feet, but instead, I was slowly, and surely, becoming an alcoholic.

One day, I was standing in the doorway of my house, facing the backyard, staring blankly through the glass door. I don't quite remember what I was saying, but I know I was praying to God to help me. As I kept mumbling, I started to feel tension building up in my heart. Then seemingly, out of nowhere, Corenthia walked up and hugged me from behind, and laid her head on my back and asked ...

"Sonny, what wrong?"

At that time her voice, the way it vibrated through my body, activated a release valve for my troubled soul; then the tears began rolling down my face like a river, as I started crying uncontrollably saying ...

"Baby, I'm tired of all of this, I'm jus tired, I need to change my life, I need God to help me, and take dis mess away from me, I'm tired baby."

No one had to convince me to see a Root Lady, I sought one for myself. I never went back to the Lady Corenthia had introduced me to. I tried to find her phone number, but I realized I didn't give her anything for the reading she gave me, in spite of the fact that she was telling me the truth.

My mother took me to this Cuban Lady. She was supposed to be good, so good that she would have whoever had stolen my money, running back to give it to me, with interest. Of course, that never happened, but she did hook me up with a Cuban fellow named Pablo.

I didn't have any friends, so I felt I could confide in Pablo. He used to tell me ...

"Don wori bout its Poppi, in a few days I'm gonna give ya someten, all ya gotta do is be straight wit me."

A few weeks had passed, and while Remy Martin was consoling me, the vibration of my beeper startled me. I didn't recognize the number, but I called it back anyway. When somebody picked up the phone, I said ...

"Yeah, somebodi beeped Sonny."

"Wassup mi friend, are you ready." A voice said through the phone's receiver. I immediately recognized the voice, it was Pablo.

"Yeah, um readi," I said. I sobered up quick. That same day Pablo brought me five bricks, and just like that I was back on my feet.

Ty and I picked up right where we left off, as far as I was concerned his investment in me was still valid. And although Sweet was still suspect, I buried those ill feelings I had for him and got back on my grind.

When Ty and his long-time girlfriend got married, Sweet, Block and I went to his wedding. We were dressed in white silk Tuxedoes, wearing fresh Red, white, and blue Kango hats. I'd never forget that the people who didn't know us thought we were a part of the mob.

They say things change when people get married, and things changed drastically with Ty and me. He told me ...

"Sonnyboy, the next time we get ready to bust down, I want all the money I invested, and I'm not selling drugs no mo, man my wife is trippin."

I couldn't believe Ty was just going to give up the game when we were making so much money. It wasn't like he was out there taking chances, but Ty made me a believer, he walked away from the dope game.

Shortly after Ty left the drug game, he started selling all his material possessions. He sold his 5.0 Mustang, Bronco, and his Rolex, to P-man Sam, but he didn't sell any of his wife's possessions. When the money stopped coming in like his wife was used to, she up and walked away from him, the same way he walked away from the dope game.

The Business

Miami was known for having Jams, that's what we called them back in the day "A Jam." Today you may hear people call a Jam a block party. Even going to, Calle Ocho could be associated with a Jam. In the city of Miami, we jammed in the middle of the hood, from one end of the street to the other, within a quarter mile radius. If you heard someone saying they were jamming on the Ave, not only did they mean somebody had their DJ equipment on the corner, playing the finest rap and urban music, it was also like hearing Spring Fling in South Carolina, or the Freak Nick in Atlanta. In the hood is where we jammed nearly every weekend.

I love going to Jams, so much so that I bought a DJ system with 48 base speakers. I liked the idea of having jams and seeing people come out to have a good time.

Since I wasn't a DJ, I would let Uncle Al use the equipment. Uncle Al was known in the hood as one of the hottest DJ's. He was young and spirited, and he knew how to rock the mic. I gave the DJ equipment to Uncle Al, and he renamed his group from The Sugar Hill DJ's too, "Sugar Hill-Rolling with Rush DJ's."

We would throw small concerts and provide big jams in the parks and on 15th ave., on the weekends and on holidays. I could still remember how the girls would come out in their cat's suits and tight miniskirts, trying to catch the eyes of the ballers that strolled through in their fly whips.

Sweet and I were into fly Whips, and we were one of the first ones to get a Wet Look on our cars out of the hood. A Wet Look was a paint job so perfect that the cars always looked like they were wet. Perfect Paint and Body Shop was the master at putting Wet Looks on cars. When they sprayed Sweet's and my convertibles, I couldn't believe how raw the paint job looked.

Sweet had a Root Bear color on his Delta 88 Convertible, and my Delta was painted Candy Apple Red. Our cars were so pretty We used to put up money during jams to anyone who thought they had a prettier car. We would let the girls be the judges, and nobody ever won.

At the time I had a few businesses, Campbell's Landscaping & Lawn Service, Stomp & Grind Records, Sonny Daze Publishing, and Sugar Hill-

Rolling with Rush DJ's. So, it's fair to say, I wasn't just your average drug dealer. I had businesses and business sense to run them. But there was always business that I had to take care of involving my drug empire.

Brenda started a relationship with a young, up and coming, hustler, that sold drugs a short distance from my spot on 73rd Street. I figured since we weren't all that serious, there was no need for me to sweat her. Not on that tip, anyway. When I found out she was hitting me up, the way she used to hit QB up, I became mettlesome into her business. To even think she was stealing drugs from me and giving it to her lover had me hot. I would search Brenda's house sometimes and find three to four thousand dollars in drugs and money. Her and one of my lieutenants used to get together and put their lick down. I couldn't really do anything to Brenda because her and her mother helped me when I first started out. Brenda and my beef grew thicker by the day, so I decided to leave 73rd Street and concentrate on my spot in Atlanta.

CHAPTER ELEVEN

MY BROTHER'S KEEPER

Early one morning, around the time Corenthia takes our daughter to school, I heard her screams invading my light sleep.

"Sonny, Sonny, dey out here!" Immediately my eyes popped open. When she said dey, I knew exactly who she was referring to. We had been discussing them ever since I was arrested in the Pork-n-Bean Projects with those guns. These were the people the Root Lady had mentioned, that was watching me.

I went to the front door to see what was going on. I could hear Corenthia arguing, telling whoever it was to get out of her yard. When I got to the door, I saw about four or five men with A.T.F. letters on their jackets.

"Come out with your hands up," they yelled simultaneously, pointing their weapons in my direction, as I stared at them blankly. I was still half asleep. At first, I thought I was dreaming. I only had on boxer shorts and a t-shirt, so I yelled back ...

"Let me put some pants on!"

"Come out now, with your hands up." I walked back into the house and got dressed.

When I finally went outside, they swarmed all over me. One of the Agents was asking me where was the 9-millimeter handgun that I purchased a few days ago. I yelled to Corenthia...

"Bae, bring me dat gun that's sittin on da dresser." Within minutes, she came back outside with the gun. In the few minutes that she was gone, one of the agents handcuffed me. He and another agent were moving with me, so fast, on our way to their car, that my feet barely touched the ground.

Twenty minutes later, we were pulling up in the back of a plain looking building. I would have never suspected it to be a Federal Sub-station. The agent parked and both of them walked to one side of the car and opened the door. When I got out, they briskly walked me through the back door of the building, up two flights of stairs, and into an office. Then one of them uncuffed me and ordered me to sit in a chair, while they sat behind a desk.

"Did you know; you could get three years for a gun?" One of the agents asked. He was nearly screaming while staring me directly in my face. Since I heard about some of my homeboys getting three years for possession of a firearm, I nodded my head yes.

"Well, what's twenty-one times three?" Before I could make the calculation, the agent wrote the numbers down on a piece of paper and shoved it in my face. All I saw was the number 63 with "years" written behind it. I started sweating like crazy, and my knees buckled, even though I was sitting down. I was so nervous and scared, and it felt like I could hardly breathe. When the officer that was yelling at me got up and walked out of the office, the other officer said.

"Okay just relax." His stare never faltered.

"I want to help you, just tell me, do you know anyone that has any guns or drugs in their house? Don't worry about my partner, he can be a jerk sometimes." I was just about to answer when the door swooped open, and the other offer walked in.

"No sir," I said, shivering.

"Do you freken see this." The mean officer said.

"Yes sir, but I don no nobodi, wit, no, guns. Dats why I brought mi guns from da gun sto."

"You freken liar, you do know somebody, play hard, and you are going to do some hard time buddy."

"Put this idiot in the cell." He scoffed.

They put me in a cell not bigger than the size of a small bathroom. There was a metal bench along the wall, a stainless-steel toilet, and a sink. The cell was cold and damp, and there was an eerie silence lingering around the walls.

The agents decided to stand by the cell to hold a conversation on their investigation. I couldn't see them, but I scrounged down by the door where I could hear everything they were saying. They started mentioning names of people that sold drugs for me out of town, including Willie Bain. They even called the names of some of my lieutenants, and workers I had in different spots. Every time they mentioned a name that I was familiar with, a frown would appear on my face, and I would wince. When I heard all that, I knew that I was hit. I was drenched in sweet, despite the fact that the air-conditioner was on full blast, I was freezing. While I was still scrounged down, the door swooped open, and I wobbled to stand upright. "Are you ready to talk now or are you ready to serve 63 years in prison; because if you don't cooperate with us, I promise that you'll get 63 years' sentence.

"Sir, I don know nobodi, dat sell no drugs, and I don know nobody dat got no guns," fighting back the urge to burst out crying.

"Okay, tough guy, you're going to the Big House.

The agents transported me to MCC Miami Federal holding facility. The commute was swift and burdensome. In the short time we drove I thought about family and just how they were holding up. I knew whatever I was going through, that it was going to be rougher on them.

As soon as I got there, I came face to face with a reality that I had no way of knowing existed. I saw big time Columbians, Cubans, and I even conversed with one of the biggest cocaine dealers in Miami, Bo Dilly. He was in the housing unit that I was assigned to. Just seeing their faces, and knowing they had been zapped out of society, made me feel uneasy. I thought if the Feds had them behind bars, facing life sentences, then having me was nothing. For me, I just knew I was about to get those 63 years the agents had promised. I was just getting prepared to do them, because I wasn't about to tell on nobody.

The next morning, I went to Bond Hearing and listened to the judge read off my charges. I thought she would never stop explaining each type of weapon they said I bought, from different Gun Stores, within the last couple of years. I couldn't figure out how they knew that, but I guess the Gun Store's owners, where I'd purchased the guns from, turned me in. When she was done, she set my bond at one hundred thousand dollars.

I was ready to post bail that same day, but my bondsman ordered me to wait until they dropped (lowered the price) the bond. I didn't want to wait, but I took his advice. After a week had passed, and the court still hadn't lowered my bond, I told my bondsman to get me out. I posted the bail after nine days in jail. The judge required that I turn in the guns before they would release me. I asked my mother to go to my house, get the guns, and bring them down to the federal building.

After my mom got all the guns together and turned them in, I was released. I stepped out of jail, and it felt like a million pounds had been lifted off of my shoulders. I still couldn't believe "The Feds" had come to arrest me. I thought the feds only arrested big time drug dealers. People like Bo Dilly, the Cuban that supplied him, and me, I thought, were on different levels. What were they saying, was I now in the big times category as well? I mean, I did have a fleet of nice cars, a couple of cribs, and the fame that came with being hood rich. So, I guess I was a big timer too.

My bondsman referred me to a lawyer that he knew. He was supposed to be good, but apparently, he wasn't good enough. He told me straight off the bat that it was going to be hard to beat the case because they had my signature on the gun's receipts. That was his take on the case, but he told me he would talk to the agents to see what can be done to resolve the matter.

A few days later, the lawyer told me that the agents wanted a bust, to make them look good. When I started looking crazy at the lawyer, he told me all I had to do was put some drugs in a car and leave it somewhere that the agents could find it.

"Man, I keep tellin ya' 11, I don't have any drugs to give, and I don't wonna talk about me having drugs anymore." I snapped.

The next day the lawyer called me and said, the Agents told him that I had another gun that my mother didn't turn in, and if I didn't bring the gun in my bond would be revoked.

I thought the agents were gaming me at first, trying to figure out a way to put me back in jail, because I wouldn't help them. When my lawyer showed me a list of all the guns I had purchased, and the serial numbers, with the missing AK-47 highlighted in yellow, that the agents were referring to, I immediately began to stress. I just couldn't remember where any other gun could be. I thought about it, and thought about it, and nothing registered to me. Something told me to call Sweet and ask him about the AK-47 he had, so I called him.

"Aye Sweet read me da serial numbers of dat AK ya got."

Right, then a light clicked on in my head. I remembered that Sweet gave me money to purchase the gun for him. The numbers that he called out matched the serial numbers of the missing gun that was listed on the paper.

"Aye man, me and da bondsman comin ova dare ta get dat gun." I heard some commotion on the phone, but I didn't pay it any mind. I just hung up the phone and headed to his house.

When the bondman and I pulled up in front of Sweet's house, he ran out of the door towards us, with the AK in his hand.

"Dis ain't yo gun," he yelled at the top of his lungs, as he pointed the AK-47 at my face. His eyes were bloodshot red, and he acted like he was a time bomb, about to explode. When it dawned on the bondsman and I, what was happening, we just froze dead in our tracks.

"You think everythang is yours, you talkin bout I broke in yo house, and stole yo stuff, I'll blow yo brains out!" He shouted. When he cocked the AK-47 the bondsman ran and ducked behind his car.

The Dope Game

I didn't really understand what was going on with Sweet that morning. I didn't have time to think about how to approach him, but I know if I approached him the wrong way, that would cause his ego to flare up at me. All I know is that the whole ordeal caught me completely by surprise.

"Boi, um tellin ya, don't make dis a homicide.

"Come on Sonny let's just leave." I heard my bondsman yelled. He had a terrified look on his face. I turned around and stared at him for a moment, then I turned back to face Sweet.

It looked like Sweet was high on cocaine. I really couldn't tell, maybe I was looking for a reason to justify his erratic behavior. I was trying to avoid my bond from being revoked, and here he was tripping. If he wanted to shoot, then let him shoot.

I wasn't about to stand there looking crazy, while he waved a gun in my face. So, I just walked up and snatched the gun from him. I threw the gun on the ground, and we started fighting.

For the life of me, I couldn't understand Sweet's actions, because if he was in this situation, I would go all in. I would've sold everything I owned, if I had too, to keep him out of jail. Why didn't he feel the same way about me was a mystery?

On the advice of my lawyer, we chose not to go to trial. He kept telling me that we couldn't win, and I was convinced that he was telling the truth. If my signature was all that they needed to prove their case, then I was already convicted. I was still out on bond, but I knew that I was going to do some jail time. The only thing about that was, I didn't want Corenthia, and Samantha, living in the same locations they were living. I had some reserve there; knowing that people would think they had money in their homes, and try to rob them, or even possibly' arm them, so I relocated both of them. I bought Corenthia a place near the Joe Robbie Stadium, and Samantha found a condo in Miami Lakes.

On the day I went to court, a large number of my family members took off from work to support me. There were about twenty of us in all. We had breakfast that morning at the Howard Johnson Hotel Restaurant near the courthouse. The food was terrible, none of us enjoyed it, but we had a lot of fun together. Until the Billy Bob came, that's when everybody's faces balled up in a knot. The Billy Bob was one hundred and twenty dollars. When my grandfather saw the Billy Bob, he went off and said ...

"Son don pay for dat food, I'll just go ta jail today, it just ain't worth paying fo." My grandmother tried to cool him down, but he continued to protest his disapproval. Corenthia paid the Billy Bob after my aunt walked my grandfather outside. The rest of us walked slowly outside, got in the van, and headed to the Courthouse.

The judge told my lawyer that I wouldn't be detained that day and that she would allow me to spend time with my family for the holidays. I was Christmas time, and Corenthia was seven months pregnant with our second child. The prosecutor didn't even want to prosecute the case. I was elated when I heard her say ...

"Your Honor, the Government move to dismiss the charges against Mr. Campbell, on three grounds, One: He wasn't selling weapons, Two: He wasn't converting the weapons into fully automatic, and Three: The weapons were turned over in a timely manner. The Government rests its case." I felt another burst of happiness when I saw the judge shaking her head in agreement.

"While I agree with everything that the Government presented, I'm going to reject the offer. If the Government lets Mr. Campbell walk out of the courtroom today, a free man, he would have missed out on an opportunity to learn a valuable lesson." The judge said as she moved some papers around on her desk.

"Tell me, Mr. Campbell, why did you buy so many weapons anyway?"

"The Guns are a hobby of mine."

"Well, you had better find another hobby, because if you come before me again with weapons charges, I'm going to sentence you to twenty-five years, is that clear?"

"Yes, ma' am. "

"The Government hereby commit Mr. Albert Campbell to the custody of the Federal Bureau of Prisons, to serve a sentence of twelve months, and upon his release, three years Supervised Release.

"Government do you have any objections?"

"No, Your Honor."

It took me a few minutes to comprehend the judge's language, but when the Federal Marshals started walking toward me, it dawned on me that I was going to be detained.

"Counsel, do you have any closing statements."

"Yes, Your Honor. Your Honor, you stated to me that you would allow my client to spend the Christmas Holidays with his very pregnant girlfriend.

"Yes, I did mention that, but I have the right to change my mind, and this is exactly what I choose to do." Marshals escort Mr. Campbell out of the courtroom.

My family took the matter rough; they started crying and doing all types of things, that showed their disapproval of me being detained. I was cool with that. I mean, it wasn't but twelve months. I'd be home in no time. All I could think about at the time was how the agents tried to scare me into being an informant. I know snitching wasn't on my mind, but I couldn't help but to think, how messed up it would've been if I'd snitched or fell weak, just to avoid going to prison for twelve months.

After staying at MCC Miami for a month, I was designated to FCI Tallahassee. At twenty-five years of age, I was on my way to prison for the first time. I had done those little County Jail stints of thirty days or less. Now I was heading to the "Big House." The thought of going up the road to prison was something to think about. I remembered when I was young, I always used to hear people say prison was rough. I never slowed down enough to think about going to prison at the time, but now I was giving it some serious thought.

During the long bus ride to prison, it felt like my heart was racing. I kept thinking about what prison life was going to be like. Would I have to fight in order to prove to other's that I'm not soft? The thought lingered in my mind. I heard stories about how you should hit the biggest inmate you see, so the other inmates will know you're not afraid. I just knew it would be rough, with my temper. I had to get mentally prepared for the worst.

After I got finished with all the medical screening, and briefed on questions like, did you cooperate with the Government, is there any reason why we shouldn't release you to the compound, are you gang affiliated etc, I made it to my unit around three O'clock am. Later that morning, I awoke early for chow, and to prepare myself to prove my masculinity if I had to. I tried my boots tight and took several deep breaths in order to maintain my composure.

On my way to the Chow Hall, I was specifically looking for the two biggest inmates, so I could size them up, the only problem was, big inmates were everywhere. I was like, okay what now? Do I have to fight all these convicts?

By the time I reached the Chow Hall, I saw two guys I thought I knew. I didn't know if I was looking crazy, or scared, but one of them spoke to me.

Aye, Sonny wassup? It was at that very moment all the strength and courage I'd garnered in the hood formed inside me. I was ready to fight with all I had and would be satisfied with the outcome.

It ain't notin Playa, I responded with an attitude. Their faces looked familiar, so I just played along like I knew of them. I later found out the guys were from Liberty City, where I was born and raised. Lil Eric was from 56th street, and Kenny was from the Graveyard. When we finally got back to the dorm, they supplied me with snacks and some personal hygiene products, to hold me down until I got the chance to go to the commissary and shop.

Lil Eric, Kenneth, and I started doing mostly everything together. We worked out together, ate together, and exchanged war stories to pass time together.

The prison in Tally wasn't as bad as I thought it would be. A few days after I got there, they were celebrating Memorial Day. Food Services had set out the barbecue grills, they barbecued chicken, hot dogs, and hamburgers. For the side dishes they served macaroni and cheese, and baked beans. They even had their own DJ set playing loud music. To me the event looked more like a family reunion, everybody seemed to be having so much fun. I enjoyed myself also, but I would soon become acquainted with a harsh reality.

In FCI Tallahassee, there were people there convicted for drugs charges, that didn't get caught with any drugs. Some were sentenced to twenty years, some thirty years, and some of them got sentenced to life in prison. Most of the people I met, during my short stay in Tally, played a minor role in a complex scheme we so often called "THE DOPE GAME."

It didn't take long before I got homesick. I truly understood the fact that anyone could adjust to prison life, depending on what they got involved in. They could totally forget about life on the other side of the fence, but no matter how intriguing I found Tallahassee to be, there was no place like home. After about seven months into my sentence, it started to weigh heavily on my mind, even though I befriended a few brothers that seemed to be handling their life sentences pretty well. I'd say to myself, that's their reality, I figured mine was just as hectic. The thing about it was when you're in prison, your loved ones are in prison too.

All type of things started happening that made it hard for me to go about the day in ease. I remember calling home one night, and Corenthia told me somebody tried to rob Sweet. When she told me that I couldn't sleep for a few nights. When I finally talked to Sweet, he told me he didn't know who the guys were. All he knew was when he pulled up to his house and got out of the car, some dudes jumped out of the bushes on him and his girl. He said ...

"Dog, dem cats wasn't tryna rob me, dey was tryna to kill me. I'm lucky dat I got away; man it was like I was out runnin all doze bullets."

"Boi be careful, I'll be out dare inna minute."

"I'm straight, I' mma chill up dare in dis new spot I got in Georgia, its jumpin too."

"Okay, I'mma holla at chu."

I met a guy in prison whose name was "Easy". When I told him my name was Sonny, he looked baffled.

"You Sonny off 15th?"

"Yea."

"Man, my homeboys told me dey tried to kill you da otha day!"

On And Poppin

Easy and Samantha knew each other extremely well, in fact, they grew up together Overtown. Samantha was my mistress, who at the time didn't mother any children from me, but we were working on it. Samantha had a son from a guy named Perm, who got killed during a shootout. Months after he had passed, word got out that he'd left her with a lot of money and drugs, and that she had given everything to me. They also said that I was wearing Perm's clothes and his jewelry. For that reason, they wanted to kill me. Easy told me the guys' thought Sweet was me. They didn't know that I was in prison and that I'd left Samantha's old house with Sweet.

Listening to Easy moved my temperature to boil, especially when he said ...

"Dogg, I only been in here for a few months, when I was out there Bonkey Brown called a meeting with all of us who was working for him. He told us that Samantha had given you all of Perm's stuff, and he ordered us to kill you."

Here I was having a conversation with a guy that was ordered to kill me, and a few days ago his homeboys tried to kill my brother, thinking he was me. After hearing that my blood pressure rose so high that I was dizzy. I wanted to grab Easy by the head and bite his throat out of his neck. The only thing that kept me from doing that was I didn't want to make my stay in prison any longer than I had too. I figured I'd get revenge when I got home.

After being in Tallahassee for a few months, I kept reflecting on the dream I had when I was eighteen years old. For some reason, I couldn't shake it. It just kept rewinding in my head, and even woke me up in the middle of the night, saying ...

"You think you're smart, all your homies keep going in and out of jail, but not you. One day you're going to get caught, and get a lot of time, but you're not going to do it all."

Somehow, I knew coming to prison wasn't just a dream. In that dream, I saw the inside of a prison cell, unlike the cells I saw in Tallahassee, and I didn't get a lot of time.

On the morning of my release, moments before I left, I gave my cellmate a heart-to-heart talk, saying ...

"Man, I wish I knew what to say to you, it hurts me to know that you have a life sentence and will never walk out of this place. You got my number dog if you need anything hit me up." Then I turned around to exit the cell on my way to freedom.

Before I crossed the door's hasp, I spun around and said ...

"Hol my bed for me dogg, I'll be back." Then I walked away, confused about that statement.

I still could remember the day I left prison. I got my property and stepped off the prison compound and gazed into the sky. The air smelled different, and even the sun had another shine to it, that gave me a sense of freedom. Even the ride to the airport felt special. I know I was only gone for twelve months, but it felt more like twelve years.

As soon as I got home, I called Pablo. We talked for a while about prison life, and afterward I told him to bring me a kilo of cocaine. When he told me it would be a couple of days, I started putting plan B into effect.

Before I went to prison, this guy named Murf, and I had the corner from 63rd to 64th Streets locked down. Anyone that tried to put down on those corners was met with violent force. When I went on the Ave., I noticed the game had changed. There was a lot of cats hustling in my spot, and it looked like Block was overseeing them. I stepped to Murf and asked…

"Man, why ya let dem cats put down in my spot?" He could tell I was pissed.

"Why ya steppin ta me Playa? Yo, brotha da one left da spot wide open, ya needz ta holla at yo boi." When he said that, I walked away shaking my head.

I felt like the new hustlers and Block were trying me. I wanted to go off and start gunning them down in the streets. I felt like at least they could have offered me a commission for selling drugs in my spot. They didn't know me, but Block knew me well. At first, I thought they were working for him, but when he saw me come back on the Ave., I didn't see him come around anymore. I don't know what happened between Block and Sweet, but he knew how this story was going to play out. I thought that, since I was waiting on Pablo to break me off, I might as well chill out. At least they kept the spot going.

One day, I was sitting in front of Mr. Wonderful's Store for hours, scooping out the spot when my beeper went off. Immediately I recognized the code, it was Pablo. When I called him back, he told me to meet him on 36th Street and LeJune Road, to pick up my package. After I met him, I went home and cooked up the whole brick, and gave half of it to Sweet.

Sweet was hustling in Brunswick Georgia while I was in prison. He had fell on hard times just before I was released. So, I figured that I could jump half of the cocaine here in Miami, and he could jump the other half in Georgia. It was a win/win situation, because with the turnover Sweet would make, he would bring back enough loot to purchase a whole brick. That would leave us a half of brick to the good. A couple of quick flips like that, and we would be back on our feet in no time.

After I finished bagging up the work, I took the drugs to a friend's house that lived around the corner of 15th Ave. Then I put my oozie nine-millimeter in my waistline and walked to the spot. I walked up to one of the guys who was selling drugs in my spot and asked him …

"Whachu sellin dogg?"

"Raw halfs and weed."

"Who you workin fo?" When I asked that a frown appeared on his face, then it disappeared when I drew my weapon on him.

"I work fo Lime."

"Where Lime at?" The guy pointed behind me across the street. When I turned and looked around, I saw Lime sitting on a car, looking in my direction. I put the gun back in my waistline and walked briskly over to where he was, with my gaze glued to his face, and said ...

"Yo Playa, I thank it would be best if ya get yo man outta my spot, fo I put him ta sleep."

Lime beckoned for the guy to come over to where we were. As I was headed back across the street to my spot, I heard the guy yell ...

"Raw halfs, and sense, we open!" I was thinking that he was still too close to my spot. I didn't sweat it, though, I had a couple of other knuckleheads to deal with. The other guys started walking across the street as I was headed towards them. As soon as they were gone, I hired two guys that were standing around, and just like that it was back on and popping.

Sista Soldier

By the end of the week, I had put eight grand aside for Pablo, and caught up on some bills with the rest. Sweet had phoned me, saying that he was on his way to the crib, and I was excited about that. I called Pablo and told him to have me five bricks ready by the weekend. Sweet, called two days later saying ...

"Man, I'm on my way, I got all da bread."

"Okay, when you get back its on and poppin."

"The few days after that, Sweet called again me saying ...

"Man, dem cats up here dun stol da moni, I'm finna kill some fo dem."

"Boi you been tellin me fo dayz, dat you on yo way, now ya called me wit dis foolishness, jus come on back home."

I called Pablo to the house, and when he got there, I said to him ...

"Mi friend here's eight grand, my brotha lost the rest of da money up da road, we'll make up in da next package."

"Sonni, mi friend, the people that I work for want all their money.

"Pablo, stop trippin, before I went to prison you was giving me twenty bricks at a time, and we never had a problem, right?"

"I know, but they don't play about their money, and you need to take care of it immediately or its going to be a problem."

"Okay Pablo I tell ya what, you and yo boss man come around here and get yo money, I'll kill all of yall. All of a sudden you don trust what I say!"

"Okay mi friend, calm down, we are family."

"Well stop trippin and bring me two bricks tomorrow."

"I see you tomorrow mi friend."

Sweet and I started working the spots together again, and everything was running smoothly. One day while I was standing on the Ave., watching the flow of traffic, Sweet walked up to me with an older looking guy and said ...

"Sonny dis Bill, he was da one moving most of the work for me in Brunswick Georgia, he straight, give him some work." Later that night, I fronted him three bricks.

The good thing about it was that Billy Bob was always on time, never faltering in his payments. He and his wife would come to my house, and he would drop a big bag of money in my hand once a week like clockwork. We had only been working together for a little over a month, but it felt like it was much longer than that.

On one occasion, when Billy Bob came down to re-up, I was at the Carwash, getting my car waxed and buffed. He called me and said that he was at the Embassy Suites Hotel and asked me to come and pick him up. He said he wanted to kill some time, while his wife and her friend went shopping. I called Pablo to put in my order, while I was on the way to pick up Bill. When Billy Bob saw me pull up in my Mercedes Benz 500SEL, with the flip-flop candy apple red paint job, sitting on dubs, his eyes light up. When he sat inside of the car, the first words that came out of his mouth was...

"Man, you got to sell me this car. This thang is cold blooded." His eyes roamed across the dashboard, and his hands touched over the interior like it was gold. When I saw how he was acting, my face lit up too. I said to myself... WOW! This cat trippin like dis ova a car."

"Give me twenty grand, and it's yours."

"You fo real?"

"Look, I tell you what, you drive the car back to Brunswick, and if you like it pay me when you come to re-up". "Can I take it now, so I can show it to my wife?" "It's yours, you can do whatever you want to do with it."

"Okay, I'll be back later to pick up the package." He said then drove off. The night before Billy Bob left to go back to Brunswick, he was complaining about his age, and that he was thinking about getting out of the dope game. I told him that I was thinking along those same lines. I let him know that he should find someone else to do business with, because that very thought had been haunting me for the past year. I told Billy Bob that this would be my last time doing business with him. I let him know that if he wanted to buy my Mercedes, to send the money back to me along with his last payment. Right before he left, I told him to be careful, and that I was going to pray for his safe return to his house.

A week had passed before word got back to me, that Billy Bob had got caught with drugs. Apparently, the Feds had raided his house and found an ounce of cocaine in his truck. I heard he was on his way back to his house and the Feds stopped him, while he was driving my Mercedes Benz.

The first thing I thought about was, since it wasn't nothing but an ounce, he'll be right out of jail. I decided not to sweat him about the money for the bricks. I figured he could use the money to handle his legal fees.

I found out that his issues were a little thicker than an ounce of cocaine. Billy Bob was a big drug dealer, who the Feds had been after for quite some time.

I didn't want anything else to do with Billy Bob or the Mercedes-Benz. I changed my beeper and phone numbers, thinking that would be the end of it.

Early one morning Corenthia and I was awakened by the sound of our doorbell. Corenthia got out of the bed to answer the door, and then came back within seconds and said ...

"Sonny, it's some lady at the door, I thank she wants you." I got out of bed, walked to the door, and stared through the peephole. When I saw Bill's wife standing on the other side, I got nervous. All type of things ran across my mind, nevertheless, I invited her in. I kept a wary eye on her the whole time. She was talking about how she came down to get some drugs from me. The whole time she talked, I sat quietly. When she paused, I stood up and beckoned her to follow me using my finger. I took her into my music studio, and turned the music up loud, so that if she was wired, our voices would be inaudible. Then I put my finger to my lips and made a shhhhhhh, sound. I then walked over to her and started frisking her to see if she was wired. When I finished, I said ...

"Girl, you comin down here to get drugs from me, while yo husband is locked up in da Feds fo drugs?"

"Yea," she said, with her arms folded across her breast.

"I don have nothin right now."

I assumed she didn't believe me because on our way taking her back to the airport, she asked ...

"Did you think I came down here to set you up?"

"I don't know."

"Well, I want to letchu know, I'm not that kind of person."

You Believe it's a Game

It seemed like I'd led one of the most lavished lifestyles in the spotlight of the ghetto dictatorship, of my time. You heard me correctly, I did say "ghetto dictatorship". That's what I called the whole thing, looking in retrospect. I mean, the drug industry is a billion-dollar industry, and there I was the low man on the totem pole, raking in peanuts, yet running for dear life, and the dear life and mercy of my kinsman and lady. Unbeknownst to me, all my life as a hustler, a bread winner, a soldier in the way of "poverty, was about to change". I'd stopped eating with God at the very minute I started believing-up-on my own warped understanding-something Great. Like the pursuit of freedom and happiness could be obtained without a struggle. What happened to me, is more simplistic than unusual when I sat at the table with Satan and let him convince me through idolatry- that he could give me fame for an eternity that he could give me life, freedom, and the pursuit of happiness if I'd eat with him, was an illusion. He was the one who coaxed me into believing I could not live off bread alone. And never minding my self-accusing spirit telling me otherwise, I believe Satan on facevalue. Now it seems as though my fame had run amok of the fifteen minutes I had to shine. This book is for the game, for whoever is so naive to believe it's a game. Read closely as these last pages turn towards the end, and so does my life.

CHAPTER TWELVE

THE FEDS

I had been working for Dade County Parks and Recreation for about three years. On this particular day, I heard one of my co-workers say ...

"Sonny, two white guys out there in the parking lot wanted to see you."

That wasn't strange, white guys often came to my job to visit me. Many of them provided different services for my Record Company and other business endeavors. But at the moment he told me that, a strange feeling settled in the pit of my stomach.

I was on the phone talking to Corenthia. At that time, she was venting her concerns about all the things that had transpired in our lives, over the past few years. The strange disappearance of the money in the condo, the gun incident with Sweet, followed by the small break away to spend a year in prison, and now the dilemma with Bill. All of this had somehow etched a mark in our lives, that we couldn't just erase away as if nothing had happened. For some reason, it seemed like every breath we took, and every step we made, something or somebody reminded us of those events.

"I'll call you back baby; somebody is here to see me."

"Bye Sonny."

"Bye Sweetie."

After I hung up the phone, I looked around the corner to see who wanted me. It was two big burly white men staring in my direction, they looked like football players. When I saw them, I knew exactly who they were. One of the agents approached me and said ...

"Are you Albert Campbell."

"Yea." As soon as I answered, both of them flashed their credentials briefly in my face. The feeling in the pit of my stomach stirred.

"Do you know Billy BobNoble."

"Billy BobNoble, ahhhh, yeaaaa, I, I know 'em."

"Well did you know that Mr. Noble went and got himself caught up in a big drug conspiracy."

"Ahhhhh, yeaaaa."

"Why didn't you come to Georgia and claim your Mercedes Benz."

"Be, cause, I didn't, won't, ta, get, caught up in his mess."

"We know, you're not involved in his drug conspiracy, but he was in possession of your car."

"I was sellin him my car, I didn't know he was goin ta take it ta Georgia. "We need you to come to the Grand Jury and say that Mr. Noble purchased your car with drug money."

"He didn't pay me, and I can't tell a lie." My eyes darted around their faces. I could tell they were getting upset with me, but I was only telling the truth. After a few more questions they finally left with these words: "we'll be in touch." One of the agents said with a strange look on his face.

A few weeks later, a friend of mine, who had family in Brunswick, called and told me his family said ...

Marvin, Samantha, I, and some other people I didn't know, were in the newspaper. The article stated that I was in charge of distributing millions of dollars of cocaine, and cocaine base in Brunswick Georgia. A warrant for my arrest, as well as everyone else names had been issued.

As the plot thickened, the word spread, throughout the counties of Brunswick and Miami, that Sonny was being sweated by the Feds.

I couldn't see how Billy Bob could snitch on me; he was only caught with a small amount of drugs. Not only that, but I didn't even know him that long before he got knocked off, so the millions of dollars' worth of cocaine was a bunch of crap. What I didn't know was how the federal system worked. I just couldn't fathom their fabrication, that somehow, me and Butler Campbell, AKA Uncle Butler, of the infamous Crew, had been implicated as an organization, that controlled one of the most sophisticated drug empires, using Record Companies as a front. WOW!

I was home in my studio listening to some music, relaxing, and trying to filter through the debris in my life when I heard pounding on the door…

"Bam… bam … bam" The knocks had to be loud because I had the music cranked up, and I still heard the door cry out loud and clear. I peeped from behind the blinds and saw federal agents, impulsively, I dropped too the floor. I picked up my cell phone and called Samantha. I tried to talk to her, whispering every word saying ...

"Sam, dey out here."

"Who Sonny."

"THE FEDS!"

Nightmare

I don't know how long I was laying on the floor before I decided that I needed to get up and see what was happening outside. Sweat was popping off of me like crazy, and I knew I couldn't lay their forever. My eyes darted around in the studio for a few seconds, and then I eased up and peeked out of the blinds. I was surprised when I didn't see anybody. For a minute I couldn't understand what was going on. I wondered why did they leave, and why hadn't they heard the music I was playing? All I knew was that the whole thing seemed suspect. No matter if they were there or not, I still felt like someone was watching every move I made. I walked around the house as if I was constantly ducking and hiding. I figured I was going to wait for a while, before leaving, but I had to get some clothes on before I could do anything. I only had on a pair of boxer shorts, and a Stomp & Grind Records T-shirt.

After I got dressed, I waited about two hours before I left the house. I was glad that Corenthia and our children weren't home. Right before I left, I heard the phone ring, but I was too paranoid to answer it. For all I knew, it was the Feds calling, trying to see if I would answer. I thought, whoever it was they could call back when Corenthia comes home.

Later on, I learned that the federal agents who visited my home were there to serve Corenthia a subpoena, to go to the Grand Jury. When that was happening, I knew it was just a matter of time before they came to get me, so I went on the run. During that time, it seemed like every time my sky-pager wet off, it was someone paging me to let me know that they had been subpoenaed. The Feds subpoenaed everybody, who they suspected had purchased cars in their names for me. They even subpoenaed my jewelers and other people I'd met through my record company. It was like a nightmare, only I wasn't asleep.

I didn't want to accept the inevitable, that my game had come to an end. I got dropped off from hotel to hotel, sleeping days, and traveling at night.

Most of the time, I had my Lieutenant Tank taking me to different hotels, or wherever I needed to go, but that soon played out. Tank started coming to pick me up late, sometimes as late as two to three hours after my hotel reservations had expired. I used to have to sit in the hotel lobbies, with my head, cast down, because everybody, no matter who they were, looked like federal agents. I figured the only reason Tank started tripping was because he had gotten paranoid also. So, I decided to tell Tank, when he finally picked me up, that I was leaving town.

Samantha was pregnant with our last child at the time. She was so stressed out with everything that was going on, that we started feuding over every little thing. I knew then, more so than ever, that it was time for me to get missing. I told my Lieutenant Tank, since he was the main man who handled my business, that he was going to be the Man. I gave him a large amount of drugs, mentioned to him how much money to give Corenthia and Samantha, each month, gave him a firm hug, and I got missing.

It was a Friday night, about eleven or twelve o'clock, with a full moon rising over the ghetto dome when I hopped on the Florida Turnpike. I was hoping to disengage myself from a reality, trying to forget my dreams and memories, that I'd worked most of my life to create.

My homeboys had family in Alabama that was pumping crack cocaine like it was legal. I never questioned the guy's honesty at all. I was too busy trying to get out of dodge, before I got caught in Miami, running from pillow to post. I should have known the guys were slimy, though; they told me they used their mother to traffic drugs in her vagina. I would have never believed that until I actually saw her come to Alabama.

With an instinctive attitude for getting money, I got right into the swing of things. I called back to Miami, and had a few bricks sent up to Alabama, and things began to work smoothly. However, when the guys noticed how paranoid I was, all kinds of slimy things started happening. Money and drugs started coming up missing daily, and since no one was claiming responsibility, not even Big "C" from the hood, I decided to leave. I left and headed to South Carolina. I left the remaining drugs with Big "C" and, his brother, Kool-Aid. As soon as I was safe in South Carolina, I called to Alabama, to see what was up. That's when I learned just how slimy Big "C' s" brother was. He told me that all the drugs and money had been stolen. The cats in South Carolina did the same thing. So, with little money on hand, I had to go back to Miami.

It had only been a month since I went on the run, but I was exhausted, mentally and physically. Between the traveling, looking over my shoulder, and getting ripped off at every turn, all I wanted now was a good night's sleep.

I called Corenthia as soon as I got back in town. I hadn't spoken to her but a few times within the last month. I should have expected her response when she said ...

"Boi, I haven't heard from you in a month, where you been? Samantha tol me, you on a run. Wen you comin home. Then I called Samantha, and she said ...

"Sonny why dose people keep comin round here bothin me." After listening to their concerns, it was hard for me to think straight, and I didn't like the pressure they were under.

I knew the Feds weren't going to give up until they arrested me. I thought about all the money I'd lost, and how everybody acted as though they were paranoid being associated with me. The Feds had turned my paradise into a war zone, and it wasn't a secret who was losing the battle. There was only one thing for me to do. I decided to go home. All I wanted was one good night's sleep, but even sleep came with a battle.

After I got home and settled in, I tried to go to sleep. I think that I may have drifted off for about an hour or so before I woke up, peering blankly into the darkness. The house was relatively silent, except for the refrigerator, central air-conditioner, other appliances, and crickets outside all contributing to an unnerving hum. The thing about it, that had me so worked up, was that I felt a presence there, and it wouldn't go away for nothing in the world. I mean, it literally felt like I had a thousand pounds on my back, weighing me down. I got out of bed, stood up, and shrugged my shoulders, trying to shake it off, but that didn't do any good. I even paced the house, back and forth, peeking out of the windows every minute or so. Corenthia was asleep, and the children were in their rooms sleep as well. Finally, my body got so tired that it just shut down on me. But, it seemed, as soon as I closed my eyes, I heard someone banging on the door.

"Bam ... bam ... barn. bam ... "The knocks went on furiously. As soon as I heard them, I jumped out of bed. I was in complete shock. I didn't know what to do, but the knocks were getting louder and faster.

"Baby, go, go see who dat is." I stammered. In the back of my mind, I already knew it was the Feds. They were the thousand pounds that I felt on my back. They were all around my house, so there was no chance of escaping.

"Sonny, da Feds out dare," Corenthia said as she walked back into the room.

I had a puppy look on my face, but I knew what I had to do. I walked into the living room and looked out of the picture window. As soon as I peered out, I saw that one of the agents was getting ready to throw a brick through the window. My heart plummeted, as I watched the agent lean back to throw the brick.

"Hey, don throw dat brick through dis window," I yelled. I was waving my arms in the air.

When I opened the door, I saw agents ducking behind vehicles, with weapons pointing in my direction. Then seemingly out of nowhere, agents stormed in my house brandishing their weapons. At that point, I got lost in the rapture of the moment. My eyes suddenly blinked, and I saw this little boy, frozen in place, as an army of men raided his apartment. Instinctively, he began to run past them. Then one of the agents skillfully subdued him and slammed his face into the wall.

"Daddi, daddi, leave mi daddi alon." I blinked my eyes and turned my head in the direction of Shakevia's voice. I shifted my head slightly to the right and saw Katrevia's pale face. She was staring into my eyes as if she was in a state of shock.

"Take my children outta here, I don want dem to see dis," I shouted. Then I noticed Corenthia standing behind our daughters, our gaze locked into each other. My eyes communicated to her the unspoken words that said ...

"I'm sorry baby The Game Is Over!"

Uncle Butler

While my face was glued to the wall, and blood was trickling out of my nose, an agent whispered in my ear ...

"What do you know about Butler Campbell." At first, I was stunned, they were raiding my house and asking me about Butler Campbell. I knew Butler, and we had broken bread together over the years. Then it dawned on me. 'Billy Bob Noble had implicated me and Butler Campbell in his drug conspiracy with that, there came about accusations of this elaborate conspiracy, that Butler and I sat at the core of. For the most part, I'd instantly regretted conversing with Billy Bob about affairs dealing with my Record Company. Had I not done that, I wouldn't be going through this horrific ordeal. Now I was paying the price for my naivety.

To add insult to injury, I had some backstage passes to some of the concerts that Butler, my rap group, and I had attended. Since we were all performing in the shows, and after parties, it made sense for me to have the passes. But the agents had a different take on the matter altogether. They gathered around the passes like they were drugs. In their minds, the passes were their solid link that mended Butler and I, at the hip, like Siamese twins. Shortly after their questions, without any answers from me, they shuttled me off to jail.

Moments after I was placed in a holding cell, I was served with a Federal Indictment, and Samantha's name was on it, among others. In the cell I was in, I could see Marshals bringing in women as well as men. The whole thing made knots form in my stomach. I kept my face pressed up against the bars, watching everybody that came in. I was praying that I didn't see Samantha wobbling through the door, with her big stomach. Thank God for answering my prayer.

A few weeks later, I was extradited to Brunswick Georgia. Up until that time, I'd never been to Brunswick, but that didn't matter. The law said, in a conspiracy, you could be held accountable for your co-conspirator's actions, without being knowledgeable of their acts.

The first few days there I sat around and listened to guys telling me everything about my case. The funny thing about that was the guys who were telling me things didn't even know me. There were some guys on my indictment that I'd never seen, or heard of, in my life. I remember a guy arriving in Glenn County Jail in Brunswick Georgia. He had been arrested on drug charges. They placed him in a holding cell for a few days, before he was released to the general population. While I was in the holding cell, I overheard the guard call a name that sounded familiar to me. The name was Rodney Walker A.K.A. "L.A. Law". I thought that name rung a bell. When I heard that name, I jumped up and ran to look at my indictment again. Sure enough, his name was on it. The next morning, I went to his cell, and the first question I asked him was ...

"Do you know me Playa?"

"Nah I don no you, wassup?"

"I'm Sonny," I replied swiftly.

"Sonny!" The guy yelped.

"Man, I don know why da Feds holding me on yo case, dey, dey just picked me up,"

I told Rodney that I would pay for his lawyer, so he could get off of my case. Over the next couple of weeks, my case slowly developed and drew closer to trial. Rodney and I had developed a good relationship, and with his testimony, I was certain I was going to be victorious. Rodney and I stayed up late nights, rehearsing what we'd say on the day in question.

I found out, in an Evidentiary Hearing, that Rodney Walker cold flipped the script. He testified in court that I tried to pay him off, to lie for me. After that day, they separated us. I made a mental note, from that point forward, not to talk to anyone else about my case, at least not in those terms anyway.

When I arrived in general population, I was immediately faced with other people I'd never seen before. I used to sit around and listen, and none of the guys even knew it was me they were talking about. I had guys giving me detailed information about me and trying to convince me and other inmates to get on my case. A guy named Shawn said to me ...

"Um tellin ya dogg, just say ya know Billy Bob Noble, an da prosecutor will call ya ta testify. Now uma run it down ta ya again, Billy Bob use to go ta Miami, and get bricks from Sonny and Butler. Sonny gave Billy Bob a Benz wit da candy paint, ya used to go by Billy Bob house an get drugs from em', ya got dat." I nodded my head.

"Okay den, here go da prosecutor number, call em in da morning." It was just that simple, this was how the prosecutor built a nothing case into a sure-fire winner. He'd asked any number of inmates in the county jail did they get drugs from me, Sweet, Butler or Billy Bob. All they had to say was yes and just that easy my witness list went from one-character witness to a hundred and one in a matter of days. All he had to do was entice them with a sentence reduction and that's it. It was just that easy. I had the sole intention of getting in touch with Butler and letting him know what was going on, but I could never get in touch with him. So, after a while, I gave up. I already knew the drill, once the FED'S arrested you all of your closest friends tried as best, they could disassociate themselves from you. That was customary. If they could cut off all means of contact, it would help prove their position that he or they didn't know you. So yes, I had the feeling that Butler was avoiding my calls especially when I sent him messages and he never answered any of them. It was nothing to it, though, I'm a soldier, one who wasn't about to snitch on anyone. I watched the making of my case materialize right before my eyes and there wasn't anything I could do about it.

The sad thing about the whole situation wasn't about the actual events because I'm taking my Fifth Amendment right to silence as I did then, but as far as them stating that they knew me, or Butler when in fact they didn't. Didn't' know what, I beg to question, didn't know me, nor did they know Butler Campbell, but they did know Billy Bob Noble, I have no idea. I do know that once the information, however, big, or small, was somehow leaked to the inmate population, inmates facing a lot of time and some not facing any serious time, that just wanted to go, started rehearsing the information to make it appear as though they knew all of us their entire lives. To the jury, it seemed genuine but to all of us who knew better there were no words to describe the abuse or miscarriage of justice practiced on citizens in the United States of America.

All I know is that before my experience with the federal government I had a lot of respect for them, I at least thought that they were honest, and had, a system that sought out justice for all. I didn't know that justice was bargained for, and not a right.

Evil Plots

There was this preacher that would come into the county jail on Sundays, to spread the Good News. By that time, going to church had become a ritual for me, rather than an option just to Pass time. Everywhere I went, I had my Bible in my hand. Every time I stopped, for any reason, I gripped it tight and said a short prayer. I used to pray so much, till I would start feeling spasms in my face. While other inmates laughed, joked, played table games, and indulged in other activities, I was trying to talk to God, about helping me fight against my adversaries.

"Please Lord, help me fight against those who fight against me for no weapon formed against the righteous shall prosper." I prayed, while, at the same time, watching my situation go from bad to worst. I couldn't understand how things were going so bad for me, but I stayed steadfast in prayer. Never questioning God's method, just begging, and pleading with Him to save me. I even confessed my sins to Him and turned my life over to Jesus Christ. I ignored the rumours that I heard that God didn't exist in the Feds. My cellmate told me a story, that my judge told everyone that came into his courtroom, carrying a Bible he'd say ...

"I run this courtroom, not God. You should have thought about Him before you violated the federal law. The only mercy that you'll get, if any, would be from me, and the jury."

Somewhere, during my trials and tribulations, I let that rumour influence me to start thinking crazy. I had learned that he sentenced most of the people, that went before him, to life in prison.

My trial had begun, and it was expected to last at least two weeks. The prosecution had a host of witnesses, and there were plea negotiations going on, between my attorney and the prosecutor, regarding my cooperation against Butler Campbell. There were also other things being discussed, about indicting other members of my family, if I didn't cooperate. So, we still had a lot of preliminary hearings to go through, of which left me with plenty time to think about whether or not I was going to testify on Butler.

One day, I found myself so tired of going through the struggle, and the roller coaster ride that my emotions were on, that I prayed to God that He would take my life. I just couldn't fight any longer, I was getting weak, while trying to keep my sanity at the same time. I figured that it was the only way out of the quagmire, I'd gotten myself into. I also figured, out of all things, that this was a prayer that God would answer, because of my sincerity.

When I awoke the next morning, I was in shock. Immediately, I found myself, for the first time, questioning God; uncertain if there truly was a God at all. Or, that it is a God, but He didn't exist in the Feds, as I'd heard. I think at some point after that, I started developing bad vibes about life and death. I felt if God was omniscient, omnipresent, and omni in love and compassion, how could He let me suffer on the account of lies, envy, betrayal, and deceit; while He's sitting up in heaven, on His throne, looking down, and laughing, at my cursed black skin. WOW! Can you see how messed up my thoughts were?

On one occasion, the preacher, who usually came into the jail to preach the word, and I had a bad experience. I was listening as best I could, but my attention span wasn't focused. On this particular day, I was actually feeling that me being there was a waste of time. I heard the preacher chanting ... "Thank you, Jesus," before he started handing out pamphlets for us to read. When he got to where I was, he looked me in my eyes, like he was in a daze. Then he walked away from me like he'd just remembered that I was contagious. At first, I thought he was acting funny because of my case, but when I heard him whisper to the guard, that he couldn't preach because he felt bad spirits in the place, I felt bad knowing he was talking about me.

The following Sunday we had a new pastor, his name was Mark. As soon as we entered the room, where we held Bible studies and church, I felt uncomfortable. I made up my mind that, after that day, I was never going to attend church again. I headed towards the door before service was over. Before I made it out of the door, Pastor Mark called me to come have a word with him. He told me, that God had sent him to the jail, with a message to give someone. He said he didn't know who that someone was before he came to the jail, and he never questions God. He said he just believed, once he got in here, that God would show him that person, he'll tell that person whatever God wanted him to know.

"That someone is you, Sonny, and God wanted me to let you know that He is going to do something special in your life." He looked me straight into my eyes and said ...

"And I know that's true because, not only is this my first time coming in a jail, in all my thirty years as a preacher. I know all that you're going through right now. You just be strong son, it's going to be some hard long years ahead of you, but I feel like you already know that." He continued to say ...

"I won't be visiting this place again, there's just too many bad spirits for me to preach here. I just want you to pray with me son before you leave." Pastor Mark smiled at me, and we stood right in the doorway and prayed together.

Three days later, I got the news that Pastor Mark had passed away. The guard said Pastor Mark had a massive heart attack. I felt bad for him, but I thanked God a ca-zillion times for sending him to me and identifying the bad spirits that the other priest claimed were present. Pastor Mark let me know about the bad spirits because he'd felt the same things when he entered the room. He said the bad spirits didn't come from me, but from all the other inmates in the service, who'd been using God as a crutch, to wipe away their evil thoughts they were plotting against me.

Eee-oow

I used to talk to Sweet on the phone, while he was on the run from the Feds. I'd often tell him to stay off the streets, at least until the case was over. I figured, if they did catch him, and I had been tried already, he'd stand a better chance of winning his case. I wasn't surprised when I listened to him, stressing, about how difficult it was being on the run. I knew from firsthand experience, it was rough. What I was trying to get him to understand was until he came to jail, he hadn't seen rough yet.

I was on lockdown for getting involved in an altercation with an officer and another inmate, I saw the officer threw the young man on the ground and began to press a finger into his ear. When the inmate started screaming, I heard the officer yell...

"Everybody, go to your cells now!" It was about fifty of us, and no one bothered to help the guy.

"Officer in need of assistance?" I heard the officer yell into the radio for back-up.

As I walked up the stairs I looked down and saw the officer punishing the guy, who was giving him no resistance. I don't know what happened, but without warning, my body spun around and headed back downstairs.

"Getch yo hand off of him, now!" I yelled at the top of my lungs, while squaring off on the officer. When he turned around and looked at me, he jumped off of the guy. Then he squared off on me and said ...

"Turn around and put your hand up."

"I'm not doing a damn thang." Then another officer walked up to me, and ordered me to put my hands up, I complied. Afterward, I was handcuffed and escorted to solitary confinement for inciting a riot.

While I was on lockdown, I heard Sweet had gotten caught. I was wondering where they going to bring him here, where I was. One day an orderly came to my cell and said ...

"Ai, yo brotha in da front lobby, getting booked in." I stayed peeking through the small crack in the door for hours, until I got tired and laid down, and dosed off.

There was this distinct sound our crew used to make, sort of like a code. When I heard the sound ...

"Eee-oow   eee-oow." I ran to the door and responded.

"Eee-oow   eee-oow," and we yelled back and forth to each other.

Sweet stayed on lockdown for about a week, and then he was released to the general population. It took me a while longer before I could actually see him because I had to stay locked down for sixty days before I was released back into general population. Nonetheless, since the jail administrators had received orders from the feds, to keep us separated, we couldn't communicate with each other. The way we worked around that was both of us got orderly jobs. We used to come out of our units every night to talk. It had been rumoured, Sweet was snitching on me, and I was snitching on him, but he and I never entertained the thought of discussing such nonsense. It was just another piece of information the feds had released in the jail. In an effort to cause confusion among us.

I'm Rolling with Rush

Sweet and I sat on the backdrop of life getting ready to face the ultimate moment, that moment, which would determine who and what we are, and more importantly our place in life. It was the moment Sweet, and I had to assume our manhood. If there ever was a time in life, where the next move we made had to be accurate, it was this time. Never before had our lives been more serious; it was more serious than all the gun battles we had, all the drugs, all the fights, and it was more serious than the childhood struggles we witnessed our mother and stepfather go through. To put this ordeal in perspective, I thought that God had delivered us to Satan, for him to do whatever he wanted to do with us, except take our lives, just to show him that we are God's faithful servants, and to test our faith.

Sweet and I sat in silence for a moment, both of us had run out of things to say. We had just about covered everything, and we also renewed our love for each other. But there was something stirring inside of me, that I had to tell Sweet. I, like Pastor Mark, didn't know what that was that I had to tell him. I opened my mouth, and let the words come out, destined to rest on his wooing soul.

"Man, I have been tellin ya what to do for most of yo life, but dis time ya have ta do whatever it is ya feel is right fo ya ta do. I've given dis a lot of thought, and I've decided ta go ta trial. Dey want me ta tell on Butler, and believe me I'm tempted ta do just dat, being as doe he is jus as guilty as you and I is, but what would I stand to gain by doing dat. Butler is a good man, and fo dat alon, I'm not goin ta destroy his name, because of our hardship. I believe dats what God would want me ta do." Sweet looked me in my eyes and said ...

"Man, I'm rollin wit Rush." Then he hugged me and kissed me on the side of my face.

My Lawyer

I would call Samantha and tell her everything that I heard involving our case. I even told her to send me her paperwork, so my lawyer could look over them. She never sent me the paperwork, and I thought that was strange. Then it dawned on me, that she wasn't communicating with me, in regard to her case, period. I assumed her lawyer had told her not to talk to me. So, I called her one morning and asked ...

"Why didn't you send me your paperwork, like I asked you to? Did your lawyer tell you not to talk to me about your case?"

"Yea."

"So, you gonna let somebody that you have never seen before, come and tell you not to talk to me? I asked with an attitude.

"I'm jus scared Sonny."

I couldn't understand how she would let a complete stranger, come in between us. I called to vent my frustration.

"They were talking bout takin our kids, but whateva happens, let it happen, we'll jus have ta deal wit it," she said as soon as she answered the phone.

I had to let Samantha know, how I felt about her burst of energy. "I'm proud of you girl." I had been thinking about Bill.

"He never seen you Sam, and if there was any way he could involve you, in this case, I would tell you to cooperate with the government, cause it's not yo case, its mind."

The first lawyer I had, got off of my case because we didn't see eye to eye, but the new one was no better. Besides, him not knowing anything about federal law, I used to hate it whenever he came to visit me. He always had bad news. He would tell me that, the feds had statements on my mother and Corenthia, stating that they were present at different times when I transacted drugs with other people, namely Butler Campbell.

"Man, what are you here to do, help me or help the government!" I snapped. The lawyer had me so mad, I just told the guard our visit was over. A few days later, I heard the guard yell out my name, "Campbell, you have an attorney visit." As soon as I heard him, I started thinking, what bad news he had to tell me now. I didn't want to see him anymore, but I had to at least go let him know how I felt. As soon as I walked into the room, I stared into the lawyer's face, like I was crazy. I want to say that he read my facial expressions, because when he saw me walk into the room, he got up and stood near the door and said ...

"Am I still your attorney?"

"Hell No!" I replied. The lawyer started pressing the button, so the officer at the control booth could let him out of the room. He must've thought I was going to jump on him, by the way, he was fidgeting, and how I was looking. He was correct, I just never got the opportunity.

I didn't have a lawyer for a couple of weeks. I knew the courts would appoint me another attorney, so I did a little investigation on my own. There was a guy in jail who referred me to, supposedly, one of the best lawyers in Brunswick Ga. His name was Mr. Grayson Lane. When I spoke to Mr. Lane, he told me that he'd represented Billy Bob Noble in the past, and, if I didn't want to get a life sentence, it would be in my best interest to hire him. Mr. Lane was talking arrogantly when he said ...

"If you want to retain me, my fee is fifty thousand dollars. I want all my money at once, and I'm going to report to the government how the money is paid. If you want to retain me, call me tomorrow, if not go get your life sentence."

Just listening to Mr. Lane, made me sick to my stomach. I had never met the man before, and I already had a dislike for him. I let him know that I wouldn't be hiring him, because as soon as he finished talking, I hung up the phone without saying bye.

The same guy that had referred me to Mr. Lane referred me to another attorney, his name was Keven Gough. I called Mr. Gough that Friday, and he came to visit me on that following Monday.

Somehow, Mr. Gough must have had access to my case files, because he told me it definitely looks like we're going to trial. He said ...

"My reason is based on the fact that the people that the government wants information on, sounds like the kind of people that if you cooperated on, your phone would just ring when you called home because everybody in your house would be dead."

Mr. Gough's fee was ten thousand dollars. Even though his fee was substantially lower than Mr. Lane, he, nevertheless, assured me that, he was going to report the money to the government. I called my friend named P-man; he was a prominent figure in the ghetto. He was the main DJ for the Space Funk DJ's back in the day. He also was down with the Triple M DJ' s, but that was just one of the many hats P-man wore. I used to cop several bricks from him when things got a little rough on my end. And since P-man knew a lot of people through his DJ persona, he had various connections.

Since P-man and I were good friends, I thought he would be the best person to deal with, in regard to cleaning my money up. When I was sure the feds didn't have my house under surveillance, I told P-man that he could take charge of my studio and remove it from my house. I had the studio built were my two-car garage was. I thought it would be wise to let P-man take it and do his thing before the feds came and took it out of my house. I still had a couple of groups left, and a project I was working on with Joey Boy Records, with their new artist Uncle Al, that I needed to complete.

So, I sent P-man ten grand, to take to his friends in the record business, in exchange for a "cashier's check". After we spoke P-man called Mr. Gough and assured him the money was on the way.

"Well, Mr. Campbell how are you doing today." Mr. Gough asked, buoyantly. Mr. Gough had paid me an unexpected visit at the jail. At first, I thought it was more bad news, but I soon found out that wasn't the case.

"I'm alright, sir, is somethin." I asked nervously.

"No, no, everything's fine. I just wanted to let you know, I spoke to your friend, and he has assured me he'll spend the money, so I'll start working on your case immediately. Mr. Gough said.

Over a weeks' time, Mr. Gough and I covered some extensive grounds on my case. I thought we were making leeway because we found out a way to discredit most of the government's witnesses. The only problem was, we still had the statements made by Billy Bob Noble. His statements were the most damaging to me and my case. But that wasn't my only problem. Now I was feeling like I'd finally met the lawyer, who was willing to knuckle up with the government.

The Double Cross

I got a visit from Mr. Gough on a Saturday afternoon. I should've known something was wrong because he never visited me on the weekends.

"Albert, I think we have a problem." He took short spurts of breaths, in between his words.

"I didn't receive the money from your friend, something must have went wrong. I didn't think, the guy was playing games, I talked to him, and he sounded sincere."

"I'll get in contact with him, and I'll call you tomorrow," I said.

Three days had passed, and we still didn't hear anything from P-man. I had run out of excuses to give Mr. Gough, and he had run out of patience. He told me point blank...

"I'm going to stop working on your case if I don't receive my money by next Wednesday."

I got in touch with P-man the next day.

"Man wassup, why you ain't pay da lawyer?"

"Sonny, I gave the money to Betty Bright, to get the check for me, and she don left town ta do a concert. As soon as she get back uma send it."

It took me a moment to comprehend what P-man was explaining to me. At first, I couldn't understand, why he would give Betty the money to get the check, but I didn't say anything. At least he wasn't telling me anything crazy. The moment I got off the phone with him, I phoned Mr. Gough and let him know, that if he hadn't received the money from P-man in a couple of days, that I'd have someone else send it.

I waited another week before I called P-man. Every time I called him, people kept telling me he wasn't home. After three or four times, when I'd called to no avail, I sensed that I was getting the runaround. I left several messages for P-man to get with my girl, but I still didn't hear back from him. I thought that was messed up, how P-man had run off with my lawyer's money and kept my groups from getting into the studio. When I called his house, all I got was the answering machine saying ...

"This is P-man Production and Studio, please leave a message."

There was nothing else left for me to do. I knew P-man should have known better than to play with a man's lawyer money. He had done federal time before, so what was his problem, it was beyond my comprehension. But to get back at him or them, I was going to tell the government all I knew about Butler, and how he'd built his production company. I was going to tell the government all I knew about P-man, and all the drugs he peddled in the community throughout the years. I was so hot, that I was even willing to drop dirt on Betty Bright, whether it was true or not, for being associated with P-man. There was no need for me to be concerned about them, it was way bigger than me anyway. My mind was made up. If they wanted to play slimy, I was about to show them what real slime is, from the Grand Jury box, and be ready to deal with the consequences of my actions.

After the end of the week, I came up with ten grand for the lawyer. I finally reached P-man one day, utilizing a three-way call. By that time, I was so hot, I'd forgotten all the things I wanted to say to him. All the threats I wanted to tell him, about revealing what I knew about him and Butler, just never came out.

"Man wassup. I been tryna call ya for da longest!" I shouted through the phone's receiver.

"Dude, I know ya hot wit me, but I been tryna get things together. I sent dis cat up da road wit some work, and it didn't work out right."

"P-man ya playin wit my life like dat? You know dis case is serious."

"Man, jus give Corenthia my studio equipment, an uma leave it at dat."

"Alright man," P-man said. He had a tone in his voice, that- made me feel like he wasn't going to do it. I wanted to let him know, one thing before I hung up.

"Hey, P-man."

"Wassup."

"You know, don nothin beat the cross, but da double cross."

"Whatchu mean."

"I'mma holla at chu."

It didn't take a rocket scientist to learn that P-man was bucking. I knew this to be true because he kept giving Corenthia the run around when she tried to pick up the studio equipment. I wasn't about to lay down, and Corenthia wasn't physically capable of getting with P-man, but she had brothers. One of them was named Crab. In my opinion, Crab wasn't all that wild, so I told him to call one of his police friends and take him around to see if they could get the equipment, I thought the sight of the police would make P-man cough up the equipment. But P-man wasn't budging. He told Crab, he wasn't giving him nothing, and that if he called the police again, that he was going to get with him. I started thinking, this joker is crazy. That was my equipment, and he was just going to take it. He had already taken my money, now he was going to take my equipment also. I had one last option. I figured since P-man was on federal probation and given the fact that he could get violated for something relatively small, I could get Corenthia to contact his probation officer, and explain the situation.

P-man made a move after I did that, that revamped all I was doing, and I decided that I'd have to deal with him personally. He threatened Corenthia that he wold kill her if she ever called his probation officer or the police again, when she came to his house to pick up the equipment ...

"And if you think I'm playing Trick, try me!"

After Mr. Gough received his ten grand, his whole tune and tempo of the case changed. We went from, the government is going to have one difficult time proving their case against me, to the possibility of excepting a plea agreement. I never thought Mr. Gough was selling me out. I just figured it was his duty to inform me of the government's offer. I think, since he'd witnessed, with his own eyes, how my friends had left me, in a den of hungry wolves, to be eaten alive, he felt that I had ample enough reason to do whatever that was necessary, to save myself.

We're All Convicts

This is how I look at the matter and listen to me closely out there because I'm only going to say this once. I suggest you all let these words soak in your minds deeply.

We're all "CONVICTS" P-man Sam, Uncle Butler, Home Team, and even TI, and Young Jeezy, you name them we're all convicts. The thing is that none of us had been convicted for our actions; whatever they were or are that defined us, under judicial standards, as such. The thing about that was, that depending on how each of us played our cards, we could escape our criminal conduct, from ever being punished. From a G's perspective, I saw Uncle Butler and P-man escaping from ever being formally called a convict. The thing about it was, was I going to let them escape after all they had done to me? That was the million-dollar question, one I have never answered until this day? Why! I'll never forget the visit from my lawyer. This guy and I were wrapped up in a game of chess. He only had one move left with his bishop and then I was going to checkmate him. What he didn't know was that I'd already set him up, by lining up my queen and locking up the line so his king couldn't cross over. I knew he saw the move and was only stalling, trying to figure if there was a way out. The fact of the matter was, there was no way out, and his every moment of concentration only prolonged the game.

"Come on move sucka!" I quipped jokingly.

"Hol up man I gotta thank of a way out," he said. But there was no way out except the possibility of hell freezing over and, he might stand a better chance if that happened.

I had no time to ponder the fact that I was playing my life out in the same manner as this chess game. Each move I made was answered by karma with a counter move. The thing was, thus far I'd been winning until I came face to face with the federal government. We were at a standstill, and I was planning my next move like my opponent was doing. The government was telling me to grab my sixteen pieces and go to jail because the game was over. And I, like my opponent, was telling them to let me look at the board. The game was not over, could not be over!

Before my opponent made his final move, I heard the guard call out my name, "Albert Campbell ... get dressed ... you have an attorney visit," the guard yelled down the hall.

As soon as I heard my name called, I froze for a few seconds, got up and walked away from the table.

"Man, you forfeit." I heard my chess opponent say. But I didn't respond. I felt a sudden sense of uneasiness overwhelm me. I was just wondering what it was my lawyer was coming to tell me now. I was also wondering if I would stand by everything, I'd promised myself I'd do. I know I had talked all that mess about this and that, but it wasn't that easy when it came down to it. I wasn't a snitch for one thing, regardless of what someone did to me. That's just not how I carried it, from being raised up from a long line of flat foot hustlers, who instilled in me: "You do the crime, you do the time."

A Lifetime Of Regret

On February 27, 1995, I was awakened by a mixture of keys clanging from somebody's hand along with a voice calling a list of names. My name was included in that list; I already knew what time it was too. The morning light was gradually chasing the night away to make way for a brand-new day. A new day of challenges, one of promises and possibly, if things went in the way the government wanted them to go, a lifetime of regret. My lawyer promised that if my brother and I were found guilty I would get a life sentence and my brother, 35 years. A life sentence? Thirty-five years? Can you believe that? I couldn't, I had to see it. I was like how I was going to get that much time when the government hadn't found any drugs, and I was Sonny, the man, the myth, the legend.

Supposedly, in the scrutiny of law and order, my brother was less culpable than I was, but allegedly both of us along with Butler Campbell had orchestrated this sophisticated-elaborate-massive conspiracy that to hear them tell it, flooded the streets with cocaine and cocaine base and made millions of dollars in the process. This was the government's opening statement. That my brother and I ran this humongous drug network that destroyed hundreds of lives and communities around the country. This was the same government that iterated and reiterated to my lawyer that they didn't want some guys, like Sweet and I who was running up and down the highway with a couple kilos of cocaine. And that they would give me corroborating testimony to get Butler Campbell A.K.A. Uncle Butler indicted and convicted. To drive their argument home the prosecutor told the jury ... "Society is fed up with people like these. This case is about rap music and the drug trade, ladies, and gentleman. And the United States of America is prosecuting this case this morning and you have been selected to sit as jurors. Your job is to determine the faith of these defendants. You and only you will determine who is guilty and who is not. It is my belief that you will return a guilty verdict for all four of these defendants. Because you'll see the pictures of homes, cars, and jewelry that was purchased from drug proceeds; you'll see why our streets are filled with crime and violence. To help the government prove its case you're going to hear testimony from other criminals involved in the case but not charged, how these defendants on trial today manufactured, distributed crack cocaine, and had turf wars."

The minute I saw how the government was putting on their case I knew we would be found guilty. They put on a real show, and they blew us up so big that I couldn't believe it. Half of the time I wasn't even present. I drifted back and forth, in and out of consciousness. At times I even sat in the jury box and listened to the evidence against me. It was overwhelming and I already had my verdict. He or I was guilty.

Samantha also went to trial with us along with my brother's friend Tyrone Butler. We all stood before the firing squad, or the legal lynching machine, waiting to get strung up.

It took two days and a wake-up and a whole lot of tears and pain; that is watching the expression of my family faces, and it was all over. The jury returned a guilty verdict for me, my brother, and Tyrone. Samantha was set free. After her name was brought up only in the context of her being my girlfriend, her lawyer entered a Rule 29 Motion (for insufficient evidence), and the judge granted it while the jury was in recess. I was happy for her. Out of all of us, I felt she deserved to be set free. She should've never been drug into this case in the first place. I can't say my lawyer didn't fight for me. He did, he fought his butt off. His main argument was, where were the drugs the government was talking about. There wasn't one gram of cocaine or cocaine base in court, but the government used pictures of our houses, cars, jewelry, and other material possessions as assets garnered from drug proceeds. Two months later it was time for us to get sentenced. My lawyer came to visit me in the County Jail the day before sentencing to do some last-minute preparations. He said... "You know they're going to give you a life sentence, Albert. They're going to give your brother 30 years, maybe 35, and Tyrone 27." He looked me in my eyes like he was waiting to see me break down. But I stood firm. I was scared as hell, even more so now of white people. I thought they were some serious creatures. But I wasn't about to let them see me sweat. I just stared back at my lawyer like, ya'll crackers bring it on! That's may have been how I was looking but all the while I was thinking how I could get myself out of this mess. "I just want to let you know ... if it's any consolation to you ... "My lawyer preached, "I never had a client like you before. Anybody else would have told everything they knew and whatever the government wanted them to tell." about. There wasn't one gram of cocaine or cocaine base in court, but the government used pictures of our houses, cars, jewelry, and other material possessions as assets garnered from drug proceeds.

Two months later it was time for us to get sentenced. My lawyer came to visit me in the County Jail the day before sentencing to do some last-minute preparations. He said... "You know they're going to give you a life sentence, Albert. They're going to give your brother 30 years, maybe 35, and Tyrone 27." He looked me in my eyes like he was waiting to see me break down. But I stood firm. I was scared as hell, even more so now of white people. I thought they were some serious creatures. But I wasn't about to let them see me sweat. I just stared back at my lawyer like, ya'll crackers bring it on! That's may have been how I was looking but all the while I was thinking how I could get myself out of this mess.

"I just want to let you know ... if it's any consolation to you ... "My lawyer preached, "I never had a client like you before. Anybody else would have told everything they knew and whatever the government wanted them to tell."

Sequel 2

www.ingramcontent.com/pod-product-compliance
Lightning Source LLC
Chambersburg PA
CBHW051209290426
44109CB00021B/2390